I0816428

Decolonization and Humanism

The Postcolonial Vision of Rabindranath Tagore

Decolonization and Humanism

The Postcolonial Vision of Rabindranath Tagore

HIMANI BANNERJI

Published by
Tulika Books
44 (first floor), Shahpur Jat, New Delhi 110 049, India
www.tulikabooks.in

First published in India in 2024

ISBN: 978-81-958394-4-5 (hardback)

Printed at Chaman Offset, Delhi 110 002

for Manab

in memoriam

Contents

Previously Published Articles

Most of the chapters in this volume are thoroughly revised and rewritten versions of the articles and book chapters first appearing in the publications below:

'The Idea of the Self in Rabindranath: Notes on Modernity, Decolonization and the Becoming of a Poet', *Bangla Journal*, Year 12, Issue 20, December 2014.

'Rabindranath Tagore's Postcolonialism: A Vision of Decolonization and a Modernist Idealism', in *History, Imperialism, Critique: New Essays in World Literature*, edited by Asher Ghaffar, London: Routledge, 2019.

'Home and the World: Women and Nationalism in the Novels of Rabindranath Tagore', *Jadavpur Journal of Comparative Literature*, 43, 2005–06.

'A Transformational Pedagogy: Reflections on Rabindranath's Project of Decolonization', in *Tagore: The World as His Nest*, edited by Sangita Dutta and Subhoranjan Dasgupta, Kolkata: Jadavpur University Press, 2015.

'Beyond the Binaries: Notes on Karl Marx's and Rabindranath Tagore's Ideas on Human Capacities and Alienation', in *Marxism: With and Beyond Marx*, edited by Amiya Kumar Bagchi and Amita Chatterjee, London: Routledge, 2014.

Acknowledgements

For a collection of essays which were written over a long stretch of time, writing an acknowledgement is near-impossible. In those years, during which I lived and worked in both India and Canada, so much happened, so many institutions and conference presentations were involved, and so many readers and critics helped by commenting on the earlier versions of the papers that were published in various places. I need to thank the primary ones, as well as some of the people who were crucially involved in securing and facilitating my research and presentations on Rabindranath Tagore. I need to remember the late Swapan Kumar Majumdar, then director of Rabindra Bhavan, who awarded me a research fellowship at the start of this project. His illness and passing was a great loss for many of us, for both personal and intellectual reasons. I cannot thank enough Supriya Ray, the chief librarian of Rabindra Bhavan, for her great interest and sincere help in the development of my research. Herself a scholar of Rabindranath, she contributed many insights into his writings. The library and archival staff always provided help with a smile when I could not locate material I was looking for.

The Departments of Women's Studies, Comparative Literature and Marxian Studies of Jadavpur University, Kolkata provided the necessary support by urging me to give talks on my research and take part in conferences that they organized. The discussions at these events were extremely important for developing and refining my ideas and critical approach to the material. Especially I must remember with great respect the late Professor Jasodhara Bagchi, herself a writer on Tagore, for the valuable time we spent discussing Rabindranath and social reform in Bengal/India. Amiya Kumar Bagchi, the founder of the Institute of Development Studies Kolkata (IDSK), also earned my gratitude by taking a deep interest in my views on Tagore, particularly in relation to his views on education and my comparison of Tagore and Marx. In Canada my appreciation and thanks go to the Department of Sociology, York University, for allowing me to arrange my teaching schedule to accommodate part of my time for archival research.

Outside of the academy, from a time long ago when I had no intention of writing on Tagore, my attention was drawn to him by two people: my late brother, Sukhamoy Chakravarty; and late friend, Manabendra Bandyopadhyay. The ideas of the humanist enlightenment that orient my reading of Rabindranath found in every one of these essays were clarified by my brother, who embodied them for me. Manabendra Bandyopadhyay helped me to recognize the beauty, the joy and sadness in Rabindranath's poetry and songs, and the psychological complexities of his novels. Without their presence in my life, I would never have recognized the link between true decolonization and universalist humanism, which I subsequently read through the lens of historical materialism. It will be my lasting regret that neither of them is present to see the publication of this volume.

For shaping and producing the actual manuscript with infinite patience and helpful suggestions, I am indebted to my wonderful editor, Stephan Dobson. My gratitude extends to Indu Chandrasekhar of Tulika Books for her great patience, which encouraged me to complete the manuscript.

Finally, once again my deepest gratitude is reserved for Michael Kuttner, my life's companion, for his loving and dedicated support for my work. The people mentioned above, and many more unnamed but valued, have all given me their best help. If errors and incompleteness of thought remain, they are solely my own.

Introduction

The essays in this volume were written on separate occasions over a long period of time, during which much has happened in India. Socio-economically and politically India has undergone a sea-change, especially through the ascendance of an ideology whose long pre-existing elements dating back nearly two centuries came to be synthesized into a religio-political idea of '*hindutva*' as the preferred national identity for India and intended to be inserted into the governing aspects of the state.[1] This hard right-wing ideology, gleaned from an essentialized communalist reading of polymorphous hinduism, has thrown up a powerful challenge to the humanist secularism enshrined in the Indian constitution. For many, such as myself, the urgency for exploring the writings of Rabindranath Tagore arises from this situation, in a search for a powerful countervailing resource against *hindutva*. My resolve to undertake this task was strengthened by a shocking event.

I had been well aware of the vigorous activities of political mobilization of the Bharatiya Janata Party (BJP) and its parent civil society organization, the Rashtriya Swayamsevak Sangh (RSS), through country-wide campaigns and various acts of violence perpetrated against muslims, christians and dalits,[2] especially from the 1990s onwards.[3] So, what I heard on the morning of 6 December 1992 came to me as no surprise, that the Babri Masjid under dispute in Ayodhya, Uttar Pradesh, was demolished. This project had been planned for a few years, and now the volunteers (*karsevak*) of the RSS had finally achieved their goal. That long-established fifteenth-century mosque was now in rubble. Victorious RSS militants showed their great masculine prowess, and their leaders were cheering.[4] In the days and weeks following this event, a scorching wind blew over north India. That wind not only has not died down, but has spread across the country and taken strong hold of the Indian state. Large numbers of people, mostly muslims and dalits, have been threatened, injured and killed. It was at this time, then, that a turn to Rabindranath seemed necessary in order to go beyond a narrow and particularist approach to politics and society.

However, before we examine the social and political thought of Rabindranath we need to discuss, as a context, the political synthesis of *hindutva* (meaning the 'essence of hinduism'), an essentialist cultural nationalism anchored to an invention of India's purely hindu civilizational past. We should also note that this ideology, a distorted cultural construct of a multifaceted hinduism, from its beginning involved no contradiction between religion and colonial capitalism. In fact, in keeping with capitalist development in India and elsewhere,[5] it now rests on and stimulates an advanced state of neo-liberal economy. Through ideological sleights of hand, it reconciles colonial modernity and imperialism with colonially fabricated Indology and orientalist invention of tradition.[6] This invention of 'India' as an ideological category intends to change the overall Indian polity, particularly the secular and multicultural criteria of Indian citizenship, into a majoritarian ethnicist one, leaving us with the question as to how an exclusive demographic state can be democratic. *Hindutva* provides legitimation for a pseudo-democracy of citizens and subjects[7] which conceals authoritarianism, constraining the multiple claims that all citizens should have, even within the limited scope of bourgeois/liberal democracy.

From its inception in 1925, the RSS and its original and fraternal bodies, such as the Hindu Mahasabha (1915) and Arya Samaj (1875),[8] relied on the European, especially British and German, ideological composite of the aryan myth, which provided an essentialist interpretation of hinduism as a brahminical, caste-based religion out of which emerged the socio-political ideology of *hindutva*. Thus, a hard right-wing/fascist cultural-political project was born. This ideological twist continued to manipulate emerging and pre-existing antagonisms felt by caste hindus towards the religio-cultural communities they considered their inferiors and others. These views were fostered by some of the strands of the pre-independence nationalist political movements, leading to the partition of India in 1947. The bloody memories of great loss of life and massive displacement of this period became a source of stimulation for further animosities. In particular, the BJP, the political arm of the RSS, has strengthened brahminical caste and anti-muslim and anti-dalit political, economic and cultural practices throughout the last decades of the twentieth century up to the present. Its long-tried method of creating hegemony through cultural propaganda and organizational practices has centred on hindu epics and puranas in order to diffuse casteist norms and extreme violence. Organized pogroms, riots and general violence against muslims, lower castes, dalits and christians have intensified over the years. Through this process, various modalities of exclusion have been put in place, coalescing into notions of the 'enemy' and the 'other'. For the lower castes and animistic believers as well as for the poorest muslims, for buddhists and christians also, cooptive or pacificatory incorporation has been sought through re-conversion or religious rehabilitation, thereby solidifying the claim that India is a 'hindu nation'.[9] The presence of Pakistan as a 'muslim nation' next door has further strengthened the idea of the enemy. Lives, property and socio-political participation on a democratic basis are increasingly under threat through this attempt at engineering a demographic shift in cultural and social terms. Given this situation, it is no surprise that secularism, rationalism, humanism, communism and diverse movements for social equality, rights and justice have further consolidated the idea of 'the enemy' for the BJP, the RSS, and their affiliates and allied parties.

Even while this state of affairs is taking shape, there has been and still is a concerted search for secular, modernist and humanist options for resisting *hindutva* and its fascist tendencies. For this reason, Rabindranath is seen as a resource for countering *hindutva* hegemony. Many of us have returned, particularly, to his social and political thought, which is of course inextricable from his cultural critique, his literature and his other artistic creations. As his productivity was voluminous and multifaceted, a selection has had to be made. We have turned especially to his prose writings (such as his essays, novels and plays), leaving aside his vast wealth of poetry and songs on account of the linguistic difficulties and amount of work that these would entail. His prose writings, including correspondence, are being read through new critical lenses to meet the needs of our times. Three aspects of Rabindranath's socio-political thought become especially relevant from this point of view: his critique of nationalism and imperialism, including his assessment of various modes used and proposed for eradicating these; his universalist and humanist understanding of the politics of freedom and civilization; and lastly, the connection between the previous two issues and his modernism, as expressed by his philosophy and his projects of social reform. These concerns embrace his critiques of quotidian norms and forms of patriarchy, caste, communalism and pedagogical repression widely prevailing in the capitalist colonialism in his time.

At this point we need to trace the intensity of Rabindranath's presence in our lives prior to this period of crisis. As with numerous Bengalis, Rabindranath has been with me since my childhood in the 1940s. I not only learned from him my Bengali alphabet and spelling, read my earliest poems and short prose pieces – *Sahaj Path*, with lovely illustrations by Nandalal Bose – but also memorized his poems from *Katha o Kahini* which my father wanted me to recite. For quite a while Rabindranath shaped my literary taste, finessed my sensibilities. But in my late teenage years I lost touch with him as I discovered the power of contemporary 'modern' Bengali poetry. Its tone of disenchantment, jagged lines and hard-edged romanticism befitting to the teeming, claustrophobic, narrow convoluted lanes of the city of Calcutta expressed much about young people like us. When new trends were introduced in Bengali literature emphasizing urban living, and when the poetry of T.S. Eliot as well as translations of Charles Baudelaire, Rainer Maria Rilke and other European modernists by Buddhadeb Bosu, Sudhindranath Dutta and others, plus the political poetry of Sukanta Bhattacharya and translations of Nazim Hikmet's poetry by Subhas Mukhopadhyay came into our hands, Rabindranath's finely crafted, melodic poetry lost its magic, though his songs – poetry carried by the vitality of their music – continued to capture us. Rabindranath's dance-dramas and plays, lacking new interpretations that made them relevant to us, seemed manneristic and caught in a cultural warp restricted to his school of music.

In the decades following the second world war interest in Rabindranath went into relative decline, both in Bengal and abroad. Modern Bengali literature had initiated and developed different kinds of poetics and prose genres having a sense of dissonance with and discontinuity from the pre-war times.[10] The biggest change came with the partition of India. The emerging shortcomings of the new Indian state in coping with the resulting political, economic and religious issues and resistances to them became quickly evident. These experiences impelled Bengali/Indian readers to search for and create new contemporary voices. The paucity and difficulty of translating Rabindranath's work might have also been a major issue in the rest of India, though he still remained a magisterial cultural and ethical figure.[11] Of his voluminous prose writings the short stories retained their popularity, while most of his novels, challenging traditional mores of the genre, with little interest in storytelling, composed with montages of fragments, interior monologues, and explorations of dark emotional recesses and critical reflections, had a limited readership as before. His plays, unusual as they were, textured with music and dialogue, with deep ethical explorations and dilemmas rather than conventional plots, were performed on a minor scale.

But the genres to mainly suffer from neglect in the post-independence period were Rabindranath's non-fictional Bengali and English prose, in which he expounded his socio-political and cultural criticism as well as his philosophical/spiritual and aesthetic judgements. Both these genres, taken very seriously in his own time, especially his excoriating critique of nationalism following the armed *swadeshi* uprising against the partition of the Bengal Presidency (1905–08), went into relative eclipse. If his projects of social transformation and anti-colonialism were not popularly understood, even when he and Mahatma Gandhi expressed profound mutual admiration and appellated each other respectively as the 'Sentinel' and the 'Great Soul' of India's freedom struggle, with the advent of Indian independence and the assassination of Gandhi (1948) these projects were generally left unaddressed. For a time, Rabindranath studies became the preserve of scholars specially dedicated to his poetic and spiritual work. What emerged from these decades was an aura of mysticism that converted him into a quasi-saintly figure or sage. This is indicated by the custom of calling Rabindranath *gurudev*, meaning a great teacher of wisdom or a spiritual guide. His biographies acquired a hagiographic tone. Eventually, however, historians of colonial Bengal and India's freedom struggles as well as of postcolonial/postmodern India turned to him with important results, particularly regarding nationalism and modernity. Much of this volume's content builds upon and responds to them. Historians Sumit Sarkar, Tanika Sarkar, Ashis Nandy, and members of the Subaltern Studies (Kolkata) group made extensive use of Rabindranath's work, in agreement and disagreement. Among these scholars the reading of Rabindranath went beyond his philosophical writings such as *Religion of Man* (1930), *Sadhana* (1914) or *Santiniketan* (1908–1914), to his critical writings such as *Kalantar* (1933a), *Nationalism* (1917) and *Crisis in Civilization* (1941), as well as his novels and short stories. The writings that had been commonly seen as transcendental excursions into a vacuous idealism began to be grounded in Indian and international socio-historical realities. His universalist humanist philosophy was being explored for a constitutive relationship of difference and identity, that is, of a complex understanding of oneness or unity. It became apparent that he was not an empty signifier of piety, that his concept of 'man' was rooted in a social being. Throughout the trials and tribulations that independent India underwent, including contestations for the criteria of citizenship, increasingly Rabindranath's writings became great resources for those seeking the affirmation of social justice and human rights. Most importantly, they provided ethical and epistemological grounds for an indispensable humanist and secular world-view of Indian society and polity.

When I went to India in 1992 to take up my research fellowship in Rabindra Bhavan, Santiniketan, it was apparent that violence against non-'hindu' putative 'others' had greatly accelerated, particularly in north India. Everyday life was in disarray through anti-muslim and anti-dalit incidents, and the polity of the whole country was thrown into the whirlpool of hindu supremacism. The 'two nations' theory that undergirded the emergence of India and Pakistan, and which had been lying relatively passively in Indian civil society, had now resurfaced with a vengeance.[12] The work that M.S. Golwalkar and Veer Savarkar had put into the making of the RSS had reached a climax.[13] The seeds of hatred which had been sown primarily against muslims and non-hindus as aliens or foreign to India, in effect constituting India as a hindu country, extended the notions to include secularism and communism as a western outlook, and were now ready to be harvested. It should be noted here that this hindu supremacist climb to power and its march towards rule in Delhi had not been linear. Banned for a time after the assassination of Mahatma Gandhi by Nathuram Godse, associated with the RSS, the organization did not disappear in any substantial way, but remained as before in the interstices of Indian civil society. It continued its organizational activities in many branches, focused on creation of cultural hegemony. Over time, especially with the rising weakness and fractures in the Indian National Congress (INC), their aspirations for assumption of direct political power grew.[14] Combining elite ideological resources with common popular cultural resources, especially prevalent in the predominantly Hindi-speaking parts of India, and conducting mobilizational exercises through calls for temple building, cow protection, mosque destruction, riots, pogroms and lynchings, the RSS and its affiliates significantly succeeded in hinduizing Indian social and political common sense. In their version, with the BJP now serving as a spearhead of *hindutva* polity, the multidimensional ideas and practices of hinduism were stripped of their historical and present contradictions. This closed ideological construction of *hindutva* derived its strength from brahminical, that is, casteist, social and economic power relations shaping Indian capitalism. *Hindutva* ideology thus assumed the status of the fundamental principle through which to reshape the Indian state apparatus by altering substantial portions of a secular democratic constitution. The hegemonic content of *hindutva* was distilled from an accretional storehouse of puranic epics and legends equally familiar to the elite and common people. The much-loved epic, the Ramayana – extant in India over many centuries and in various versions, specially the Tulsi Das version relied upon by Gandhi – provided a great inspirational source for hindu communalism, though with a particular interpretation.[15] While the Ramayana and the Mahabharata served the purpose of the BJP/RSS combine's imagined hindu nation as a device for its mass cultural incorporation, for the satisfaction of the hindu elite these epics provided a pretence of scholarship and rewriting of Indian cultural history. The colonialist and the hindu nationalist projects mirrored each other in that the fascination with the putative 'aryan' identity of the hindus, so loved by far-right hindu nationalists, relied wholly on orientalist Franco-British misinterpreted versions of the Vedas and the Puranas and orientalist historiography. The identity construction of the 'hindu' proffered by RSS/BJP was none other than the mythical German indological 'aryan'.[16] This aryan identity gracing the *hindutva* ideology relies for its social and political effectiveness on a brahminical world-view and looks to casteist rituals to create grounds for social cohesion. The ideological constellation that shapes *hindutva* as the natural essence of India relies on 'others' who are non-hindus and comes with invented enemies of the ideal of India. This social view insinuates itself into the pores of daily and cultural lives, and, further, operationalizes itself with promises of rewards and advancements for those who wish to belong within the *hindutva* purview. Here we have the fascist nationalist ideological device, replete with the notions of a legitimate self or social actor and an 'enemy' to be objectified and acted on.

For these reasons, Rabindranath's critique of nationalism from the standpoint of universalist humanism becomes important for us. His vision, demonstrated in his entire opus, provides grounds for a necessary humanist outlook. Rabindranath's rejection of nationalism as a means to decolonization developed over a period of time, progressively clarified through his encounters with various aspects of colonialism and imperialism. Shedding the ambiguity of the earlier period, he pointed out and warned against continuous threads of religious identitarianism embedded in the nationalist project. Bengali cultural nationalism was constituted to a large extent by these threads and influenced the Indian National Congress at an all-India level. It should be noted that the Congress at this time was not a political party with a defined univocal ideological platform, but rather an ideological complex with a character of social movements having both secular-liberal and cultural-religious strands within it. These strands continued to coexist in an uneven balance and saturated the political consciousness of India's freedom struggle. The strain of hindu religious sentiment for a time was subordinated to the idea of a nation as envisioned by liberal, progressive members of the INC, to the extent that it even accommodated the social-democratic views of Jawaharlal Nehru. In spite of occasional confrontations and riots, and constant political rivalry between hindus and muslims, quasi-socialist liberal values won out for a long period, right into the moment of Indian independence. Thus the Indian constitution, its writing presided over by B.R. Ambedkar,[17] manifested itself in a most inclusive idea of citizenship. This new nation state, embracing diversity, chose a humanist song by Rabindranath as its national anthem. The idea of Indian citizenship found its resonance in Rabindranath's world-mindedness, his universalist humanism. Without a doubt, then, I felt that we would need now to strongly reassert the legacy of Rabindranath. My own marxist social analysis and politics saw his secular humanism as no hindrance. A full critique of class, caste, and patriarchal social relations and ideologies could not dispense with his social vision.

Through the decades of the 1990s and post-2000, Rabindranath's relevance has only increased for us. Indian politics entered a quickly expanding era of *hindutva*, until the BJP securely won central political power, though there were sporadic periods of weak Congress rule. Very quickly the democratic institutions of the Indian state were used for a communally partisan rule or were assaulted up to the point that the social-democratic constitution of India began to be dismantled. The hindu right sought to literally replace the neutral geographical understanding of Hindustan, as the land of the people of the Indus river valley, with the notion of a country for hindus. They also claimed the legitimacy of hindu rule by indicating India as the domain of a legendary hindu king, Bharat (*Bharatvarsha*). The deadly consequences of the political ascension of the BJP, both nationally and provincially, were manifested in 2002 in the pogrom against muslims in Gujarat. This pogrom not only terrified the muslims and deterred their citizenship claims, but also mobilized a great number of hindus, as evinced in Narendra Modi's overwhelming victory in the Gujarat elections after the

Godhra attacks. The hindu right triumphalism continues into the present era since the demolition of the Babri Masjid.

Despite an archaic pre-capitalist appearance through the use of *hindutva* ideology, the BJP/RSS remaking of the Indian state and society is by no means an anti-modernist project.[18] A reactionary modernism, it is congruent with neo-liberalism and western imperialist projects and the cult of consumerism. In fact religion itself has become commercialized, blending into the retail and corporate ventures of capital in India. Anti-modernist only when it comes to humanist enlightenment ideas of civil and human rights, some forms of socio-economic equality and secularism, the state of reactionary modernism rests on xenophobia, religious bigotry, superstition and casteism. These provide the necessary groundwork for a highly acquisitive and destructive form of capitalism. The hindu majoritarianism that has introduced hierarchy into the idea of citizenship constantly removes support from under the feet of any oppositional politics. This essentializing and fundamentalist version of hinduism, overtly active from the third decade of the twentieth century, has worked like a mole in the soil and crevices of Indian civil society and culture. It has introduced religion as the dominant vehicle of political agency and has sought to ensnare other political parties into their ideological playing field. Hindu extremism is now taking the upper hand and forcing other political projects to play to its tune. At this point, the political and social thought of Rabindranath can provide us with the groundwork for a resistant culture.

The broad rubric of decolonization comprehends the essays in this volume. They explore Rabindranath's critique of nationalism and culture within the organization of colonial capitalism in Bengal/India, and also in the imperialist societies of the west, through the lens of humanist universalism. Though Rabindranath himself did not use the expression 'decolonization', a term that is generally known to have been first used by Frantz Fanon (1968), I have adapted it as a conceptual and organizational term to comprehend the different ways in which colonial capitalism is understood and challenged. Decades have passed since both Rabindranath's and Fanon's time, but debates have persisted since then regarding what it means to decolonize, whether it is a pertinent critical concept for our postcolonial times – that is, what conceptual and political interpretations we might invest it with. There are a number of current critiques and reflections on colonialism and its aftermath asking particularly whether the notion of decolonization is applicable beyond the context of colonization to include indigenous and caste oppressions, slavery and patriarchy. That is to say, it asks whether or not the notion is applicable to all societies constructed through power relations homologous to colonial occupation and violence. These questions have gained great urgency at the present time, when indigenous and anti-racist movements as well as movements against land occupation have gathered strength, and have incorporated in their theorizations the issues of colonization, nationalism and cultural identity. Thus, colonization or decolonization are no longer limited to territorial occupation, economic exploitation and ruling by external forces, but include internal social relations of power, cultural practices and political ideologies within the occupied spaces themselves. Decolonization remains an imperative and holistic project, not only in political-economic dimensions, but also in an overall hegemonic sense in the matter of social subjectivities, agencies and forms of consciousness.

The essays here explore Rabindranath's understanding of colonial hegemony, and the proposals and social visions he developed towards a world apart from and against it. To consider these only in terms of a political counter-hegemony would undermine the universalist humanist scope of his vision. It would be better perhaps to consider Rabindranath's social project and vision in the Gramscian sense, which extends beyond a historically specific colonial moment to the principle of a fundamental change not only in the sphere of politics but of deeper forms of consciousness. Thus, considering decolonization only in politico-economic terms would be a reductive effort and could not satisfy the criteria for a 'true' decolonization,[19] which would have to heed Fanon's warnings about the 'pitfalls of national consciousness' since the colonial native elite and petit bourgeoisie aspire to achieving leadership roles, sidelining the colonized masses. Fanon's warning echoed the reasons for Rabindranath's rejection of nationalism, which he saw as possessing strong elements of self-interest on the part of the native ruling classes. In fact Rabindranath went beyond Fanon in jettisoning the idea or imagination of the nation as the core of anti-colonialism. He felt that nationalism essentially suffers from the particularisms of interests of distinct social groups which tend to elect themselves as vanguard. Though a larger space of social organizations and relations may open up in the course of anti-colonial struggles, ultimately the scope of national consciousness remains territorially bound and immediate in its concerns. Thus, Rabindranath goes beyond Fanon's awareness of the perils of nationalism to an unqualified rejection of it.

Among the whole host of issues and critiques of colonization and nationalism that have accrued since Rabindranath's time, his concerns and questions concerning decolonization endure. In keeping with his holistic vision of social transformation, Rabindranath posed the fundamental question of the processes that would bring about the change; what would be the right means to achieve a true decolonization? In conceptualizing the problematic of decolonization in this way he eliminated a dualist idea of means and end, because at each step in his conceptualization of decolonization as a process – rather than a political event – the means becomes a step of the end. Thus he brings to the fore the moral and ethical questions and dilemmas inherent in the notion of decolonization as they shape in an ongoing way subjectivities and agencies that would not sabotage the original intent for a *true* decolonization. If this were to be neglected, an anti-colonial project would fall prey to political and economic reductionism, or would convert decolonization into a cultural identitarian project unmindful of the material nature of historical social movements. In other words, we have to recognize that colonialism is not simply the project of an abstract power but an amalgam of domination involving socio-economic life and forms of consciousness. Neither Rabindranath nor the latter-day thinkers have reached consensus regarding answers to these vital questions, nor have they resolved the dilemmas of decolonization. It remains an ongoing project, extending beyond common conceptual uses, anchoring decolonization in history and particular property relations. No matter what answer we come up with, colonialism and decolonization remain as signifiers of power and freedom in a holistic humanist sense. The most critical aspect of decolonization lies in undoing historical relations of power and in the making of a revolutionary democratic history. To better understand what decolonization means, we need to be more concrete than simply offering wish-images and metaphysical statements, and selectively demonstrate them in particular instances. The social and political thinking of Rabindranath, his creative and pedagogical practices for decolonization, as well as his location in a colonized space, offer us this opportunity.

When we turn to Rabindranath for a critical understanding of nationalism and resources for decolonization, we should not think of him as an all-knowing figure who thought seamlessly without contradictions, revisions and inconclusiveness. It would be wrong to create an iron-clad portrait of him, making him into a sage-like construct who knew of his future thoughts from the early stages of his life as though he had a ground plan according to which he directed his personality, ideas and future concerns. The temptation to see him in this way comes easier for people who mainly read Rabindranath in his mature phase and deduce the past from the present, or who work primarily from anthologies and are unable to read his writings in their original language. In this lies the danger of bypassing the dynamism of his development and according him a linear trajectory. A close scrutiny of his opus will show that Rabindranath does not come in one whole piece, that he contradicts himself periodically and at times even holds simultaneously two opposite sets of sentiments and social views. Thus, if one tendency or approach becomes uppermost, a struggle with it by the opposite is also vividly evident. This can occur to the point whereby the struggle leaves an indelible impression of what he ultimately rejects on the attentive reader. From this point of view Rabindranath is a master of sublation, whose creative work in particular is textured with a fruitful irresolution, leaving readers to assess the text in their own way. Though he matured towards a principle of hope in universalist humanism and a faith in 'man', he consistently captures in his work an ever-present tension between the local and the extra-local, the particular and the universal.

A good place to explore the non-linear trajectory of Rabindranath's thought can be found in the shifting meanings he attributes to the tropes of 'East' and 'West'. Tracking the changes in the meanings and uses attributed to them by Rabrindanath, sometimes sequentially and sometimes simultaneously, shows that the path to universalist humanism is strewn with obstacles. Signally important is to note how these conceptual devices are employed in understanding historical and social reality. These notions can be used in two epistemological ways: one that grounds them in historical and social/material reality, and the other which disconnects them from lived time and space. In the latter case they become ideological in Marx's sense, as outlined in *The German Ideology* (Marx and Engels 1970). In their ideological application, as done by many European writers since the era of colonization, they provide a reifying cultural understanding. Rabindranath and other Asian writers were not immune to this ideological understanding of culture.[20] The emergence of the East and the West as ideological categories which texture a colonial discourse arises from an adaptation of pre-colonial civilizational notions prevalent in Europe prior to approximately the seventeenth century. In that era, these notions indicated cultural differences without introducing connotations of cultural superiority and inferiority.[21] This is the discourse that Edward Said critiques in *Orientalism* (1979a), associating it with the notion of power/knowledge as articulated by Foucault (1980) and which culminated in the essentialist civilizational argument of Samuel Huntington's *Clash of Civilizations* (1996).[22] This ideological reading confers a static character to geographical and social spaces, occluding the non-homogeneous nature of cultures everywhere. Colonial discourse of the East and the West invents two mutually exclusive cultures, and constructs through this device a barrier between Europe and its 'others'. This discursive invention affects, therefore, both the colonizers and the colonized. The general epistemological effect is to create homogenized cultural blocs or civilizations as fixed types, and to erase differences both between and within them. The core of hegemony lies in the ideological mode of thinking, extending the relations of colonization beyond the political and economic sense to the realm of consciousness and asserting a permanent cultural superiority of the colonizer. Any critique of colonial discourse has to displace ideological forms of thinking and put in their place the historically formative and socially dynamic character of all cultures, replacing categorical abstractions or conceptual essences by the concreteness of actually existing societies.[23]

The discourse of orientalism, centred on the ideological use of the term 'Orient' and entering Asia through the process of colonialism, influenced writers like Rabindranath. The invention of the discourse developed through the administrative practices of the East India Company, defining and instrumentalizing the relations of ruling. It introduced value relations of power between the cultures of the East and the West, shedding their pre-colonial perception. In this colonial project of knowledge for ruling, the civilizations of the East and the West were redefined, and the East/Orient, once perceived as great as Europe, came to be considered as decayed. The project of colonialism envisioned by the East India Company became a mission of returning the East to its former greatness. Thus, the ruling apparatus of mercantile colonialism textualizes 'India' as a constellation of cultural categories into which are embedded ethnicism and religion, demonizes muslims as invaders and foreigners, and attributes to an essentialized hinduism the status of a national culture. Through this sleight of hand the ideologues of the East India Company deflected attention from their own status as foreigners and their encroachment and invading activities in India in the name of rescuing Indian civilization. The current aspiration of the BJP for the creation of a hindu *rashtra* (nation) based on *hindutva* relies on and replays this earlier trope of the orient, and seeks to create a polity fabricated on an ideal 'ancient India' as its 'historic' legitimation. This invention of India by the East India Company, with its civilizational mission to restore it on its former grounds, was however depreciated by the developing colonial state through the de-chartering process of the Company in 1858. The new colonial approach of the British state itself had less use for the orientalist invention of India's past glories. Though the utilitarian approach brought in with it a discourse of backwardness and barbarism, traces of the earlier orientalist discourse seeped into the culture of ruling for reasons of administration and social control.[24] These varying ideological approaches of the state had their influence on the subject population.

These changes in the modalities of British rule in India, adumbrating utilitarianism with orientalism when necessary, industrial with mercantile capitalism (along with a plantation economy involving deindustrialization of the colony), and exalting British culture over the indigenous, created great socio-cultural upheaval especially in Bengal, the epicentre of colonialism. Colonialism created new classes of landholders (*zamindars*), professionals, and businessmen and white-collar workers (*bhadralok*) within its orbit, many members of which identified with aspects of orientalism and others with colonial modernism. This situation of multiplicity and fluidity, a mixture of old and new social forms of consciousness and practices, resulted in a crisis of cultural self-identification. It catalysed new subjectivities and agencies for political projects in response to colonialism. Self-making and self-identification therefore became major undertakings of the pre-*swadeshi* cultural and political development in Bengal. It is in this conjuncture that Rabindranath's life and work must be situated. He and his family were an intrinsic part of this struggle for national cultural identification, and as a young man he was involved in the project of the transvaluation of values along orientalist lines that characterized a large strand of the emerging nationalist ideology. For colonial subjects, this implied a situation of irresolution and double consciousness, a simultaneous exaltation of orientalism and an internalization of the values of colonial modernism. To this mix entered continuing practices and beliefs of pre-colonial times, all of which created a crisis of identity on the one hand, and on the other, a great yearning for the development of a sense of self and individuality. The problem that this situation introduced in the project of national self-identification could not be resolved by the creation of new norms and forms of a simple hybridity (Bhaba 1994). Protean forms of counter-hegemonic consciousness began to emerge with their changing politico-cultural common sense. Thus belief-worlds were created which were in states of coexistence and contradiction. As progress was made towards the formation of a nationalist ideology, a sense of self-assertion or even superiority began to spread among the colonial subjects. An adequate reading of Rabindranath would have to be sensitive to these formational impulses, as he too felt the pulls of different counter-hegemonic projects.

Exploration of some of these issues brought about by the colonial incursion in Bengal forms the content of the essays in this volume. Critiques of nationalism, racism and the situation of women in Rabindranath's novels, involving his views on sexuality and the social organization of the family, are vital parts of his general social thought (Bannerji 2020a). The development of his thought, however, was not linear. Instances of contradiction can be found, for example, in the period between 1905 and 1908, which culminated in his writing of *Gora*. Battling against orientalist cultural nationalism and trying to devise a critical platform against both colonialism and imperialism, he drew his inspiration from universalist humanism. But the effort is not yet fully successful in creating a third critical space, as he displays a reactive raw response[25] to the racism experienced by himself and others and which drew him towards cultural nationalism. In his western correspondences he remarks on the discrimination meted out to a poet from the colonies by the British/western literary and political world. His general effort is to be truthful about the immediate experience of racist colonial violence while trying not to act in a reactive manner on the same principle as the colonizer, that is, by responding to racism with racism. This conflict, though mostly resolved over a period of time, remains in a constant search for the third space. This element introduces a restlessness which afflicts Rabindranath in all aspects of his life and work. The partially resolved contradiction largely explains his at times desperate efforts to stay grounded in an empathetic humanist understanding of the 'other', both indigenous and foreign. In *Atmaparichay* (Of Myself), he states that his only authentic identity is: 'I am a poet' (Tagore 2009a: 1). This realization, however, is constantly invaded by an equally powerful realization that he is not only a poet, but a poet of a colonized people. He does not want to disavow this socio-historical and existential truth. In his unease about his reception in the west – for example, about the Nobel Prize awarded to him in 1913 – in his angry self-deprecation and condemnation of others regarding the matter of translations of his works and his efforts to write in

English, we find the same unease regarding his identity. It is imperative for him to create an identity that is both specific and universal, which he does by assuming an identity that goes beyond being a colonial subject to one of being human in universalist terms. This applies as much to himself as to others, both colonizer and colonized. This is possible by discovering points of commonality and intelligibility between human beings irrespective of their spatial location and outside of relations of oppression and exploitation.

The universal human identity, which Rabindranath also calls 'man', implicates the self to an 'other' and is reliant on the principle of shared capacities at the levels of production/creation and communication. This 'being' human is not merely an idea or an abstraction, but rather necessitates embodied selves in interactive relations. Such a human identification of the self is cognizant of both commonality and distinction between subjects. This socially relational humanist lens fundamentally changes the meaning of the 'individual' away from its bourgeois definition, and thus from atomism and power relations to one of enabling co-constitution. Challenging as this ontological and epistemological shift may be, for Rabindranath it is the essential basis for the assumption of *human* identity. It is this shift that enables the achievement of the goal of decolonization of those living within conditions of colonialism, slavery, and other oppressive and exploitative relations of class, gender, caste and race. Being human, therefore, is not a passive state of existence, but demands conscious and social activity. Humanization can thus only occur through conscious practical activities within specific concrete formations, their modes of organization, cultural and institutional norms. A homologous sameness can only be constituted with a weaving together of specific differences. This process implies the necessity of acts of translation involving various discursive and linguistic levels for constituting a dialogical whole. What underlies them are shared expressions of sensuous, active human capacities, making human survival possible.

This conceptual position establishes the philosophical framework through which Rabindranath interpreted India's freedom struggle and an end of colonization. His humanist endeavours had to contend with the fact that India was interpellated within the colonial governance and which made it into a composite of two nations, namely, hindu and muslim. The construction of 'the hindu' and 'the muslim' as constitutive devices for ruling stood as the most dominant obstacle in the path of forging a fully decolonized India. A truly human or even national identity irrespective of ethnicity necessary for an independent India was only partially achieved by the freedom struggle, leading to brutally partitioned political entities. This false decolonization is not solely to be blamed on the British manoeuvre of divide and rule, but has to be acknowledged as the work of that part of the elite of Bengal/India which seized the opportunity provided by colonial rule to call for hindu revivalism and a hindu state. This was followed by muslim nationalist demands. The hindu politicians on their part took up the colonial discourse and advocated the return to a mythic past invented by orientalists in the composite idea of 'aryan civilization', whereby the colonized sought an affinity with the colonizer and saw themselves as a superior 'race'.

The question of national identity became further complicated through the rejection of religious revivalism by social critics and reformers who tried to synthesize the notion of 'Indian' both for the nation and its people. Rabindranath personally grew up in this humanist reformist environment, and he found in the Brahmo Samaj a strand of a humanist third path.[26] It is from this that he evolved humanism not only as a philosophical idea, but as an identity for true liberation. This broader approach, inclusive of social ethics, rested in a secular humanism which could accommodate an imaginative and philosophical spiritualism. Rabindranath's idea of 'man' emerges from this base of a dialogical encounter between an Indian philosophy of oneness and the humanism of the earlier phase of the European enlightenment. In his version of humanism, Rabindranath eschewed the dogmatic insistence on rationalism, abstraction and scientism, and nuanced the ideas of knowledge and truth. His social approach privileged imagination and spiritual (not institutionally religious) awareness. His point of departure for social criticism and reform lay in this, and simultaneously accommodated a critique of particularisms within a universal sense of human belonging. Rabindranath evolved a syncretic modernism synthesized from Indian philosophical and cultural traditions and tenets of European enlightenment uncaptured by capital's expanding colonial project. Though not always or entirely free of various particularisms or abstract idealization, his conception of freedom was constructed through a universalist humanism. Decolonization embodied for him this, rather than a merely political freedom.

The trajectory of Rabindranath's thought moves between an orientalist trope of India on the one hand, and on the other, a socio-historically grounded understanding of past and contemporary India. Furthermore, his orientalist view of India is a divided one. Thus, he sees 'India' as an idealized construct derived from a philosophical standpoint which conveys an essentialist and static view of the past, and equates the repetition of this past as the imaginary of freedom. But his idea of India holds within it a humanist world-view that resides and persists at the base of all civilizations. In this view, the past is neither static nor radically cut apart from the present, and the idea of Indian civilization contains no connotation of superiority over others. The element of power/knowledge which defines colonial discourse is absent here. As such, this idea of India/the East serves as an imaginary of humanist universalist values to which the rest of the world could turn. But at times we also find in Rabindranath a conventional form of orientalism, in which the idea of India/the East becomes a reactive or defensive one, responding in kind to the binary framework of Orient and Occident. In these instances, India/the East is constructed through a power/knowledge lens of civilizational superiority and inferiority. While India is imagined in terms of pure idealism, the West/Occident becomes an essence of crass materialism. In this interpretation, Rabindranath relies on a version of enlightenment in its adapted aspects of capitalist colonialism which emphasizes hyper and instrumental rationalism, mechanization, consumerism and greed for money. In contrast to this ideological depiction of the West, the essence of the East is construed as renunciation, as a search for the pure self and salvation of the soul, while the West is projected as a parable of a fall from grace and a substitution of the spiritual self by possessive individualism.[27] In a similar vein, he saw christianity as an essentially Eastern phenomenon and the life of christ as an embodiment of renunciation, sacrifice and love, which he considered Eastern qualities that did not sit well with the modern industrial, though christianized, West.

Interestingly, Rabindranath makes a critical use of the East/West trope not only to offer an ideological civilizational condemnation, but also to present a social critique of both the contemporary West and the East/India. Thus, idealism provides him with the point of departure for an urgent material project of social reform. Just as he constructed the East as an ideal type of purity and a degraded actuality, he saw the ideal type of the West as similarly divided. The present-day crass materialism of the West, which he severely castigated, was balanced by Rabindranath's deep appreciation of the West's enlightenment humanist values uncontaminated by capitalism. Thus he made a distinction between two aspects of modernity encoded by the enlightenment, of a humanist modernism and the values of modernization of capitalist colonialism. He revered and protected the key enlightenment concepts of the equality of humans, the socially individuated individual (as opposed to possessive and competitive individualism) and the outlook of universalism. The idea of freedom implied in the enlightenment's universalism, understood ethically in terms of justice and equality and thus promoting a critical consciousness, became his own goal, the cornerstone of his vision. In this vision, developed through the last decades of his life, he found the possibilities of universal coexistence at the level of the human, and rejected the binary colonial discourse of East and West.

Rabindranath's idea of freedom is connected to the idea of the individual, of 'man', which is rooted in universalist humanism. Just as he extended the definition of colonialism to include all forms of domination, so too he expanded the notion of freedom beyond the boundaries of the conventional political and economic scopes. This expanded freedom included all relations between the self and the other and nature, and their expression through creativity, material production and art. Thus understood, freedom becomes an active process, a way of be-ing[28] in the world which is constantly renewed by changes of consciousness, society and history. It is this understanding of freedom that I identify as Rabindranath's decolonization project, aspiring for a truly free and world society. It illuminates his anti-colonialism and his ideas of the self, personality and individuality, and provides the fundamental criteria for his rejection of nationalism. In his poetic moral vision for the elimination of colonialism he was not seeking a *national* community, but rather a *world* community and a meaningful internationalism.

For contemporary scholars brought up within the ambience of postcolonial studies, reading Franz Fanon and associated anti-imperialist writers such as Aimé Césaire, Ngũgĩ wa Thiong'o and others, Rabindranath may seem an unlikely choice for exploring the idea of decolonization, being considered too romantic, quaint and old-fashioned. But the currency of his post-second world war image as a poet and a sage, along with his association with the late nineteenth and early twentieth centuries, occludes very important aspects of his life and his social and political thought. He was a highly controversial political thinker and figure in his own time, particularly regarding the eradication of colonialism and imperialism. His life spanned the Indian freedom struggle, in which he was always actively engaged. For the purpose of an in-depth anti-colonial critique, in my opinion it is crucial to understand this once world-renowned figure who pitted his humanist/universalist philosophy against capital's aggression and imperialist wars. His response to the Russian revolution, Japan's imperialist ambitions, the rise and development of nazi and fascist ideologies and the attempts of South Asian and East Asian countries to overthrow colonialism becomes a window to anti-colonial and anti-imperialist struggles, offering a prescient and critical vision for an authentic decolonization. The essays in this volume show that Rabindranath was a more than life-sized figure who had the ambition to create a new, syncretic and substantive Indian culture, for which he drew on the available cultures of his time. The contribution of his political and social critique pre-dates the foundation of the Indian National Congress (1885). Even before the advent of Mohandas Karamchand Gandhi in Indian politics in 1915, Tagore was considered a major figure by all political parties and groups involved with India's freedom struggle. Thus, he was both an insider and a contributor to the different shifts in what the freedom movement (*swadhinata*) and nationalism (*jatiyatabad*) as well as self-rule (*swaraj*) came to mean. His contribution signally lies in developing an alternative vision of society based on humanist principles and corresponding institutions. The following essays suggest that Rabindranath's idea of universalist humanism was not at the cost of the specificity of the social individual. His works provide us with a thoroughgoing understanding of social and political crises with potential catastrophic implications on a global scale. The same crises, which continue into our dark and chaotic present times, call for a re-reading of Rabindranath. He is a historical figure who flashes up, to paraphrase Walter Benjamin, in our moment of danger.

Rabindranath was, to my knowledge, the earliest globally known writer from *within* a colonized society. Thus his consciousness, imagination and critique are grounded in the perspective of anti-colonial resistance. Being pressured to become a colonial subject, he could testify from his personal life to the violence of colonial hegemony on himself, and on India and other colonized societies. In fact he detected elements of violence and corruption that entered into resistance to colonialism through the ideology of nationalism, the context and formation of which he found in European imperialist aggression within and beyond the Indian subcontinent. Rabindranath's legacy in decolonizing consciousness and society is not only relevant for those who are at the receiving end of colonization, but also for the remaking of the colonizing/imperializing societies themselves. His interpretation of decolonization thus contributes to a global legacy of critical thought on individual and collective human freedom. Though critiques of colonialism and imperialism, notably by Vladimir Lenin or Rosa Luxemburg, made vital contributions to understanding the integrity of colonialism to capitalism, it is not until we consider the contributions made by Rabindranath and other later political thinkers, such as Fanon, that we can truly apprehend the overwhelming human cost of colonialism. The harm that is done is not only in terms of economic exploitation, but in the very terms of human consciousness and human existence on earth.

Another compelling reason for exploring Rabindranath's idea of universalist humanism in relation to decolonization is that his view contributes to present-day social movements a way to transcend the goal of a nation state, and introduces a dimension of self-identification with others, going beyond mere political freedom, to an ethical self–other relation. Rabindranath rejected a simplistic form of anti-colonialism based on the idea of the west and the rest, and centred on a privileged ethnicity. Nationalism, the conventional instrument of anti-colonialism, was excoriated by him as a twin of imperialism/colonialism. While remaining wholly cognizant of oppression, he did not accord to victimhood an automatic moral superiority. As decades later Audrey Lorde would say, one cannot destroy the master's house with the master's tools, Rabindranath sought to create other tools made from critical and ethical premises unconnected to any form of domination, imperialist or nationalist. Thus, for him, postcolonialism would not merely bypass colonization as a specific historical phenomenon by seeking to return to the stage when colonization intruded – thereby idealizing the past and going against the grain of history. Rabindranath created a new problematic of decolonization by eschewing the ideological binary paradigm of modernity versus tradition, which has exerted such power on postcolonial and postmodernist studies.

Rabindranath is also an important subject of study because significant thinkers on colonialism and imperialism in the vernacular literature of South and Southeast Asia were, and continue to be, unknown in the metropolitan countries as well as to each other due to existing language barriers. But he could be accessed a little more by those who do not know Bengali, as some of his writings were originally in English and others were translated, providing a supplement to his Bengali writings. Scholars could also draw on his diaries of his European and non-European travels as well as his public lectures reported by journalists in those countries. His vast correspondences with western intelligentsia and creative personalities have come to light. For all these reasons, with the help of this supplementary literature as well as his Bengali writings available to knowledgeable people, Rabindranath can be seen as a prime candidate for a serious consideration regarding the problems and positive potentials congealed in the concept of decolonization.

This collection of essays is not a monograph on Rabindranath, but rather is meant to concretize and clarify ideas central to his work. The epistemological approach organizing them questions the relationship between the notions of postcolonialism and decolonization. In what ways can we get past colonialism into a truly 'post' stage of decolonization and not perform a simple conceptual reversal which projects an anti-colonialism based on nationalism? The essays also question the affinity conventionally perceived between postcolonialism and postmodernism. We need to ask why modernism is seen as necessarily a part of colonial discourse and thus as an enemy of 'true' postcolonialism in thought and practice. If postcolonialism involves a critique of colonialism, we need to inquire whether any critique is at all possible outside of a historical and rational social analysis, that is, outside of modernist thought. To totally reject modernism would be to conflate critical thinking with colonial discourse, which is patently absurd. This volume, therefore, proposes a postcolonial critique which embraces a version of critical modernism while rejecting postmodernism as the indispensable epistemology of postcolonialist thought. The core themes of this volume consist of subject formation and socio-historical agency in the context of colonialism through an exploration of Rabindranath's opus. Given the multidimensionality of his life's work, I make a choice and exclude much of his literary, artistic and musical creations. The essays particularly speak to capitalist colonialism's hegemony and common sense from the standpoint of resistance, that is, the development of counter-hegemonic subjectivities, cultures and politics. The essays move away from the Hegelian master–bondsman paradigm often used in postcolonial studies, and also from the thematic of recognition and reciprocity found in much of the literature concerned with colonialism and social relations of power in general. Decolonization as understood here involves not only a transcendence beyond these frameworks, but actually begins from the premises of a new social critique, premises based on a humanistic universalist perspective as the point of departure.

Here something must also be said regarding the critical potential of humanism/universalism, because in postcolonial studies both hold a questionable status. They have been considered as abstractions or idealist devices for the concealment of actual socio-historical power relations and thus as inimical to authentic forms of anti-colonialism. As such, the notion of the human, or 'man', has been perceived as a colonizing epistemic instrument. We need to stress here that while a deployment of the concept of the human and of philosophical universalism has sometimes been incorporated in projects of colonialism and hegemony, this is not inevitably the case. Humanism and universalism cannot be considered as mere ideological occluding devices, but rather can hold significant critical possibilities. Rabindranath himself uses them as a philosophical stance for critique, but he was certainly very aware of colonial capitalism's annexation of enlightenment thought. He interprets the notion of the human and deploys universalist epistemology as elements of the enlightenment which survive capture by colonial capitalism. Furthermore, though idealism has served the purpose of a cartesian dualism of mind–body relations, Rabindranath's idealism is non-dualist and inter-constitutive through the mediation of shared human capacities, imagination and empathy. His approach certainly has a utopian dimension and conjures a wish-image, a category of desire. But in that capacity utopian idealism serves a critical purpose, because it becomes a referential horizon for projects of a fundamental critique of the nature of society and attempts for social transformation. By using idealism as a standing critique of the actual, Rabindranath rejects a positivist empiricism. What could or ought to be our utopian desires then become a receding horizon towards which we advance.

This kind of idealism is not the only content of Rabindranath's humanist understanding of society, culture and history. His humanist idealism also emerges from his deep awareness of his own location in colonial hegemony and his general understanding of inequality across the world. His approach thus inter-constitutes the social and the individual, the present and the past, the here and hereafter, in an epistemology that I call idealist modernism.[29] This implicates the idea of the universal human as a conceptual move towards 'decolonizing', thus making decolonization a part of universal history. Rabindranath's idealist approach is accompanied by an empirical rather than empiricist dimension, thereby placing India in the contemporary world, showing how the freedom of India is part of decolonizing history. His philosophical and critical framework, which begins in and with India, is necessarily extendable and applicable everywhere. It creates the problematic of decolonization in terms of the full development of the human, calling for a fundamental/radical transformation in consciousness and society. His idea of transformation goes beyond political economy and rejects the instrumentality inherent in nationalism as well as its unmediated, nativist, spontaneity. This view of decolonization is not to be bounded by the bourgeois notion of rights and laws of nature and state, but rather is rooted in the truth of the self, the development of a full personality and individuality, which Rabindranath sees as indispensable to the idea and project of freedom. In sum, the freedom of India relies on the same freedom aspired for and actualized in the rest of the world. He sees capitalist colonialism as a version of the same power relations that construct social reality everywhere.

What follows is a brief overview of the content of the essays in this volume in the light of its full scope. The first essay, 'The Self, The Individual and the Question of Modernity', scrutinizes Charles Taylor's claim in *Sources of the Self: The Making of the Modern Identity* (1989) that the ideas of an inner self and of an individual set apart from a customary collective belonging, as well as the ideas of humanism and freedom, are typically phenomena of modernity dating back to seventeenth-century Europe. If we are to take Taylor's argument seriously, then the presence of modernism in any form in non-bourgeois colonial India should be seen as a variant of colonial discourse, and therefore as civilizationally inauthentic. So, the use of these enlightenment/modernist ideas by subjects inhabiting colonies could not serve the project of genuine decolonization. I make here a distinction between subjects living in colonial spaces and an ideological construct termed 'colonial subject', in which it is assumed that the entire consciousness or being of those living in the colonies is reshaped by colonial hegemony. Taylor's assertion is contradicted by the way in which these 'modernist' concepts play out in the writings of Rabindranath. In all the genres of his writings and correspondence, these so-called modernist concepts actually serve as the epistemological and critical core of his transformational project. From his critique of nationalism and imperialism to artistic expressions of personal and spiritual fulfilment, Rabindranath develops a humanist philosophy, incorporating within it the ideas of an inner self, of being and becoming, of individual subjectivity and agency. Decolonization, understood in humanist universalist terms, rests on a deep sense of self and social awareness that evolves into an actively defined socio-historical identity. For Rabindranath, no antithesis exists between modernity and decolonization, since a substantive notion of self, human be-ing and a praxis of freedom can emerge in the colonized condition as in any other society based on relations of power. It is this sort of self-development and identity that is explored and expressed in Rabindranath's autobiographies, letters and critical reflections, culminating in the idea of a poet's identity. His idea of a 'poet' is a specific one: it does not only involve imagination and a romantic sensibility, but a critical and ethical dimension within its very aesthetic. A poet's freedom, or *swadhinata*, is therefore not qualitatively different or set apart from that of others. His idea of the human is not of a passive character of being, but rather of an individually active modernist one with the concreteness that comes from a struggling individual and social existence, which cannot be disconnected from an expanding sense of the world.

The second chapter, 'Rabindranath's Postcolonialism: A Vision of Decolonization and a Modernist Idealism', further explores the theme of modernity. It challenges the conventional assumptions of colonial discourse associated with modernism evident, for example, among postcolonial critics of Indian Subaltern Studies. In their view, Rabindranath's universalist modernist humanism cannot be the source of an authentic decolonization. In contrast, I explore Rabindranath's use of the ideas of modernism and identity as a complex of different types of modernity. Prominent in this is a particular type of modernity in the service of colonialism and another in the service of humanism, a universalist identification of the self or the individual. The latter is a critical anti-colonial modernity which I have termed idealist modernism. Even though Rabindranath is susceptible, at least in the earlier period of his work, to colonial modernity, he develops into his stance of idealist modernism by drawing on resources founded in Indian pre-colonial philosophy and ethics. This essay makes the point that the kind of modernity postulated by Rabindranath cannot be seen as either a spontaneous reaction or a mimicry, a repetition, of colonial discourse. Modernism and rationalism as practised either in India or in Europe cannot be qualitatively differentiated, dubbed pre-modern and modern (as in Charles Taylor), because Asia and Europe, conceived as Eurasia, have been historically, materially and creatively connected over many millennia. Therefore, we can recognize the absurdity of thinking that the definition and use of reason, its deployment in rationalist and universalist thought, should be the epistemological prerogative of any particular geographical space.

'Always Towards: Development and Nationalism in Rabindranath Tagore' considers further the two faces of modernity discussed in the previous essays. It harks back to the idea of modernity as having both a humanist and a capitalist colonial sense. The critical idealist or universalist understanding of the notion of the human in Rabindranath's works is a composite of Indian Vedantic, Greek philosophical and islamic rationalist tenets found in India, as well as of the principles of the European enlightenment, which can be directly connected to both Greece and islam. This perception is opposed to colonial modernity, in which reason is captured by militarized, mercantile and industrial capitalism, and in which it is converted to empiricist technological and instrumental rationality. This type of modernity Rabindranath identifies as a device for dehumanization, putting profit before people, prioritizing narcissism and greed and lust for power over human well-being. In this context, Rabindranath's approach to science and technology is unlike that of Gandhi. He does not reject science and industry per se, but encourages both when they serve human needs in production and creativity and relieve the dehumanizing aspects of labour. Science in its best sense of human inquiry into nature and the material universe in general, he supports wholeheartedly. The engagement of human capacity with nature and the material world does not exclude, for him, imagination and spirituality. This understanding helps Rabindranath in avoiding the ideological pitfalls of equating all forms of modernity with colonialism and all forms of tradition with anti-colonialism. Thinking outside the binary logic of colonial discourse, he dislocates the notion of the human from that of being a European, in the imitation of which the rest of the world cultures must devote themselves. The human for him is an embodied ethical and aesthetic being who is present everywhere. It calls for and exercises a moral imagination that is historically, but not unilinearly, evolving. Here Rabindranath works on two registers: that of ideality/possibility and actuality/the empirical. While recognizing that human beings have shown the capacity for any atrocity on each other or nature, at the ideal level Rabindranath's humanism expresses a trust in instances of compassion and empathy. Latent in human capacities, he sees possibilities for emancipation in a holistic sense. Thus, his view of modernity is to be distinguished from capitalist modernization in relentless pursuit for profit. Development here means human development, and it contains the connotation of always moving towards human well-being beyond the bounded horizon of the here and now. This view of human 'being' involves a perpetual 'becoming' and renewal.

'Home and the World: Women and Nationalism in the Novels of Rabindranath Tagore' offers us Rabindranath's critique of nationalism in socio-political and psychological terms. It brings out the complexities of Tagore's ideas of political subjectivities and agencies in the context of colonial Bengal and in other non-colonial social relations of power. It exposes how the politics of nationalism involves a mediatory relationship in social organization, especially with regard to the private and the public through the psycho-social embodiment of gender and sexuality in the figuration of the fictional protagonists. His criticism of nationalism here is expressed through his critique of patriarchy and narcissistic possessive individualism. The same narrowness and particularism for which he rejects merely political nationalism, he finds in gender relations and the family. For genuine freedom or decolonization ideas of nationalism and possessive individualism are rejected, since both neglect the development of a social individual and the emergence of a personal and creative identity as fundamental elements for the fashioning of a new individual and a new society. This stance clarifies Rabindranath's modernist humanism by contrasting the universalist 'new man', the bearer of a genuine freedom, with a narcissistic and anti-human nietzschean ideal of man. His rejection of nationalism as a psycho-social and political process posits a concurrence in the narrowness of reaction and the substitution of one ruler by the other. The ideal of freedom, which is the opposite of any relation of power and control, is the key to his vision of fundamental transformation, and it assumes a relational equality between the self and the other.

The next chapter, 'A Transformational Pedagogy: Reflections on Rabindranath Tagore's Project of Decolonization', explores Rabindranath's ideas and practices of education in the broad sense of social pedagogy, understood also philosophically. It examines these ideas and their institutional expressions in Santiniketan, established in 1901 for the schooling of children and adolescents that included programmes for art and music, and subsequently in the curriculum and teaching methods of the university Visva Bharati (established 1921). The essay also touches on the sister institution of Sriniketan, a centre of research and training for agricultural and horticultural sciences, as well as handicrafts. Thus, his idea of holistic education is realized by bringing the arts and sciences together, and it disarticulates education from the conventional service it provides for the production of commodities and the administration of wealth, as well as social and state control. Instrumental and institutional sense is replaced by a pedagogy for the transformation of social consciousness that only a humanist education might bring about. A better grasp of Rabindranath's idea of decolonization can be achieved by reading his interpretation of education in Gramscian terms of knowledge as hegemony, and also by referring to Paolo Freire's similarly transformational view of education as social conscientization. The essay further widens the scope of Rabindranath's philosophy of education by drawing from his visit to and positive assessment of the educational project of the then newly formed USSR.

The final chapter, 'Beyond the Binaries: Notes on Karl Marx's and Rabindranath Tagore's Ideas on Human Capacities and Alienation', brings together the basic themes of the previous ones. It particularly concentrates on relations of power which inflict harm in the shape of an overall alienation, preventing the full development of human capacities in the cognitive, practical and creative sense. The idea of alienation prompts us to consider Rabindranath and Marx comparatively. For neither of them is alienation considered an intrinsic aspect of the human condition. Nothing is predestined, as in the christian myth of the fall or the myth of 'human nature'. For both thinkers, alienation is socially produced and incumbent upon conditions of inequality at all levels, and is generated by historic relations of domination. Existence within conditions of domination makes it impossible to consider productive activity as being creative, joyful and self-fulfilling. Even when the process of the creation of objects and the final product has sensuousness, beauty and practical satisfaction for those who make and use them, they are ultimately distorted through market relations and money. Under these circumstances, the individual's sense of self and relations with others are diminished, and human creative potentials are not only actually unrealized but even prevented from being imagined. Thus considered, we find an overlap between the ideas of Rabindranath and Marx. As in Marx, Rabindranath also holds the view that social production and reproduction of any kind, when performed under oppressive circumstances, alienate people from what they make, from nature, from each other and, finally, from themselves. Their existence becomes one of securing survival. They live to work rather than work to live, and their creativity is subject to the necessity of generation of wealth for a social few. Neither Marx nor Rabindranath disconnects productivity from creativity and ethics. This situates the individual securely within a collectivity of others, and, as both point out, alienation is a result of a social organization which also shapes the natural environment in which we all live, whether rich or poor. They both require a thoroughgoing change in the mode of social organization that has placed people in a totalizing alienation.

Thus, Rabindranath and Marx share a radically emancipatory social vision, which also requires creating new imaginaries and types of human beings. Freedom, then, is freedom from conditions of alienation. Such freedom contains freedom from oppression, but also freedom to create non-oppressive social relations, ideas and practices. At this point, Marx and Rabindranath part company. While Rabindranath's modernism is idealism and understands the subjective aspect of the problem of alienation, Marx's historical materialism differs substantially in being able to comprehend both the subjective and actual material agencies and practices. They differ, therefore, in the way they understand the construction of alienation – one as a systemic mode of production, and the other mainly in ethical terms. Thus, how to achieve a substantive freedom or create a decolonized society through social analysis, and the consequent political practices based on the modes of mediation necessary for transforming the existing society into the ideal one, is missing from Rabindranath's transformative ideas and practices. Marx, however, grasps through his historical materialist method this principle of mediation and formulates a dialectical concept of class which results from that understanding, establishing thereby the connection between forms of consciousness and (existing) modes of production of capital. Rabindranath, though deeply aware of poverty, has no relational and productive understanding of class, but uses 'class' (*sreni*) in the Weberian sense of hierarchic stratification. He has no relational explanation connecting poverty and wealth. However, he severely denounces the dehumanization resulting from poverty and ongoing relations of power. Unlike Marx, Rabindranath does not think of and criticize private property in the means of social production, but he does question large-scale agricultural and industrial development connected to profit motives. In his economic thinking Rabindranath was a proponent of small and middle-sized agricultural cooperatives and productive enterprises. As a substantial landlord, he himself experimented with these economic models with some success. Though initially unaware of colonialism's ineluctable connection to capitalism, through his travel experiences in Europe, the United States, the Soviet Union, and Southeast and West Asia, as well as his experiences of the first and second world wars, he saw this truth clearly. Though many traditional marxists would dispute the attribution of humanism to Marx's thought, I would claim that his ideas of radical social transformation were animated by it. If it were not so, then there would be no point in advocating self and social emancipation through communist revolution. Rabindranath shared with Marx such a humanism, rooted in the real lives of people throughout history and enlivened by an ethical imperative. This would be the goal of decolonization, a movement towards a society based on true individual freedom and creativity.

Notes

[1] See Irfan Habib (2007), which has an excellent and most comprehensive introduction on the role played in general by cultural practices, especially religion, in the Indian polity. See also Romila Thapar (2017).

[2] Dalit, literally meaning 'oppressed', is a term referring to those who are outside of the four major castes in hinduism. It is a term created and adopted by those referred to as 'untouchables' in the 1880s to indicate their oppressed condition, giving it a political connotation of resistance to brahminical hinduism.

[3] See Tapan Basu *et al.* (1993); see also Achin Vanaik (2017).

[4] For a close study of the development of the Babri Masjid destruction, see A.G. Noorani (2014). Film director Anand Patwardhan documented the build-up and aftermath of this incident in his 1992 documentary, *Ram ke Nam* (In the Name of God). See also the 1994 sequel, *Pita, Putra aur Dharmayudha* (Father, Son and Holy War).

[5] Consider, for example, Israel and Iran, where state religion and neo-liberalism coexist.

[6] On the idea of the 'invention of tradition', see Hobsbawm and Ranger (1984). On the invention of India as an ideological category for ruling, see Himani Bannerji, 'Beyond the Ruling Category to What Actually Happens: Notes on James Mill's Historiography in *The History of British India*', in Bannerji (2020b).

[7] See Mamdani (1996) on the distinction between citizens and subjects. Though Mamdani explores neo-colonial states in Africa, his general critique applies across the board.

[8] Of the three, only the Hindu Mahasabha became a political party, in 1935. Regarding the ideology of the Arya Samaj and its dependence on Indological/ European orientalism, see Romila Thapar (2017). For the role that the aryan myth played in the nazi and other fascist parties, see also Uma Chakravarti (1989).

[9] '*Ghar wapsi*' (coming home) is a religious reconversion programme aimed towards dalits and the scheduled castes, initiated in India first by brahminical hindu right-wing organizations. This programme was intensified by the Vishwa Hindu Parishad (VHP) and the RSS from the last decades of the twentieth century. It serves the purpose of establishing the claim that islam, christianity, buddhism and sikhism were originally alien to hinduism, and of realizing the claim that India is essentially a hindu nation.

[10] The shift was evident in writers such as Jibanananda Das (1899–1954), Sudhindranath Dutta (1901–1960), Bishnu De (1909–1982), Buddhadeb Basu (1908–1974) and Subhash Mukhopadhyay (1919–2003).

[11] His songs spread extensively all over India, however. Two of his poems became the national anthems for India and Bangladesh respectively.

[12] The 'two nations' theory, in my opinion, emerged from the way British colonialism constructed the political constituency of colonial subjects in India, dividing them in two communities both governmentally and ideologically. The Muslim League made it a key principle for demanding Pakistan because hindus had been constructed as the majority population in India. A better understanding

of this hindu majoritarianism can be gleaned from the 1932 controversy between Gandhi and B.R. Ambedkar (1891–1956). See also Kancha Ilaiah (1996); Anand Teltumbde (2018); Irfan Habib (1995, 2011).

[13] For the major works of the founding figures of the RSS, see Golwalkar (1939, 1966) and Savarkar (1923). For a thorough discussion on them and their civil society organization, see Tapan Basu *et al.* (1993).

[14] The RSS family (*Sangh Parivar*) branched out in political party forms, eventually culminating in the Bharatiya Janata Party (BJP).

[15] The Ramayana, attributed to the sage-poet Valmiki around 500–100 BCE, was written in Sanskrit, but many regional versions developed in other Indian languages; see Romila Thapar (1992). The dates of the Mahabharata, an accretional Sanskrit epic attributed to the sage-poet Vyasa, are not precise. Third century BCE to fourth century CE is the probable time-span.

[16] The discipline of indology originated in the eighteenth century through the work of officials of the East India Company, the chief figure being William Jones, who founded the Asiatic Society of Bengal in then Calcutta in 1784. This is a branch of Oriental Studies spread in Europe through Persian scholarship which then shifted to Sanskrit, especially through linguistic studies in Germany. The work of Max Müller (1823–1900) had the most substantial influence on the development of the 'aryan', marking a shift from linguistics to territories and social groups, leading to the myth of aryan history and invention of a brahminical tradition.

[17] B.R. Ambedkar (1891–1956) headed the drafting committee of the constitution of India. He, along with Jawaharlal Nehru and others, entrenched equal citizenship and secularism in the constitution. He also emphasized that India must go beyond mere political democracy to social democracy. This view was also supported by the Indian National Congress.

[18] This type of modernism, which relies on the invention of tradition and use of popular religious myths and lore, has been a common device of civilizational/ cultural nationalists and is termed 'reactionary modernism'; see Herf (1989), which explains in the context of the role played by culture/ideology in politics, how the rejection of the rationalism of the enlightenment can also be a modernist approach. This ideological position uses religion, myths and so on as a hegemonic device, while being concordant to fascism, neo-liberalism and all other forms of capitalism.

[19] Here I draw on Fanon's distinction between 'true' and 'false' decolonization.

[20] See Goldberg (1993) for an in-depth formulation of a political-cultural discursive process.

[21] See, for example, in the plays of Shakespeare or Christopher Marlowe, the use of the cultures of the East signifying high culture and wealth.

[22] See Aijaz Ahmad (1992) for a critique of Said's ahistorical application of 'East' and 'West', though he agrees with Said in seeing such a discursive construction as a hegemonic device of capitalism.

[23] The other aspect to the essentialism of the hegemonic process is that, equally ideologically, it can resort to illicitly extending a discrete part or fragment of social

reality to substitute for the whole. For this paradoxical function of ideology, see Marx and Engels (1970).

[24] William Macaulay and James and John Stuart Mill, among others, with their utilitarian and liberal philosophy and political economy, were united in this view and devised suitable administrative and educational policies for ruling India.

[25] Especially in his letters, where he can be more private and direct.

[26] His grandfather Dwarakanath Tagore (1794–1846) and father Debendranath (1817–1905), along with Raja Rammohun Roy (1772–1833), founded the Brahmo Samaj as a strand within this third path.

[27] In keeping with this, Rabindranath's disappointment with Japan emerged from his rejection of imperialism and technological militarization, as well as his perception of it as a civilizational space mutating from eastern spirituality to western capitalist materialism. His dream of pan-Asianism ended with Japan's aggression in 1932 against China.

[28] This hyphenated way of representing 'being' introduces an active aspect of the notion of 'human'. It exceeds a static view of the human, found in people as they are, and includes within it an idea of becoming. To attain humanity requires an ethical aspect to living.

[29] See Himani Bannerji (2018) for my formulation of this idea, which I find subsequently being used by others. While the concept has been used since at least the 1980s mainly in art criticism, to my knowledge, my coinage of this term analytically in the social sciences was new.

1

The Self, the Individual and the Question of Modernity

> So we come to think that we 'have' selves as we have heads. But the very idea that we have or are 'a self', that human agency is essentially defined as 'the self' is a linguistic reflection of our modern understanding and the radical reflexivity it involves. ... But it was always not so.
>
> – Charles Taylor, *Sources of the Self* (1989: 177)

In reading Rabindranath, one constantly comes across ideas of the self and the individual, two ideas which he considers connected but not identical. Treated as philosophical and experiential notions, they serve him variously as sources of reflection, critique and creativity. These ideas are central to Rabindranath's emphasis on the sense and idea of an inner self as vitally necessary for the development of individual identity. In the above epigraph, however, Charles Taylor presents the idea of an inner self and its conceptual correlates, such as the individual, as components of 'modernity', a complex of socio-cultural and political beliefs and practices which he particularly locates in and identifies with seventeenth-century Europe, the era of bourgeois development. He makes an equation between modernity, an interiorized sense of self distinct from the christian notion of the soul, and the emergence of the individual. He emphasizes the novelty of this development, even for Europe, by stating that 'it was always not so'. His *Sources of the Self: The Making of the Modern Identity* (Taylor 1989) explores the proposition and the emergence of the idea of a self-possessive individual subject who should be considered 'a linguistic reflection of our modern understanding'. The whole text recounts the long and complicated journey that Europe made in arriving at this stage. Such an exclusive association of the inner self and its elaborative constellation of ideas with a bourgeois European world-view and sensibility, however, is reificatory and fixes the notion of modernity to an exclusive spatio-temporal zone. This prompts us to question the exclusivity and the fixity of this association, and the very meaning of the concept of modernity. The literary, cultural and philosophical presence of ideas categorized as modern by Taylor enjoins us to engage in a thorough scrutiny of the idea of modernity itself, and to search for alternative and/or supplementary sources of genealogies tasked for understanding it.

In fact, Europe itself needs to be examined socio-historically for variations and complications of this theme of modernity and its discursive modes. This is important because the notions of an interior self, the individual with a self-conscious reflexivity and specific personality, as outlined by Taylor, are also to be found in their formation or fullness in India and other non-European spaces. Resources for reasonability and creativity, for ethical relations and moral insights inseparable from ideas of a self, of a personal and social subject, of an individual and collective identity, all qualities generally associated with modernity, provide the bases and points of departure for radical social transformation everywhere. This version of modernity includes the idea of the 'other' in compounding the notion of the self and relies on the assumption of shared sensuous, including intellectual, capacities. Thus, endowed equally to all humans, these same human capacities, which are susceptible to socio-historical variations, produce similar content in Europe and elsewhere. This ubiquitous presence of human capacities encourages us to think of the particular or the individual in a relation of mutuality with the universal, and as such the inner self and the social being of an individual do not contradict but are enfolded in the idea of the human. Understood thus in humanist terms, the self and the other, the individual and the universal, provide the premises of a non-narcissistic self and the claim that not all possible human relations lead to antagonism, restraint or domination. Eschewing intrinsic power relations between the self and the other in order to build a universalist understanding of human freedom, a pathway is created towards an uncompromised decolonization. To substantiate this point, I will examine Rabindranath Tagore's (1861–1941) social and political thought. Such an examination needs to be briefly contextualized to Tagore's background.

Rabindranath was born in Bengal, a region of India colonized by the British in the eighteenth century, into a wealthy and culturally elite family. He was born in Calcutta, the capital city of the British empire after London, at a time of transition when a feudal and mercantile socio-economic system, with some rudimentary features of capitalism, was caught in the grip of an ascending capitalist colonialism. This transition led to the destruction of the pre-existing economy, purposely creating a semi-feudal plantation system and commercial social relations and practices that served a thriving British industrial capitalism. Thus, the character of colonial capitalism evolving in India was distorted, uneven, inadequately differentiated, exclusive of Indian participation in important sectors and under-capitalized.

But even under these deformed colonial socio-economic circumstances, Rabindranath's philosophical and social thoughts on the self, the individual and society, as well as his vision for a humanist or true decolonization, are substantive and modernist. They are multidimensional and compounded with both non-European and European thought. They are not primarily derivative of colonial discourse, as suggested by the logic of Charles Taylor's argument or, for that matter, argued by Indian Subaltern Studies.[1] Rabindranath's idea of the inner self, which is ineffable but always present in any state of individual being, as in modernity addressed by Charles Taylor, should also be distinguished from the doctrinal idea of the soul, because his sense of an inner self is imbued with a capacity for social involvement. With the accumulation of experiences of living in the world and with temporal awareness, this self is a compass for the development of a recognizable personality integral to being an individual. Such a philosophy of a socially responsive self relieves Rabindranath of the charge of being a derivative thinker engaged in the mimicry of western/modernist thought. His works show him as an Indian modernist thinker open to ideas of the European enlightenment, but selectively and without any particular affiliation with seventeenth-century Europe. It should be noted that Rabindranath's philosophy or social thought, his modernism, shows access to and acceptance of not only European ideas and cultural forms, but also of conceptual resources originating in India and other parts of Asia. The overall result is a type of modernism which, though at times susceptible to colonial discourse, is far from being that, as exemplified by his complete rejection of nationalism, caste, religious communalism and appeals to tradition in general. This kind of modernist philosophical disposition is to be found not only in Rabindranath, but also in many of his Indian predecessors and contemporaries. They were historically open to ideas and cultural forms arriving in Bengal and other parts of India from Europe, as well as from West and Central Asia. Over a very long period of history, incoming ideas and practices, which ranged from providing modalities of ruling to organizing the economy, philosophy and the arts, were historically absorbed or acculturated among the peoples living in the geographical space of India. This phenomenon may account for the fact that when a pressing time came with the colonial acquisition of power, Indians did not consider European or British thought as wholly alien, opaque or incomprehensible, irrespective of their agreement or disagreement with it.

History shows that the basis for intelligibility that was established over millennia continued to be present in the communication of Indians with diverse others, and this intelligibility is therefore not to be regarded as an immediate accidental and imitational factor. The large geographical space shared between the joined continents of Europe and Asia contained a great wealth of Greek and Perso-Arabic thought, of different kinds of philosophy, science, art, craft, religion and culture, and those traditions were a common heritage. As for the Europeans, their ideas of and relations to India changed over time as they developed their productive forces and political apparatuses, and moved from monarchic feudalism and mercantilism to large-scale industrial production and a capitalist colonizing state which captured a large part of India. The type of modernity which characterized European colonial discourse in the post-enlightenment era specifically arrived in India in the latter half of the eighteenth and into the nineteenth century. It was then that ideas such as that of the Orient, race and social darwinism, or British forms of property and administrative and civil laws, were introduced and diffused. They were indeed new and different from the earlier social, cultural and economic practices and values, and were the major means for establishing colonial hegemony. But equally, they also drew upon pre-established ruling relations, ideas and practices. Furthermore, like all hegemonic projects, their success was incomplete. Even when these hegemonic discursive and ruling devices were disagreed with and resisted, they were still comprehensible and absorbed into the indigenous social formations and cultural realms.

All of these factors help in explaining and challenging the essentialist civilizational otherizing forms of thinking and conceptual spatialization found in the philosophical and social thought of Charles Taylor and others.[2] My aim here is to explore these issues through the openings provided by Rabindranath's writings and thus to challenge the dualistic or binary epistemology articulated upon such paradigms, especially in postcolonial studies. Of particular interest are arguments constructed on the paradigm of tradition versus modernity offered as critical solutions to the problem of colonial discourse. This gesture in the name of critique leads to repeating the very discourse we seek to challenge and misleads us to the same essentialist spatial culturalism. By examining some of Rabindranath's prose writings,[3] I would like to demonstrate that 'modernism' is a highly complex – even contradictorily evolved and organized – concept. It has many registers and contains an amalgam of thoughts from different but continuous historical moments, social organizations and geographical spaces. In fact, the question of the origins of the conceptual complex called modernity, and an insistence upon the authenticity of its constructive elements, are actually immaterial or even irrelevant. What is important for a true critique is the usefulness of the synthesis of philosophical views and epistemological approaches, originating no matter where, for creating an explanatory device. What we need is a type of social and political thought that is comprehensive, and which dispenses with over-generalized civilizational essentialism or universalist claims for particularized forms of thought.

From this critical standpoint we can show that Rabindranath's world-view, with its emphasis on an individuality imbued with an awareness of an inner self, is, contrary to Charles Taylor's view, one of critical idealism rather than an idealistically disguised particularism. In this way, Rabindranath goes far in formulating a project of humanist freedom, which should characterize a true decolonization, brought about by the work of self-realized individuals in the process of continual self-generation. Of course, this universalist humanism is idealist, but it is not empty of content because the notion of freedom intrinsic to it is ethical – that is, socially aware and critical rather than narcissistic and competitive. Thus Rabindranath is equally unsparing to all sides involved in the colonial project. He exposes the destructive capacities of traditionalist/casteist hierarchical hinduism, as well as of hyper-exploitive capitalist colonialism with its cultural and pseudo-scientific biological racism.

The epistemology underlying Rabindranath's social thought differs from that of cultural essentialists – such as Charles Taylor – and exemplifies signally important aspects of the modernist thought of his times. Furthermore, his views were not atypical among Indian thinkers of his period. He inhabited widely ranging milieux, in which a number of his contemporaries disagreed with him while others were in firm support.[4] He in particular provided the most significant synthesis of historically old and new and so-called eastern and western concepts and values. Relying on their familiarity with various historical and social ideas, a portion of the Indian elite were adept at mixing European enlightenment thought with the

Indian to suit their philosophical and critical needs. Rabindranath also did this, but he was particularly competent at providing critical and enduring insights into socio-political developments in India and elsewhere.

Before going any further in our exposition, we need to explore further the complex concept of 'modernity'. Intellectual history supports the case that a significant shift occurred in European social and political thought during the seventeenth century, both building on and reversing the meanings of key concepts and their deployments in the previous feudal era. Raymond Williams captures this shift meticulously in his *Keywords* (1976). He shows how in the purview and needs of rising capitalism entire discourses, and thus the meanings of words, changed radically. He provides the example of how the word 'individual' changed in meaning from indicating a person's indivisibility from the social collective or community, into one of a divided, discrete personal unit (Williams 1976: 161–65). The advent of the enlightenment shifted the philosophical tenets from the previous period's emphasis on christian community to secularism and the assertion of the individual and shared human capacity for reason. A secular humanist outlook and a rationalist and scientific world-view spread in tandem. Together, these emphases spell out the ideas of and the necessity for a personal conscience, for individualism in social terms, and for criticism for the sake of improvement and the progress of society. In religious terms, the enlightenment thinkers mostly evade the question of faith by adopting agnosticism, and occasionally atheism. The conceptual complex of modernism is constituted with these ideas and their allied elements. Reaction to these enlightenment tenets came in the shape of extreme counter-reformationist interpretations of religion, along with political conservatism, irrationalism and atavism. But simultaneously, and of equal importance, the modernist appeal to universal reason and secular humanism accompanying the demotion of institutionalized religion inspired a call for the activation of imagination and an encouragement to project into and perceive sublimity and spirituality in nature. With this came an emphasis on cultural pursuits, artistic development and the cultivation of sensibilities as well as utopian visions of social change or world-making. What we now call romanticism contains these notions, and coexists in coherence with as well as in contradiction to discourses of reason and humanism.

Returning to Rabindranath, we find that celebrating the emergence of an individually differentiated consciousness dedicated to a project of freedom from fetters of power relations to achieve a society of self-aware, self-possessing, reflective individuals, identifies his thought/philosophy as a certain type of modernism. In this, his thought contains certain aspects of enlightenment thought at a stage of its development when it was not mutated by capitalist colonialism. The largely pre-colonial era of enlightenment thought could not become colonial discourse because either practically or ideologically, capitalism had not yet become fully developed. Rabindranath's work also displays some influence of colonial discourse, given the circumstances under which his thinking evolved. We see in his work influences and uses of early enlightenment thought, as well as traits of colonial discourse. Many of his reflections and critical self-consciousness are wrangling with it. In an overall assessment, Rabindranath is a modernist thinker. To get a true measure of this modernism, our understanding of modernity and modernism needs to be flexible and comprehensive, and they need to be exposed as conceptual constellations with various traits of content and form, ranging from romanticism to reason and allied ideas, without any necessary synthetic resolution.

With many interpretations conferred upon these notions in various historical and social contexts and for various political and cultural reasons, modernity and modernism are both vast and indeterminate in their scope. Though connected at their root, the terms also have some specific connotations. While modernity indicates social norms and forms, it is primarily value-bound but not specific as to what forms or expression it has to take. Modernism, though it also shares the value connotations with modernity, is strongly connected to expressive or formal characteristics, making it into an aesthetic movement as well.[5] Of particular importance for us is the use of these concepts from the 1970s onwards, when modernity, modernism and their conceptual derivatives began to mark out a discursive colonial hegemony. In postcolonial studies, the notion of modernity was transformed from its early enlightenment character and modified into a binary paradigm in which it held a definitionally referential and opposing relationship to the concept of tradition. In this formulation the concepts of modernism, modernity and tradition lost their substantive meanings and came to be used in referential and antithetical terms in their connotations. Within this binary paradigm, modernity began to stand for subordination to colonialism and tradition unequivocally for indigenous agency/resistance. This clearcut ideological dualism gradually gave way to a more sophisticated understanding of these concepts, as necessitated by attempts of internal critique. The unity presupposed within the sphere of each concept, perceived as homogeneous faces of epistemological duality, needed to undergo fracturing through class analysis and critiques of race, caste and patriarchy. As such, modernity and tradition were both subjected to internal critique, and there were as many questions surrounding the concept of tradition as of modernity. A simple equation between tradition and resistance, and modernity and colonial hegemony, underwent changes. It was found that not only were some traditions oppressive for the indigenous population, but some had no provenance in the past. Thus, whole fields of enquiry developed around the invention of histories, traditions and customs in certain socio-political contexts. Similarly, the concept of modernity also lost its homogeneity and ceased to be equated with colonial hegemony; it has come to be seen as no longer incompatible with genuine anti-colonialism, and it may even become necessary for it. Modernity and tradition have thus taken on nuanced, complicated and even self-contradictory meanings. For these reasons, any discussion of Rabindranath's ideas on decolonization and his critique of nationalism cannot forego the ideas and practices of modernity and modernism.[6] They are constant textual presences in his social and political thought under different names. The essays here speak to many such uses and presences. With regard to Rabindranath, modernity has sometimes taken on adjectives. Other than universalist/modernist humanism, idealist modernism or contextualized modernism have functioned as synonymous with modernism. This flexibility in apprehending modernism is fundamentally connected to rethinking anti-colonialism through various internationalist, cosmopolitan and universalist world-views and politics. Anti-capitalist and anti-imperialist critiques cannot reject modernism in toto.

Focusing our attention on the notion of an inner self as a signifier of modernity, let us examine Rabindranath's writings. In exploring and expressing the idea of the self in its innermost sense in human terms, Rabindranath turns to the metaphor of the child (*shishu*). This metaphor is to be found in both India and the west. This romantically imagined child figure is not only symbolic of innocence,[7] but is also the germ of the self. In time and through interactions and social processes, this child will become what William Wordsworth (1770–1850) called 'the father of the man'.[8] The child will be gone in time, but will also be there in an organic development towards lifelong human be-ing, realizing, circumstances permitting, his capacities to their full potential. In this view, attaining humanity attributes a conscious and ethical aspect to living. This figure of the child as the essence of the self Rabindranath finds both in the Indian Upanishads,[9] and in the ideas and portrayals of childhood in European romantic literature and social philosophy.[10] It is ubiquitously present in Rabindranath's literature, music, and pedagogical ideas and practices, and allows him to work at the same time on the two registers of being and becoming of the self. Growing up through myriad social and interpersonal experiences and activities, through processes of internalization and externalization, of subject formation and expressiveness, this child is at the core of his humanism and is the existential basis of universalism. Simultaneously, this child evolves into an individual with an identifiable personality.

The child's/self's education is a lifelong and holistic one, consisting of the education of sensibilities, emotions and a discerning morality. It is endowed with aesthetic and creative dimensions. Such a be-ing of the human embraces external and internal nature, and is capacitated to create new things – that is, not only to repeat. The metaphor of the child is a governing figure in Rabindranath's philosophy, and therefore a force for radical inventiveness and innovation which connects imagination to daily life, society and expressive cultural activities. It connects social transformation with forms of consciousness and the making and transforming of art. This in-forming relationship between self, society and individual asserts an idea of freedom which is humanist or non-instrumental, and implicates the concept of freedom in reason. For Rabindranath, this desire for a substantive rather than a relative freedom, a freedom to or for instead of freedom from, is at the heart of all human be-ing and is present universally. Furthermore, conscious will and agency, rather than a compulsion and habit, provide the motive force for individual development, that is, the emergence of an identifiable personality. This making of the human, as Rabindranath put forward, is not a purely idealist excursion. Though projecting beyond the empirical, the idea of the human comprehends the existential and experiential, thereby becoming social and expanding in concentric circles in mutual relationships to others, relationships which need not be only positive or agonistic.

At this point in our discussion of Rabindranath's modernism, we need to return to the earlier mentioned metaphor of *shishu*, the child, to explore the ground zero of his idea of pure awareness as the self begins its journey towards human be-ing. As the vastness of Rabindranath's opus imposes restrictions on how much material can be drawn upon, I will mainly use some of his descriptions and comments on the child, as well as his autobiographical reminiscences, reflections and a selection of letters. They will be treated thematically rather than linearly or chronologically, tracing a loose order among his ideas of the self, individuality or personality, up to his arrival at the point of recognition of universal humanity. Within this framework, he affirms his identity as a poet, a musician and a painter, as well as a pedagogue and a participant in radical social transformation.

Self, Other and the World

We begin with a reminder of the centrality of the concept of self that pervades Rabindranath's thinking. He sees the constitution of the self as two-fold: one, a form of self-awareness residing within a person; the other, a self-awareness which is susceptible to the particular society and history in which a person lives. The first consists of a sense of the universal; the second is experiential and socially relational. His idea of the human is both imaginative and spatio-temporal. In his autobiographical writings, he depicts how the totality of the individual, consisting of these two aspects of the self, resides in a spatial sense of 'here' and 'there' as well as a temporal sense of 'now' and 'then'. This self is a composite moving along an axis of dynamic time–space intersection, with an ever-present self-awareness. This dialectic of the self emerging from these two aspects constitutes the self's individual identity. This identity reflects a given space and time, but also projects into the future, expressing an in-forming relationship between being and becoming. In this sense, the poet's being, the mode of existence of a poet, is both transient and permanent, as the poet is an actual person born in a social setting mediated by its social relations, and is steeped in the surrounding environment and culture, while also sharing with fellow humans basic sensuous capacities and needs. In this formulation, difference from others and oneness with them serve as the bedrock of human identity. Rabindranath speaks of this composite self as *atma*, implying something akin to the soul, while also using the word in the sense of possession and awareness of one's own individual being. *Atma* consists of these two aspects – an ineffable awareness and experience as *ananda* (joy), which is its originary source of self-reference and self-renewal, and *rup*, indicating both form and beauty. The aspect of *rup* is the modality of expressing *ananda* in multifarious ways and through created objects. These two aspects together constitute human imaginative and creative capacity and object-producing artistic expression in the broadest sense. Bringing about a dialectic of boundless *ananda* with a myriad of *rup* or defined forms is the core task of being human, implying a general aesthetic sense. What a human being perceives and feels, or makes and externalizes, is both bounded and free, perishable and imperishable, as every form (social or aesthetic) yields place to another. Being human consists of the *ananda* within, which is *arup* (formless), in a creative relationship with the plenitude of *rup*. Thus, just as the presence of flux is everywhere, so also the promise of renewal is ever-present.

Rabindranath's discourse of the self may give an impression of a religious way of thinking, but we need to understand that this discourse, although idealist and spiritual, is not religious and dogmatic in a ritualistic and institutional sense. It is still secular in not identifying with any religion, and it has no originary world-view. Its spirituality is philosophical, contemplative and imaginative, and is predicated upon the modernist notion of an ever-present awareness of an inner self. Here the self feels itself in a nameless way, while it can also reflect upon itself. Though idealist in one sense, it is social and material in the other.[11] It involves the shaping and making of the self and the world we live in, and elaborates a durable medium of communication with others near and distant. The socialization of the self is intrinsic to having a self. In this chapter I show how Rabindranath uncovers a notion of the self both directly as it evolves towards the identity of a poet, and indirectly by infusing his idea of a poet with a universalist humanism. As mentioned above, the core self, captured in the metaphor of the child and the growing up of the child, evolves into what Rabindranath has become now at the time of writing his reminiscences (though this child is constructed from an adult viewpoint). This is a process that all humans undergo. Its outcome is not predestined, and it involves subject formation and the emergence of an identity in every case. This hindsight through self-representation is modernist and outlines a formative history as the self or the individual subject becomes an 'object' in mutual relations with others. Such retrospective writings involve one's own self becoming an imaginative construct, an object to the author, because it is not simply a process of memorializing but the creation of an identifiable personality which is put together from the memorial components.

The writing of memoirs or interest in self-portraits is a modernist occupation. Rousseau's autobiography and other memorializing writings are secular enterprises involving a sense of an inner self and the development of an individuality in personal character traits. It is the same with Rabindranath. In *Chhelebala* (Childhood) and *Jibansmriti* (Reminiscences), the self is recuperated as a sentient experiential being, starting with the moment when the self is aware but not articulate (Tagore 1912a, 1940). A bundle of mental and physical capacities with limited practical abilities, the early self is a potential, a proclivity, a temperament. Longing to journey forth, this self stores life experiences through historical time and social interactions; thus, it is imbricated in cultural and socio-political events. These processes of development and differentiation of the 'self' are necessarily rooted in the sense of the 'other', personal and communal[12] – the world gradually comes into him as he enters the world, resulting in a content developed from experiences and activities which actualize and grow the human capacities of the child. This dialectical inter-constitution arises from the self's formative movement with the other in a plural sense, shifting at the same time the self's location and relationship with the inside and outside.

In Tagore's memoirs, 'being' is simultaneously an immediate self-awareness and an existence in lived time. It is not an abstraction, an empty signifier or a conceptual container to be filled later by experiential, cognitive and relational content. From the moment of birth, as with all children, the child Rabindranath enters into expanding self–other relations. This activates and refines his human capacities and potentialities of individuation. He gradually develops an environmental or spatial awareness and absorbs social mores. Thus, as an embodied being he develops specificities as he continues to live at the axes of historical time, and so of changing society. Ignoring this fact misleads us into converting the idea of 'being' into an abstraction unconnected to any content, in which the idea of 'becoming' and the 'making'/'changing' of the social self lacks concreteness. In actuality, the journey of the self is marked by both retention and changes, by a flowing form of subjectivity, gradually acquiring a palpable identity and social agency. In keeping with his own development, Rabindranath's conception of the child has aesthetic/imaginative aspects as well as a pedagogical one, since the child is open to the world and is intrinsically a learning being with a will and an agency for self and social transformation. The child's developmental process gives rise to the tropes of the 'new' and renewal, which Rabindranath captures especially in his literary writings. The 'child' is thus a figure of innocence with a potentiality for developing into an adult social individual, active in the world yet endowed with an innate capacity for wonder, play and creativity. The self within the child remains as a creative principle, not just a memory, at the core of the adult in all stages and changes. This dynamic creative process has been captured in European romantic literature through autobiographies and the genre of *bildungsroman.*[13]

Rabindranath's *Reminiscences* describe social mores, family relations, household organization and decor – the architecture of the life-space of the

Tagore family. The child Rabi is a memorial creation through selection of details of significant experiences and events. The energy of imagination and discernment involved in remembering fuses the details into the making of a particular child-self. This forging of a self in the crucible of experience and imagination, aided by expressive capacities, remains the subject's characteristic to the last minute of his life. The child of these memoirs is 'now' the adult Rabindranath writing about the child, the self 'then', that he remembers. This self is a poetic construction and more than a selection of details, as it involves an ongoing process of sorting, distinguishing and making which results in a collaged form of identity. Because the child in our own past cannot be directly accessed by the adult self, it is through the retrieval of his child-self that Rabindranath advances the idea of the child as true for everyone in general. All autobiographical writings recreate the past by recovering, reordering and reconfiguring memories of events and experiences from the standpoint of 'now'. The process includes both voluntary selection and rejection, but also, according to Rabindranath, involuntary memories and feelings that recollection triggers in us.[14] Lived time in the past, as well as in the present, forms a canvas on which the self-portrait of the poet is drawn. This memorial activity brings out a self from seclusion, from the protected realm of the family, from within the child's hiding spaces of consciousness and architecture where his imagination runs free.

Echoing these sentiments, Rabindranath tells us in the preface to his *Reminiscences* that 'life memories are not life history' (Tagore 1940: 6). What interests him are flashes of memory or 'memory pictures' (ibid.), and self-discovery made through the process of recuperative narration. Not mere copies of life, it is with images and feelings arranged and rearranged that he creates his child-self, which deepens with time his sense of individuality and personality until it settles into the comprehensive identity of a poet. He compares his reminiscences with paintings by an inner invisible painter who has, unbeknownst to the rational consciousness of the poet, already selected the details, colours and overall design of the painting. The memoirs (both *Chhelebela* and *Jibansmriti*) also paint the child Rabi's growing awareness of what he would later know as colonialism. Eventually, in response to this, he would write of a substantive 'Indian' culture composed of diverse eastern and western sources. The manhood of this child Rabindranath would be spent in designing this composite Indian culture, resting on the universalist idea of the human in the face of colonialism and power relations within Indian society.

Rabindranath's self-portrait contains a multidimensional arrangement of space. The inside and outside living spaces of the family household have their architectural and relational correlates. The 'now' and 'then' of time are complemented by the 'here' and 'there' of space. In this, time itself assumes a spatial quality – it is a space consisting of a remembered reality. The public and the private, home and the world, inside and outside, the individual and the social, the personal and the institutional, the national and the international, are spatio-temporal categories which play both binary and dialectical roles in his memorialization. They mark out differences and divisions between the individual and the social, as well as formative identifications and unity of perception and experience. Together they offer us the concreteness of Rabindranath's way of be-ing human evolving into becoming. Thus, Rabindranath's memoirs or life-pictures make emotional, experiential and physical spaces something other than a mere container of the self or the subject. Space in this sense is not to be treated as a box, a room or a womb inhabited by a body with a mind. This space is cultural and social, at once the inside and the outside, moving in two overlapping and concentric circles with the self in the centre. As such, the organization of the space of the life-environment and lived time is not an intersectional reality, since the memorial content is not separable from the concrete existence in the past.

This concentric movement and its concreteness are vividly presented in Rabindranath's descriptions of the child Rabi, gazing out at the garden from within the confines of a small servant's room. The child sits beside the window bars looking at the family pond, with daily activities taking place around and in it. Trees are reflected in the pond, people bathe in it and perform other tasks. The bathers' habits and quirks are described with the precision of a humorist or cartoonist. The pond's solitude also draws the child to it in the afternoon, after the day's bustle is over: 'When the pond was deserted, my attention was attracted by the lower part of the trunk of the banyan tree. Its areal roots cascading down, created a deep, mysterious darkness. In the mystery of this almost invisible nook it seemed that all known mores of the world were suspended' (Tagore 1961b: 10).[15] Looking at it, he felt that '[b]y accident a kingdom of the impossible, escaping God's wrath, existed right in the middle of broad daylight' (ibid.).

This child Rabi was simultaneously an insider and an outsider. The 'outside' in its quality of 'otherness', of 'not-here', was more palpable due to the child's location in a closed room. From his vantage point the family household itself was a divided space, though the presence of adult men, women, girls, boys and young children infused the life both inside and outside. The social organization of this familial space is described by Rabindranath thus:

> We were forbidden to go to the outer part of the house. Even within the inner quarters we [boys] could not wander freely. So, we saw the world from within a seclusion. The something called 'outside' was beyond my reach, yet its appearances, sounds and smells touched me suddenly for a moment through the openings of doors and windows. (Ibid.: 11)

As a boy child of a wealthy family Rabindranath was left, along with his cousins and nephews, to the care of male rather than female servants. Though a part of the inner world involving the upbringing of boys, it was an enclosure guarded by these male servants: 'We were under the discipline of servants. To simplify their own tasks, they nearly stopped all our mobility. But no matter how tight was their bondage, from our point of view their general neglect of us offered a great freedom – our minds were left free' (ibid.: 9). The exclusion of this young child from the 'outside' made his pleasures and freedoms seem infinite. With his gaze focused outward he was inexorably drawn to its mysterious expanding spaces. This intense feeling prompts Rabindranath to say: 'In those days the thing called the world had an intense taste.... [I]t was the earth itself, [with its] water, trees, vegetation and the sky, which spoke to me. It never allowed my mind any indifference' (ibid.: 14). The young Rabi not only wanted to range over the earth's surface, but he was struck with the desire of 'wanting to go *into* the earth, below its dull mud-coloured cover' (ibid.).

A Child in Colonial Bengal

These recollections of childhood made from the adult poet's standpoint contain the elements of a future individual identity as he emerged through life. He portrays a child in the process of gathering content for his creative and expressive powers, and thus enhancing his imaginative and formative capacities. This is a portrait of a poet in the making during the phase of a particular Bengali family at the moment of colonial encounter. The child Rabindranath grows up within the parameter of capitalist colonialism infiltrating and shaping India.[16] The history of this society becomes the child Rabi's individual experience of that reality. The particularities of these experiences are those of a child in an elite family living in a city created precisely by the needs of colonial administration, as Calcutta was the centre of British rule until 1911. An understanding of his social being or growing subjectivity requires a recounting of this social setting.

Rabindranath's own family wealth came substantially from business collaboration with the English and through land ownership. The joint-stock enterprise of Carr, Tagore and Company, launched by his grandfather Dwarakanath Tagore (1794–1846), was one of the earliest such ventures in colonial Bengal. Dwarakanath was a convinced anglophile who visited England twice and died there (mysteriously) in 1846. The familial culture of the Tagores consisted of the new Anglo-Bengali lifestyle pursued by urban upper-class 'natives'. This was particularly true with respect to their public life, including their modes of pleasure and leisure. Though with Dwarakanath's absence and death the business was bankrupted and the family lost its opulence, they continued to be the owners of vast landed estates shared across the large joint family.[17] In this they benefited from British rule, especially through Lord Cornwallis's Permanent Settlement Act of 1792.[18] As landlords living in Calcutta, they also continued to emulate some aspects of pre-existing courtly culture rooted in Bengal's aristocracy of muslim *nawab*s, whom the British defeated in 1756. This mixture of courtly and British cultures provided the template of a new elite colonial lifestyle. The religious practices of this family were also not typically 'hindu', as they rejected idol worship and strict caste practices. Dwarakanath and Rabindranath's father, Debendranath Tagore (1817–1905), were founder figures of Brahmo Samaj, which was chiefly initiated by Raja Rammohan Roy (1772–1833). Brahmo Samaj, a socially and spiritually reformed hinduism, was of unitarian persuasion, drawing on a monotheistic strand of Indian philosophy (the Upanishads) and some of the basic tenets of the kind of islam (sunni) prevalent in India. The brahmo form of worship was non-ritualistic, rejected idol worship and involved meditation on the one true spirit pervading the universe, the essence of all consciousness. The social location of Tagore's family was thus in a liminal space between the 'old' and the 'new' – between the 'emergent' and the 'residual' economic and cultural life (Williams 1985). Rabindranath himself spoke of the unique situation of his family: 'The uniqueness that arose in the family in its isolation was natural … an island cut off and isolated from a continent. So, there was a characteristic style to our language [known as] Tagore speak' (Tagore 2009a: 51). We might add here another statement regarding the family's modernity: 'Even before I was born our family had raised its social anchor and drifted away from conventional moorings. Codes and regulations [hindu ones] played little part in it' (ibid.). Their relationship to the new government was on the whole peaceable, indicated by the older brother Satyendranath Tagore's (1842–1923) employment as the first 'native' appointee of the British Indian Civil Service. With its roots in older pre-existing cultures and yet open to foreign influences, the Tagore family played an enormous role in the making of 'modern' Bengali culture.[19]

This mixture of socio-cultural relations and forms of consciousness shaped the child Rabindranath. The notion of difference and the act of differentiating were essential ingredients in his self-development. The difference between brahmos and conventional hindus became clearer when the adolescent Rabindranath was socialized into the adult male culture of his family, marked by new British and older feudal styles. Tagore's sense of temporality of the 'then' and the 'now' thus reflects the transformation of feudal ways of living and thinking in the urbanization of the Bengali elite. In *Atmaparichay* (Of Myself), Rabindranath speaks to this transitional time: 'I arrived when the old time had just retreated from this house and a new age had barely descended ...' (Tagore 2009a: 51). Initially, in his own childhood, he took imaginative refuge in the spaces of 'then' or the past to observe the moment of 'now' with more perspicacity. In the organization of the feudal household, the *andarmahal* (inner quarters) consisted of a space for women, servants and children. Within this space little had changed over time, and it offered him a vantage place for seeing the daily life of the inner quarters, as did the cast-off furniture and older modes of transportation such as the palanquin. The nature of time in the *andarmahal* and in these secret spaces for a child to hide in made him feel free, outside of the clock time of the public 'outer' quarters (*bahirmahal*) of the male world. We see a nostalgia in his memoirs at the disappearance of the inner space, gradually taken over by the modern ordering of life and by the mores of public institutions through the induction of daily discipline. He felt this un-freeness of the outer world as inimical to the freedom that the child-self needs in order to grow. In this confused setting of then and now, in the interstices of a semi-feudal, semi-colonial and emerging features of a bourgeois family, Rabindranath experienced a kind of unsupervised 'growing up'. He was largely left to his own devices, without a consistently organized 'upbringing'. His earliest sense of 'being' and 'becoming' was formed in those unsettled times of childhood, the fused diverse cultural life of his youth. Institutional education was optional, as with many wealthy families in those days, since no pressure existed for pursuing a career or a profession. Subsequently, as an adult, he managed his father's considerable landholdings and was thus integrated into the property basis of the family wealth. Income from the estates provided not just secure survival for the family, but also the financial means for shaping the new/modern mores of Bengali culture and politics. Except for the tyranny of the male servant caregivers and a short period of discipline in formal schooling, Rabindranath enjoyed the relaxed lifestyle of a wealthy family. We can see from his descriptions how in the fusion of feudalism and capitalist colonialism the form and content of daily life, arts and culture mutated, how notions of civility and ideas of masculinity and femininity were redefined.

Rabindranath's earliest memories of the 'outside' proper and of colonial public space are those of his schools. At first he attended Normal School, which was a basic primary school, and then the Bengal Academy, which he describes as a '*firinghi* (foreign and white) school', and finally St. Xavier's, a school established by the Jesuits. They were all short stints. His memories of these institutions depict the reality of colonial schooling, but they are not named as such by the child Rabindranath. Much of what happened in these schools seemed to him absurd as well as oppressive. About his second school he wrote:

> I remember one thing – when the school started, the first thing that the boys did was to sit in the gallery and recite poems accompanied by music. The idea behind this must have been that there should be some entertainment for the boys along with their lessons. But the songs were in English and their tunes all the same. We could not understand the verses that we chanted or the ritual we were performing. It was not pleasant to join every day in this boring and pointless affair. (Tagore 1940: 18)

Rabindranath's first contact with the outside proper was thus not auspicious. The enforcement of discipline, the oppressive behaviour of the teachers (including the meting out of corporal punishment), complete indifference to teaching, the absurdity of an English curriculum, and an alien and (then) incomprehensible language made him a rebellious student. He eventually left school and was home-taught. His later pedagogic conviction that a child's education should be conducted in the mother tongue has its experiential basis in his own formal schooling. At home, from his earliest days, he was taught in Bengali; his love of Bengali literature dates from that time:

> Because we studied in *Bangla* [Bengali] when we were young, our mind was moved as a whole. Education should be like eating. At the first bite begins

> the pleasure of taste. Way before satiation the stomach wakes up happily, the gastric juices lose their sluggishness. This cannot happen to Bengalis if they begin their learning in English. The very first bite rattles both sets of teeth. … After that half of life is over before realizing that it is not a piece of rock or a brick but rather a sweet stewed in syrup. (Ibid.: 31)

This introduction to reading, to the pleasures of literature in the mother tongue, joins the ideas of home, mother and interiority, and provides a contrast to that of the outside or the public sphere. It is as though the 'mother', an interior aspect of a child's consciousness, has been implanted in one's learning process and literary enjoyment. English, then, served as the 'outside' of cultural life, a foundational introduction and interruption of colonial discourse in the development of a child's consciousness. In support of my equation of Bengali with the interior of the child's consciousness and English with the public space of colonialism, Rabindranath says: 'At that time the elite of Calcutta had relegated the Bengali language to the women's house-bound world. Only English was used in public life – in correspondence, in education, even in everyday speech. In our home this aberration could not happen' (Tagore 2009a: 51). In the process of his emergence as a poet, Rabindranath's early acquaintance with Bengali literature – as folklore and vernacular epics, for example the Ramayana[20] – stimulated his imagination and musical sense through language. The rhyme, rhythm and metric schema of poetry, and even the cadence of Bengali prose, stimulated the child Rabindranath. He began making his own verses very early, and was encouraged in this by his older brothers, relatives and family friends. He imposed his verses on anyone who could be persuaded to listen.

Rabindranath distinguishes between an 'outside' of the family home and of public institutions, and the 'outside' that is nature. This world of nature lay beyond the reach of language, Bengali or English, colonial discourse and educational institutions. In his early adolescence he took a trip with his father, Maharshi Debendranath Tagore,[21] for the purpose of acquiring a new education of senses and intellect. Debendranath spent much of the year in spiritual pursuits and self-quest in different parts of eastern and northern India. This father–son relationship, the *maharshi*'s involvement in his son's education, was unusual for his time, and is worth special consideration. The holistic education imparted by his father, in its deep engagement with Rabindranath's everyday life, his learning and leisure activities, fulfils the criterion of education in the sense of educating the whole consciousness of a person, and later became the pedagogic ideal of his own school, Santiniketan. This is the period for the young Rabindranath of the development of emotions, artistic sensibilities, reflection and expression. In *Jibansmriti*, Rabindranath connects this educational experience with the sense of clarity and maturity of the inner self (Tagore 1940: 37–38). He describes this precious time he spent with his father, who had the insight of seeing him at the cusp of boyhood and adulthood and who initiated him into spiritual awareness (ibid.: 43–44). Though not neglectful of conventional education (Sanskrit, English, Botany and so on), Debendranath made Rabindranath a companion of his spiritual journey, of his meditation, and set him on life's path.

During their travels Rabindranath's relationship with nature came to be endowed with a profound meaningfulness and empathy. He sensed the presence of the divine in the landscape of the snow-clad peaks, forests and streams of the Himalayas – on every side he felt the presence of freedom, beauty and form. Through these nurturing moments which spanned his everyday life, Rabindranath developed the desire to overcome the dualism of the inside and the outside, and he established within himself a feeling of a universal creative soul which fuses nature and human consciousness and gives rise to the idea of the universal human. Freedom was an essential component in this development of individuality, and later he made it central to his idea of be-ing human. As Rabindranath saw it, his father

> never forbade [me] to do anything by raising any idea of an obstacle. As he allowed me to roam around in the hills and mountains, he also gave me a similar freedom to find my destination in the path of truth. He was not afraid of my making mistakes, nor anxious because I might suffer. He held up in front of me an ideal of life, not a rod of punishment. (Ibid.: 40)

Describing this trip with his father, Rabindranath centres the idea of 'freedom' as the essential necessity of self-making and acquiring an individuality (ibid.: 61). His father also provided him with the example of living a righteous life informed by a spiritual morality. Debendranath became for him an embodiment of spirituality, of conscience, of masculine rectitude, combined with love of solitude, daily piety and a stern gentleness. He draws a portrait of his father seeking the aura of the One and the True in a description endowed with the quality of a dream:

> My bedroom was at the far end of the house. Lying in bed, through the glass panes of the windows, in dim starlight, I saw the pale icy glow of the mountain peaks. At times, unsure of the hour of the night, I saw father. He was wrapped

> in a red shawl, carrying a lit candle holder, walking silently. He was on his way to meditate in the glass-enclosed veranda. (Ibid.: 46)

Rabindranath returned from his trip a changed person, having reached the edge of adulthood with the freedom to move at will between the inner quarters of women and children and the adult male space of 'outside'. Now the experiential distinction of an outside and inside world disappears for him. He not only reads Bengali literature, but participates in the creation of it as a writer, as a poet. His *Reminiscences* describe this making process of modern Bengali literary culture. He felt within himself the creative exuberance of the new times. Patriotism, and even nationalism, marked much of his literary output at this time (ibid.: 66–70).

The Self as 'Poet': Be-ing and Identity

In *Atmaparichay*, Rabindranath wrote about discovering himself as a poet, which was both a particular way of being in the world and the aesthetic practice of writing. In this context of self-consciousness and identity he 'introduces' (*parichay*) himself as he wants to be known by others. The memorials *Chhelebela* and *Jibansmriti* portray the development of the child into a poet emotionally, imaginatively and artistically. In a similar manner, *Atmaparichay* captures his self-understanding and observations through an arrangement of spatio-temporal tropes mentioned above. The result is a complex text which is at times contradictory and irresolute.

The translators and editors of *Atmaparichay* comment that Rabindranath considers the 'outer life [a]s incidental to the inner life' (Tagore 2009a: ii), and Rabindranath himself calls the essays 'my life-account' (ibid.: 1). Their purpose is to show how the different aspects of his self-realization solidify into his individual personality, which has the creative vision and capacity for poetic expression. He asserts with the statement, 'I am a poet' (ibid.), the very truth that lies in this realization, which he reaches after a long period of self-exploration and literary writings. He considers each of his poems or poetic writing to be a 'fragment', or segment, of a great, lifelong poetic opus. On its own, no poem or imaginative work holds 'the significance of the whole body of [his] poetry' – each is 'incomplete' in itself, but 'a single continuous significance glows through them all' (ibid.). He feels that this 'significance' is related to a universal or a 'cosmic purpose'. '[B]ut I know', he continues, that 'all my writing is a mere occasion; every piece is building up something that is yet to come, something it has not the faintest idea of' (ibid.: 2).

Atmaparichay reveals that the identity of a poet is not a fixed or static one. It is a distinction of be-ing in the world in a certain way and in a response to it, it is not a matter of producing a reified object called a poem, an occupational craftsmanship. In this self-exploration he lays bare the connection between becoming a maker and the poetry that is made. Thus the 'being' of a poet is intrinsic to the becoming of a many-sided artist, Rabindranath, who ranges through diverse literary genres, through music and painting. Emphasizing the self or the 'I' is neither narcissistic nor solitary. This 'I' is always in relation to a 'you' or a 'thou', in separation and in oneness. A song, for Rabindranath, is not only an expression of a personal emotion, of a momentary experience, but rather an expression of subsumed earlier relations and feelings in response to 'the wider world' (ibid.: 3). Yet, the creative self or I here does not know or pre-empt what it will be or make the next time, because that can only be learnt in the creative process. The poet is something like a messenger who deciphers the message in the very act of carrying it. As Rabindranath puts it, 'I have come to see that while life is being moulded, someone is weaving all its joys and sorrows, its pluses and minuses in their fragmentary process in a continuous significance' (ibid.). He names this weaver of poems, this creative life-force, *jibandebata*, the 'life-god' or life itself as god. His own self/I is both immersed in and expressed through this life-force. The *jibandebata*, in whom lies the being of Rabindranath's poetic self, is the ultimate poet, the source of all poetry:

> This poet who takes up all the good and the bad in me, all my constituent parts, the favourable and the unfavourable alike, to go on creating my life, it is he that in my poetry I call *jibandebata*. ... I know that he has brought to me the expression of the present moment. An immense memory of a long sequence of existing, continuing through this world gathers around him and lies in me, in my unconscious. (Ibid.: 4–5)

It should be noted that the word *debata* conventionally means god or lord. Rabindranath's *jibandebata*, however, serves as a life-force and has no religious connotation in the ordinary sense of the word. He himself, quoting from a letter he wrote, provides the difference between the pursuit of this 'life-god' and 'religion':

> I can by no means say that I have been able to acquire within myself, in a clear and strong form, what is usually spoken of as religion. But I can often feel in the depth of my mind that something is being created. It is no kind of particular dogma – but a deep consciousness, a new organ of my soul. (Ibid.: 6)

He repeats:

> I cannot say whether what is written in the scriptures is true or false, but all such truth is unsuitable to me. ... What I shall be able to build up with the whole of my life is *my ultimate truth*. From this it is clear that being and truth are connected, as also is the freedom needed to make *my* ultimate truth. (Ibid.; my emphasis)

Dissociated from scriptures, rituals and institutionalization, Rabindranath's idea of religion is based on the root-word *dhri*, meaning 'to hold', from which the word *dharma* is derived, commonly translated as religion but actually meaning 'that which holds us/essentially characterizes us'. It is connected to the idea of truth, which is also a dynamic life-force that permeates the identity of being human and is given a fuller expression by the poet. Writing in 1917, Rabindranath distinguishes a conventional religion into which one is born from this consciousness of an inner and unitary universal presence which can be felt by everyone. This durable presence is also fine and elusive, only partially captured by any given form. He says, '[t]he very assumption of a name erects such a screen that the *inner* religion itself escapes [one's] notice' (ibid.: 23; my emphasis). Looking back to the portrayal of his father, we can see the germination of this spiritual non-denominational sensibility and imagination. Debendranath's unitary and meditative brahmo world-view, derived from the Upanishads and the spirituality of sufi and sikh saints, profoundly influenced Rabindranath's own. In *Atmaparichay* he states this explicitly:

> Through the Upanishads the family had an innate relationship with the India of the pre-puranic era. Even when very young we used to recite *slokas* from the Upanishads every day. ... [F]rom this it will be understood that the emotional effusion that is generally to be noted in the religious tradition of Bengal did not enter our house. (Ibid.: 67)

He also writes: 'My soul and character from their shaping, their birth, were not overlaid by the scriptural tradition of a bygone era' (ibid:); further, 'When I was born our home was not bounded on all sides by walls of a dead past of social customs that had more of habit in them than truth' (ibid.).

The view of religion in *Atmaparichay* is also found in Rabindranath's *Religion of Man* (Tagore 1966) and numerous other texts. The typically modernist connection made by Charles Taylor between ideas of an inner true self, freedom and humanist universalism is present throughout.

Rabindranath's fundamental reliance on these ideas frames his notion of religion, which holds together individual consciousness and conscience. It also finds in nature some innate aspects which are responded to by the human nature of the individual self, as both share the same driving force of life. As Rabindranath says:

> An inherent religion and instinct of life builds up all that is animal and living. The animal need not have any sense of the religion. Man has another being, greater than his physical being – it is humanity. The creativity that is inside this being is his religion. For this reason *dharma* (religion) is a very significant word in our language. The wateriness of water is the religion of water. The fieriness of fire is the religion of fire. Similarly man's religion is his innermost truth. (Ibid.: 23)

Rabindranath's modernism becomes apparent in this unconventional and philosophical use of the concept of religion found in *The Religion of Man.* This capacity for appropriation of religion is the quintessential *quality* of all human beings, which cannot be quantitatively captured or precisely articulated. Rabindranath says as much when he writes:

> What is my religion? Even today I cannot say I know perfectly and clearly what it is – after all it is not scriptural creed laid out in tenets and postulates. To know and look at this religion by uprooting it from the innermost tissue of life, by exposing it and holding it up for scrutiny, is not possible for me. (Ibid.: 44)

Having considered Rabindranath's ideas of the self, of being and becoming in connection with truth and freedom, which together produce a unifying wholeness, we return to our consideration of the crucial self–other relation. His memoirs show us how the self of a person, his or her awareness of a substantive individual being, consists of a process of making distinctions. It is in interaction with others, in being able to identify similarities and differences, that the sense of the self and an awareness of the world grow. In other words, the individual self is both personal and social. As the social is a network of interactions and communication, it both binds the self to and keeps it free from other(s). The self is both a submergence in an immense, ineffable spirit the other and an identification with everyday common others who possess the same relationship to the spirit other. It is an innate quality of human capacity. This dialectical idea of a self differs from the Hegelian one, which is antagonistic towards an other and involves a demand for recognition and reciprocity in a struggle that conceives the other as a master. For Rabindranath, this antagonistic relation is accompanied by another self–other relation which steps away from the paradigm of annihilation or recognition, isolation or reciprocity. The self–other relation for him is equally positive and mutually nurturing. Here the self, in a peculiar 'I' and 'you' conjunction, has 'no pride in separate existence' (Tagore 2009a: 7). The submergence of the self in the other is not experienced as a relation of bondage or defeat, as a loss of self, but as an augmentation and fullness. We thus find in Rabindranath two understandings of the other: one that is social, which is an active source of opposition and empathy; and a spirit other, which is beyond any bounded sense of self-consciousness. They together provide a unified sense of self in the world. This unity is brought about not through a process of aggregation, but with the help of creative power. As Rabindranath says, if

> the creative power can once be felt, I can realize my own link with the endlessly created universe. … [I]n me from time without beginning a process of creation has been going on. … [W]hen I look at my own flowing life in its connection with endless world and time outside itself, then I can see all life's sorrows tied to a huge strand of happiness – *I exist, I become, I continue, I understand this is a large affair.* (Ibid.; my emphasis)

This universalist stance of the self as articulated by Rabindranath shows him enfolded not only in human others, but also in nature. Here self-consciousness is reflected in, rather than obscured by, a nature conceived as an alien entity to the human. Instead, '[t]he sense of an unbroken line between me and the natural universe, an ever-old oneness of being, has exerted a deep pull' (ibid.: 11). In the same essay, Rabindranath says: 'nature has enchanted me with her forms and essences of beauty, her colours and fragrance. Mankind with his intelligence and mind, his affection and love. And I do not distrust this enchantment, I do not criticize it' (ibid.: 17).

Thus, for Rabindranath, man's relationship with nature involves the inter-constitution of intelligence and beauty, which mirrors the merging of the masculine and the feminine aspects of being 'human'. This union of beauty and reason, nature, and human, masculine and feminine, is essential for the poet Rabindranath, for whom the idea of the universal man is a negation of dualism. Under the antagonistic condition of dualism, the experience of a self in others is impossible. As Rabindranath sees it, the main problem for becoming a 'true' self necessary for being a poet is *the ego*, which derives from a negative relationship with the social other and provides a barrier to embracing the universal other. This social ego, as distinct from the universal human, is subject to time in a mundane sense, and is textured with the particularities of the here and now, which resists the fusion of 'I' with 'you'/'thou'.[22] This fusion is essential for the poet's relationship to *jibandebata.* The poet always aspires to a unified and universal self, but this aspiration is not always possible and certainly cannot be taken for granted. Thus, the work of a poet is to be both true to and overcome tensions between personal individual life and the universal humanist one mediated through imagination and empathy. The result is sometimes successful and sometimes not. Rabindranath concludes by saying that sometimes the particular triumphs over the universal, as '[h] owever great a poet he may be, *the whole of him* is not a poet' (ibid.: 18).

The realization that an actual poet is not always an ideal poet, and not even 'always a poet' but an ordinary person living in his or her time, limited to a separated and bounded identity, makes Rabindranath's notions of 'self', 'being' or 'identity' particularly complex, fluid and elusive. In struggling against dualism, he complained about this self-division, his inability to be always in the universal mode:

> A person's *reputation* is based on the way he is known to the outside world. If this external identity does not agree in any way with his inner truth, then a split enters into his existence. Because a person is not only what he is inside himself, he exists largely in the way he is known to all. 'Know thyself' is not the final truth, 'let thyself be known' is also of great importance. (Ibid.: 24)

If this 'split' is to a large extent inevitable, what then is the way to maintain the self's integrity, its own 'truth'? I mention above Rabindranath's reliance on creative power for overcoming the self-division, along with self–other division, but it would appear that more needs to be done to create a wholeness or a dialectic of 'constancy' and 'inconsistency', 'disharmony' and 'harmony'. Rabindranath does not reject contradiction out of hand or erase it; instead, he makes contradiction an element of his poetic sensibility and sense of self; which is to say, he finds truth in a harmony of dissonance provided by the contradiction. To be truthful, then, amounts to being able to create a harmonious universal form in which difference and particularities are constitutive elements. Remarking on this, Rabindranath says: '[T]ruth has a harmony. … But the harmony is not without contradiction – it is something that embraces disharmony and is greater than all discord. … [I]f one respects the truth, one ought to have the courage to know the world as it materially is – divided between uneven fragments' (ibid.: 27).

At the age of seventy (in 1931), the issue of the self becomes increasingly vital for Rabindranath, and yet remains unclear. Any idea of a fixed identity still retains the threat of reification, of becoming a persona rather than a person. He acknowledges that '[i]t is not easy to acquire a true self-knowledge. The central thread of unity within life's diverse experience does not easily reveal itself. ... I have looked at myself in many fragments, again and again [at the] tokens of my identity ...' (ibid.: 23). In his reconciliatory efforts, Rabindranath concluded that there were both antagonistic and non-antagonistic senses of difference. They are not only empirically there, but are necessarily so, because they are needed for a clear perception and expression of the whole:

> In every man truth has a universal form and at the same time an individual form. That is his personal religion. And in that he is preserving the variety of the world. This variety is an invaluable element of creation. And so, we do not have the power to destroy it completely. (Ibid.)

He continues:

> However much I may follow the rule of 'sameness', I can by no means blot out the difference between my form and the form of others. Similarly, however much I may think that by assuming a communal label I have come to belong to the common religion of my group, still my religious soul knows that a certain individuality of my personal religion exists at the root of my humanity. (Ibid.)

He further comments that 'what is apparent from *outside* is *my non-individual religion. That common identity is my religious society*' (ibid.; my emphasis), but in his creative work and personal reflections, what he holds as truth inside of his consciousness joins him with common humanity, signalling far beyond a particular religious group belonging.

Rabindranath repeatedly discusses the pitfalls of a public and communal identity – this outer religion which threatens to substitute for one's personal understanding of religion or human conduct (*dharma*), and which exposes deeply disturbing social and political consequences. He saw that the politicization of the outer or common identity of being hindu or muslim, of 'communal' identities, had created mutually destructive relations since the time of Lord Curzon's 1905 division of Bengal along 'religious' lines. In his novel *Ghare Baire* (The Home and the World), Rabindranath spoke to these antagonistic socio-cultural differences and even extended this understanding to self-divisions within one's own personality. As far as his own 'self' and its development were concerned, though he was certain that his own identity was more than dualist and particular, he still could not entirely escape the dualism and antagonism of his social life and public identity.

Before we move on to the definitive moment of Rabindranath's self-discovery as a poet, his acceptance of a named identity, we need to review the main points about self-making and overcoming the division between the social and the universal 'self'/'I'. The 'other' of this 'I' could be anyone, or a familial or close person in the social setting of the 'I'. The 'other' is also a self-experiencing subject, and in the interaction between them the 'self' emerges in the process as a distinction and in a mutuality of identification between 'I' and 'you'. This separation and identification is an ineluctable human condition starting at birth and expanding in concentric circles until death stops the process. The concept of 'recognition' (as found in Hegel and his followers, such as Taylor and others) is an enunciation about this condition.[23] This dynamic involves not just antagonism, but also 'recognition' and 'reciprocity'. At its best, this 'I' and 'you' relationship is recognized as a relationship between two equals as and in love. In this sense, the other is socially and personally a condition for self-fulfilment.

Understood thus, the relationship between 'I' and an 'other' – the 'thou' of Rabindranath – is a beneficent relationship in an expanding awareness of infinitude. The merger of the 'I' with this other is therefore not an experience of self-loss but of self-finding. One could use a metaphor of the wave and the ocean for this relationship. The wave is nothing but water which temporarily acquires a defined form that is dissolved and recomposed endlessly. This submergence of the one in the other is a relation of joy, not of bondage or self-annihilation. The universal 'other', then, is a self which is recognizable in every face, and in it that other self and the feeling of a conscious 'I' are not antithetical. In this philosophy, humanity is not alienated from nature, and both are endowed with an enlivening 'spirit' which itself is embodied in experiential human existence. This realization brings Rabindranath to a nameable identity through a long process of active interactive living. He says: 'Now I followed this long orbit of life. … I understand that I have only one identity, and it is this: I am simply a poet' (Tagore 2009a: 48). And he continues:

> I have no doubt that within me a profound consciousness is guiding itself towards an unchanging goal, defying obstacles in its path as well as self-opposition. It is in the inspiration of this consciousness … that the homage of life can find a complete expression of its unity and individuality. (Ibid.: 67)

Our recognition of Rabindranath as a poet who has achieved an authentic and unifying self-identity is incomplete unless we scrutinize further the path he traversed as a social self in his own time. This requires a consideration of Rabindranath and modernity, a discussion of subject formation in the colonial context. The following section will explore colonial hegemony in Bengal, and Rabindranath's response and resistance to it in order to achieve the goal of universalist humanism.

The Colonial Context

While power relations are pervasive even in 'normal' conditions of growing up in any family and society, becoming an individuated self, a social subject, within colonial relations is far more challenging. Colonialism is a 'self'-destroying force for its subjects under all circumstances. Capitalist colonialism, not exceptionally, imposed a master–bondsman type of relationship between the ruler and the ruled, which was meant to be all-pervasive. Whereas in the colonizing 'homeland' there are overarching patriarchal and class relations, colonialism as an absolute system of exploitation adds a particularly deforming twist to social relations in the colony through racialization of class and patriarchy. Both colonized wage labour and unfree labour – working on plantations in conditions similar to slavery or indentured labour – exist in a social reality which is absent in the 'homeland'. Even an elite person such as Rabindranath could not but be affected by such domination, and as a colonial subject he had to struggle for 'freedom' in more senses than the personal and the philosophical. The existential and cultural life of the colonized elite went beyond direct economic oppression to one of colonial hegemony developed through administration, education and cultural activities of the colonial state. Hegemony was consciously designed as well as practically emanated from the colonial socio-economic relations and productive forces. But it is essential to note that the colonial subject, in spite of the colonizer's intent, was never entirely made over by or absorbed in the class relations and cultural forms of hegemony. In its systemic cargo-hold, colonialism in its capitalist expansion carried its own Trojan horse. We should remember that, historically speaking, colonization does not happen in a socio-historical and cultural vacuum in either the country it originates in or the country it penetrates. The penetrated countries are historical and social spaces having pre-capitalist and pre-colonial subjectivities and agencies. These components continue to be active in the social fabric even though they are mutated in the process of capitalist colonization, whose character they mutate in return. Written and oral culture, socio-economic relations and practices, cultural artifacts and histories, among other aspects of social organization and relations, largely remain in one form or another, as do collective memories, dreams and fantasies.

Colonial discourse projects a reifying vision of the society and the identities of the colonized, while in actuality the people are not stagnant, even though aspects of life and productive forces of the subject population may be rendered obsolete, discarded and mutilated, as well as diverted into tributary channels in order to feed the egos and coffers of the colonizing countries. In some cases, for example in India, pre-existing social organizations consisting of class, caste, patriarchy, laws of inheritance and ownership of property offer grounds for shaping the 'new' system. They also pose obstacles and contradict the new project. Though this pre-colonial social organization is imposed upon and pressed into service by colonialism, the society of the colonized is also continuous, an experiential space, and not amnesiac. After all, the colonized subjects are not theoretical categories; they are actual people with their collective and personal histories, memories and ways of social being. Though in postcolonial studies, 'subject' is often confused with 'object' and colonial hegemony aspires to objectify them, in actuality, the inhabitants remain experiencing and responsive subjects. But, of course, an important phenomenon like colonization does add a powerful new complication: existence within the orbit of capitalist colonialism produces a *double subjecthood* among the colonized, who are simultaneously self-affirming subjects and subsumed in the colonial process.

In this respect, Rabindranath was both a hegemonized and a resisting subject of colonialism. It created a great tension and tortuosity in the complex processes of 'becoming', though the core of self-awareness of any human being cannot be eliminated. The development of the 'self' and the formation of a relatively stable 'identity' formation entail greater complications. The double aspects of being as self-awareness, and as social participation and formation, rebound and resonate with each other, and the possibility of a serious self-bifurcation accompanies the efforts of self-making. Thus the idea of 'freedom' – of the freedom to be and to become – is ambiguously poised. The result of this situation is one in which individual desires, imaginative capacities and range of expressions are simultaneously thwarted and stimulated. Thus the individual self's 'authenticity' or assertion of self-hood must be fought for at multiple and contradictory levels.

The early stages of his development of double-consciousness[24] or self-division intensified during Rabindranath's stay in England. There he experienced an immersion in middle-class English life as an 'Oriental' among 'modern' westerners. His experiences were shaped by the colonial gaze,[25] alienating him and reifying his authentic social being. Even though he rose to the surface to breathe in the company of his relatives and Indian friends or made defiant gestures of independence, he did not succeed in freeing himself from the trap of being a negative or peculiar other of the English, and he always felt on display. A positive self-development could not happen in this un-free, claustrophobic atmosphere. Rabindranath's desires – both sexual and social – are at odds with each other.[26] He wanted to 'belong' among his English hosts, but faced with the ignominy of exclusion, he wanted to break free from this desire. Helpless and out of control, he is at the mercy of the world outside, of the unpredictable behaviour of 'others' who hold ruling relations over India. The overall experience is one of trauma to the self.

Trapped in the colonial gaze, away from his country, young Rabindranath falls back on a common defence mechanism: he becomes an expert in sarcasm and caricatures the colonizer's social life. To this mocking portrayal of his 'others' he adds a tone of moral condemnation of what appears to him as their hyper-sexualized male–female relations. He also excoriates their habits of conspicuous consumption. About the English women he meets, he says:

> They are not averse to sacrificing their happiness and health to the ritual of beguiling men's minds. They will tighten their waists like wasps – they can tolerate any amount of suffering for that. Dressing in showy clothes, sticking some feathers into their coiffure, day and night they sit like dolls. They are so habituated to acting that unnaturalness is natural for them. (Tagore 1929a: 244)

Furthermore, he adds:

> Like hunters who don't kill birds to eat them, but who enjoy their marksmanship, they derive the same satisfaction from possessing hearts. I can't stand to see these efforts to charm, putting on manners and airs, moving their bodies in certain ways, making their voices high. No one can charm me with these things. (Ibid.)

At this juncture of an identity crisis Rabindranath creates an idea(l) of India for comparison and judgment. This imagined India relies on the prevailing binary categories of the colonial discourse. As is common with this discourse and its inversion into nationalist discourse, the burden of distinction rests on a critique of sexuality and gender roles prevailing in European stereotypes of India. Typified as an eastern man, Rabindranath feels that his masculinity is always under scrutiny, as the colonizer's gaze renders the colonized male into an effeminate and queer subject.[27] In order to counteract this castrating colonial gaze Rabindranath deploys his sense of class superiority as a counter-offensive. In an act of rebuttal, he calls the English working people on the ship during his first journey to England 'servants', and throughout he speaks contemptuously of the low-class English and Anglo-Indians. He makes scathing remarks about them in his letters to his peers and relatives in India. His contemptuous condescension also takes the form of over-generous tipping and adopting textbook-correct English social etiquette. The unhappy and divided consciousness of the colonial subject wrestles with the constantly reifying and negative gaze of the colonizer, which is both refused and interiorized by Rabindranath, like other colonial subjects. His divided consciousness is the performative space in which he acts out self-objectification and his struggles for the assertion of subjective freedom. He fights a battle on both fronts – against himself (and other hegemonized colonized subjects) and against the surrounding oppressive 'normalcy' of the English world. He experiences simultaneously a longing to belong, to be recognized by 'the master', while also clinging on to a substantive and independent sense of self that he had developed prior to his departure from India. The desire for sameness with and difference from others are at loggerheads.

At this point, Rabindranath sporadically appeals to ideas of the shared condition of humanity to counteract the shock of colonialism's racializing tropes expressed in terms of culture and colour. The notions of whiteness and blackness now influence his own social perception as well. In this identity crisis universalism provides him a foothold against the fear of loss of self and his rage at involuntary subjection, thus protecting his sanity. Asserting his humanity against colonizing history and imprisonment in his skin, he fights the dehumanization of the self, and, in the process, of the colonizer. Rabindranath draws upon his inner sense of being a poet, an artist, while also drawing on his sense of humour and ridicule. Torn between his negative and positive feelings for the English and Europeans, he tries to personalize the white people among whom he lives. They become more real as he lives in close quarters with them. He senses in their behaviour towards him kindness, fairness and familial affection. He finds the women to be beautiful. He mentions the maternal care of his landlady, the brotherly relations he has with her daughters. Relying on these tokens of actual or imagined acceptance, he tries to achieve a feeling of 'sameness' underneath their 'differences'. This gesture partially relieves him of the pain of discrimination and alienation that lay at the bottom of his stay abroad. He also searches for and finds 'sameness' at the deeper levels of philosophy and culture. This is not surprising, as there have been ongoing connections and influences historically among the cultures of Europe and Asia, as already mentioned. Rabindranath himself had prior acquaintance with some of these and identified with the humanist values of the enlightenment, christianity and European romanticism, primarily of English literature. He found a sense of freedom as an authentic self in these cultural spaces, thus making the world of art and philosophy his realm of freedom. The aesthetic contacts and shared 'human' values provide him a common ground whereby the English/Europeans are perceived as more than colonizers. It is within this disjunction between experiences of rejection and objectification, and the common inheritance he shares with Europe, that the need arises in him to differentiate the English into categories of the 'good' and the 'bad'. This distinction he maintains throughout his life so as not to essentialize and demonize them or Europeans in general. Thus begins Rabindranath's lifelong attempt to reconcile the paradox of western universalist humanism and its particularist colonial and racializing discourse. 'Western' humanism is not an oxymoron for him, any more than that of an 'eastern' one, though he continues to have questions regarding who gets to define and decide 'who' actually is human and why, and he insists that the notion of the 'human' is universally applicable.

The memoirs, letters and diaries of Rabindranath reveal that he made a meticulous study of colonial relations and discourse during his many visits abroad. No detail escapes his notice. At the same time as he critically explores colonial discourse, he also carries on a scrupulous self-reflection, aimed at two sets of discursive masks – modern/western and oriental/eastern. From his awareness of the inner space of the 'self' within him he watches, as though from a distance, himself and others, Indians and non-Indians, acting out these roles which often occlude the inner self. In his reactive engagement Rabindranath changes his persona, sometimes self-orientalizing and at others embracing it as an iconic opposite to the west. Yet, his growing human awareness pushes him to reject this role-playing and these masked manoeuvres. This antinomic awareness marks Rabindranath for life. The authentic self and the mask are at times melded together and at others pulled apart. In his idealized civilizational claims for eastern spirituality, he depicts Christ as an eastern prophet and christianity as an eastern religion. Sometimes he projects himself as a messianic figure who is a redemptive messenger of the east to the materialistic people of the west. This figure, in later life, is sustained by his sartorial change as he, like his father Debendranath, dons the robes of sufi and sikh saints and *baul* mystics. This style he adopts distinguishes him from his grandfather, Dwarakanath Tagore, a worldly figure, who dressed in the style of the Mughal courtiers and of the Bengali *nawabs*. However, Dwarakanath's aristocratic image, also iconically eastern and gleaned from the monarchic courtly culture of West Asia, could in no way be seen as anti-materialistic.

Conclusion: The Self In and Beyond Colonial Discourse

> Men make their own history, but they do not make it just as they please; they do not make it under circumstances chosen by themselves, but under circumstances directly found, given and transmitted from the past.
>
> – Karl Marx, *The Eighteenth Brumaire of Louis Bonaparte* (1963: 15)

It should be noted that while growing up within the great arch of capitalist colonial rule, Rabindranath's earliest memories, noted at the outset, have no perceivable allusion to the importance of racist discourse and blackness or whiteness. Colonial reality did not impinge on him until he went to school, but even this created no significant animosity in him towards his English teachers, but rather a frustration and a baffled amusement. He does remember, however, that being forced to learn all his subjects in English was a disincentive to remaining in school. But his childhood was not marked by any sense of socio-cultural inferiority, because his fellow students were from upper-class families and of a significantly higher standing than the English teachers. This distance from the direct impact of colonialism came to an end with his first western trip, to England. As was becoming a practice among wealthy Bengalis, he was sent to England to possibly become a barrister and to become familiar with English society and culture. His writings from these times abroad during his late teen years indicate that he began to understand more about colonial modes of governance and was exposed to colonial discourse. The tacit colonial common sense he absorbed in India from the social environment became explicit and entrenched during this trip and subsequently during other English and European trips, and this enabled him to get a clearer sense of what racism and orientalism mean in an existential way.

From this time onwards Rabindranath's personal communications and writings show us his partial transformation into an oriental subject for westerners, and even for himself. There is a gradual process of adaptation to and a struggle with a racialized cultural identity or persona about which he became self-reflexive and critical. The struggle consisted of a reactive cultural essentialism which threatened his sense of self and his relations with others. The prevalence of racist/orientalist discourse in England and Europe impelled him at times into a reverse orientalism, conferring upon the west the taint of aggressive, consumerist materialism, while the east was idealized and seen as superior. Without even wanting to, he was becoming the representative of the 'east', a symbolic figure within colonial discourse. That figure had its temptations, but he was aware that it was also destructive for his innate and social sense of self. This identification as Europe's 'other' spurred him to gestures of defiance as well as of submission. His trips to England and Europe often put him in an agitated and ambivalent frame of mind, which did not decrease with time. The attributed and partially assumed persona of the east confused his sense of self and contradicted his ordinary life. His previous sense of self, developed outside of the direct colonizing encounter, was now jeopardized by his actual living in the west. In this identity crisis he returned to the notions of the 'human' and 'humanity', the 'world soul', and the principle of universality which he had encountered since childhood in brahmo preaching and as a desired way of life. This revision sustained him through his identity crisis during his earlier stays abroad and deepened through his life in future encounters with the west. Composing a universalist idea of the human from the Upanishads and other branches of Indian philosophy and literature, from Perso-Arabic monotheism along with selected aspects of European enlightenment, which subsumed within it Greek humanism, Rabindranath evolved an idealist epistemology outside that of colonial discourse. This concept of the human he expressed, as noted above, through the metaphor of the child. This metaphor is the measuring rod for judging the distance between an incorrupt self and a compromised self infused by power relations. Such idealism, contrary to common understanding, actually served a critical purpose for Rabindranath, and reveals to us a general potential for critique. Instead of being an abstraction and an avenue of escape from the material world, idealism becomes an epistemological device for distinguishing the actual from the desired. Thus, it opens a critical space for the use of imagination in envisioning a way of being in the world which always moves towards an uncompromised ideal of humanity.

Rabindranath's own personal journey towards what Charles Taylor called modernity should be contextualized to the modernity pervading in nineteenth-century Bengal. This modernity, consisting of a sense of inner self, ethics and individuality, thrived relatively independently among the elite within the ambience of colonial hegemony. An idea of the individual developing among them throughout the nineteenth century prompted cultural innovation on many fronts. Instead of being threatened by the incoming European ideas, resting on their cultural legacy, they could absorb these ideas and cultural practices selectively and voluntarily. Colonial discourse was not the only option open to them. A relative autonomy of consciousness was also possible, as Bengal had not experienced a full-scale cultural dispossession via the colonial project. Given the socially complex, culturally rich societies they found themselves in, a full-scale hegemony was an impossible task for the British.[28] With Bengali language and pre-colonial ideas and literary traditions at their disposal, the urban elite, drawing from European ideas, fashioned to an extent their own cultural life. Social reform and religious cultural revivalism – both equally modernist at bottom and in spite of an invention of tradition – resulted from these processes of reaction and synthesis. Various philosophies of knowledge and political ideologies plunged the time into ferment (Bannerji 2001b). Different strands of nationalism, cultural and economic, mark this moment. Though later Rabindranath rejected nationalism, he gleaned from cultural nationalism at its earliest and inchoate stage a passion for freedom.

Rabindranath's signal contribution in the realm of social and political thought was a critical use of idealism. He was not in the main a reactive thinker, but one who created a substantive and ethical philosophy of the individual, for which he drew on human potential for creativity. He was a philosopher/poet with a message of universal humanism, a message that he brought into daily life, his pedagogic activities, political commentaries and relations with international intelligentsia. Thus, he was very different from the orientalist-western vision of him as a guru, a spiritual missionary. He not only criticized the acquisitive materialism and war-proneness of the west and insisted on a cooperative life and pacifism, but his moral critique included Indian culture and politics. The violence of materialism that he abhorred in capitalism and imperialism, he saw in Indian nationalism as well. Rabindranath's modernist idealism, in the last analysis, was not a derivative discourse but rather, a universalist synthetic one. He explored the contradictory and coherent elements in contemporary societies that give rise to different types of modernism. His own modernism is antithetical to *colonial* modernism, a view lost to many students of postcolonial studies. For them, reason is tantamount to instrumental rationality. But for Rabindranath, reason implies a sense of the universal, and it includes empathy and imagination and the idea of social good.

Rabindranath's universal humanism is not simply a pious utterance. It is neither linear nor rapid, nor does he indulge in a formulaic idealism. It exposes a struggle in the heart of modernism between its aspirational universalism and subordination to colonial power, and we must choose between them. We cannot find a dialectical resolution of this conflict that is projected in double consciousness and a dual subjectivity. The universalism implied in Rabindranath's humanism, the imaginative and empathetic individual that he searched for, logically conflicted with the particularism of the colonial subject, both assimilated and nationalist. Nor did he hope for a positive change to take place in the imperialist west. In his lifetime he witnessed the first world war, but also the preparations leading up to the second. He saw the triumph of fascism in Europe and Japan at each step. These experiences deeply saddened and burdened him with a tragic vision. Could the individual ever get beyond the antagonistic binary of the self and the other?

Ironically, it is this violent individualism and imperialism that made it imperative for Rabindranath to look for a non-voracious, non-reductive unity among the many. The European wars and expansionism made him see the necessity for mutuality in human relations. This was not about recognition from a superior other or the wresting of concessions from a dominating force that led to a fight unto death. Under these circumstances, towards the end of his life Rabindranath could only hold on to his sense of inner self and a humanist vision articulated upon that. His vision asserted a free self which seeks no one's permission to be. In the ruins of the second world war, his sense of the human relied on the principle of hope. For this, the idea of the child, the birth of a new man, provided him with a metaphor. This child took on the figure of christ in the context of the human sacrifice demanded by wars, and hope came in the shape of renewal or resurrection. The sacrificed child would be resurrected, he thought, and return to the world in a renewal of humanity. This is the scene described in a 1940 poem titled '*Nabajatak*' (The Newborn). In this gesture Rabindranath created a figure which fused the Upanishadic view of the inner self with the child of European romanticism into a glimmer of universal human consciousness. Decolonization disarticulated from nationalism and the freedom of particular groups had to be universal, a redemption unbounded by any discourse of power.

Notes

[1] Subaltern Studies started in Kolkata, India in 1982, to become internationally influential. It began as a collection of articles in a journal of the same name. An experiment in historiography, it was an attempt to create a way of reading and writing history with a contra-marxist historiography, specially rejecting historical materialism and emphases on class as a primary analytical category, privileging culture over class and questioning class-based political organizing. When they used the term class, they interpreted it in the Weberian sense of stratification.

[2] This form of civilizational/cultural understanding of non-European societies is deeply influenced by Hegel's *The Philosophy of History*. Taylor, as a major Hegel scholar, is an example. Samuel Huntington's idea of a clash of civilizations is articulated from such a point of view. To some extent it can be applied to Edward Said's conception of orientalism (1979a), which has made a critical and historical use of this epistemology. For critiques, among many, see Ronald Inden (1990), Aijaz Ahmad (1992), and Himani Bannerji (2001c).

[3] For an extensive number of his writings on society, culture and politics available in English, see Sisir Kumar Das (1996b).

[4] See Tapan Raychaudhuri (1988); see also Sivanath Sastri (2016).

[5] For a better understanding of the relation between modernity and modernism and the possibilities of their formal variations, particularly in the Indian context, see Partha Mitter (2007). See also Geeta Kapur (2000: 299), who writes: 'Modernity is a way of relating the material and cultural worlds in a period of unprecedented change that we call the process of modernization. It is also an ontological quest with its particular forms of reflexivity, its acts of struggle. Modernity takes a precipitate historical form in the postcolonial world, while its praxis produces a cultural dynamic whereby questions of autonomy, identity and authenticity come to the fore.'

[6] See R. Siva Kumar (1997) and Elise Coquereau (2014).

[7] See, for example, Philip Ariès (1965) and Colin Heywood (2018), among numerous others.

[8] See his poem, 'The Rainbow'.

[9] Late Vedic Sanskrit texts. They are philosophical ideas put forth in a poetic form of dialogues involving a quest for knowledge. They are also known as Vedantas and became the basis of philosophy. They mark a transition from Vedic ritualism to spiritual ideas.

[10] For an originator of this trope, see J.J. Rousseau's *Emile*.

[11] My argument should make it clear that while all religion is a form of idealism, not all idealism is religious, thus bringing us to an idea of secular universalism or spiritualism.

[12] The notion of communal is used here not with a negative connotation, as found in India and where it is used to express an irrational, parochial attachment to one's 'community', which is a code word for religious affiliation, especially to hinduism and islam. This politicization of religious belonging derives from the colonial constitution, which created the identity of ruled subjects in ethnic-religious terms. This lies at the root of future Indian political development, including the partition of India on religious grounds.

[13] For the idea of *bildungsroman* (novels of formation), see Goethe's *Wilhelm Meister's Apprenticeship* (1795–96) as an archetypal example of the genre. In the English context, see George Eliot's *Middlemarch* (1871–72), also Lovejoy (1948).

[14] See Benjamin (1969c), who writes at length on the topic of involuntary memory while discussing Marcel Proust's novel *In Search of Lost Time*.

[15] All translations from Bengali in this chapter, except those from *Atmaparichay*, are mine.

[16] Capitalist colonialism needs to be distinguished from pre-capitalist occupations and conquests. Unlike, for example, following the Mughal conquest of India, in which the Mughals did not refer back to a 'mother country' and send it tribute and so on, capitalist colonization in its systemically necessary expansion of capital in endless search for markets, means of production and labour remains rooted in metropolitan capital. It involves but exceeds conquest, plunder and so on, and may or may not involve 'settlement'. But it always includes the insertion of the colony in capital's logic of administration for accumulation. The socio-cultural formation of capitalist colonialism gives rise to a 'modernity' which delinks itself from the humanist values of the enlightenment and morphs into racializing colonial discourses. Both western and non-western countries fall within its hegemony. A critique of colonialism of our time is incomplete and misleading without a refutation of capitalism and imperialism.

[17] Rabindranath witnessed Dwarakanath's business empire in decline, but he did not experience a loss of social status, which goes beyond money wealth. The shadow of feudal hierarchy hung over the present: 'We had a large and old-fashioned mansion with a portico hung with a few broken shields and spears and rusted swords' (Tagore 2009a: 51).

[18] The 1793 Permanent Settlement of Bengal imposed by Charles, Earl Cornwallis, chief administrator of the East India Company administration. This legislation created and empowered a class of landlords in Bengal who were largely loyal to British rule.

[19] On the Bengal Renaissance, see Susobhan Sarkar (1970b).

[20] An epic attributed to the sage-poet Valmiki around 500–100 BCE, the Ramayana was written in Sanskrit, but many regional versions developed in other Indian languages. In its local versions it was held very dear by common people, read out

and sung in homes and festivals. These versions contributed a great to deal to Indian common sense at different social levels.

[21] *Maharshi* is a Sanskrit word for 'the great sage', not a priest but a man learned in ancient wisdom. When used in Bengali it does not sound as pompous as in English, because it was a common attribute of a deeply philosophical thinker.

[22] Regarding the ego Rabindranath says, 'the greatest thief in the world is the ego' (Tagore 2009a: 18), because it undermines the self and the other at once.

[23] The concept of 'recognition' has been so widely discussed that it seems pointless to name names, but an acquaintance with Hegel's phenomenology is richly rewarding. There are of course other ways of interpreting the concept in terms of mutuality and ethics.

[24] This notion is Hegelian at its source and has been used with great utility by Frantz Fanon in *Black Skin, White Masks* (1967), but also much earlier, in 1903, by W.E.B. Du Bois in *The Souls of Black Folk* (1996). In Fanon, this concept is connected to the master/slave parable. A central concept in Hegel's phenomenology, this double consciousness is self-divided, part of the master–slave/servant parable of self–other relations, and it is further connected to the notion of unhappy consciousness.

[25] The notion of the colonial gaze is widely used in postcolonial and critical cultural studies and has been around for decades, deriving from Foucault's notion of the gaze. It was used in speaking about colonial ideology implicated in all social interactions. See McClintock (1995) and Alloula (1987). In the context of the male gaze as used by feminists, see Mulvey (1989).

[26] Just as in the process later described by Frantz Fanon in *Black Skin, White Masks* (1967).

[27] See Mrinalini Sinha (1995), Indira Chowdhury (1998) and Himani Bannerji (2001a, 2001d).

[28] See Bernard Cohen, 'The Command of Language and the Language of Command', in Cohen (1996). See also Hobsbawm and Ranger (1983).

2

Rabindranath's Postcolonialism

A Vision of Decolonization and a Modernist Idealism

Naming is an act of clarification, as it involves a scrutiny of the object to be named. This is important for characterizing the social thought of Rabindranath Tagore, which has been a matter of controversy for almost a century. His social thought has been considered paradoxical because, while a critic of colonialism, he rejected both nationalism as a means for decolonization and the national state as a stage towards true freedom. Consequently, he has been thought of variously as anti-nationalist and a supporter of British rule, a derivative thinker influenced by colonial discourse, a good nationalist who served as the conscience of the nation, a cosmopolitanist and a humanist philosopher, as well as a mystic and a spiritual guide. This confusion could be clarified by naming him a modernist postcolonial thinker, a position that would allow us to achieve a wider scope within which we could grapple with the complex, at times contradictory and unresolved nature of his critique.

The notion of postcolonialism has two aspects: one descriptive, and the other epistemological with political consequences. As a descriptive notion it lacks any specific content other than a reference to a historical period of colonialism and steps taken to end it. Even though the notion of postcolonialism has been generally associated with postmodernism, there is no particular reason why it cannot instead be modernist. Postcolonialism has as such no predetermined theoretical and methodological direction. It serves as a general term which takes on a theoretical valence depending on the critic's own knowledge standpoint. The idea of 'post' implies an ambiguity as to whether we are speaking about what comes after colonialism socially and politically, or about the politico-ideological methods of decolonization undertaken to end and go beyond colonialism. Thus, postcolonialism could imply both what Frantz Fanon called a 'true decolonization' and a 'false decolonization' (neo-colonialism).[1]

Here we need to provide a context for the emergence of the notion of postcolonialism and the discipline of postcolonial studies. The mid to late 1970s could be taken as the time of their emergence as a type of literary/cultural critique displacing commonwealth studies (Edward Said's *Orientalism* was first published in 1978).[2] Mainly used by academics, the term and the discipline lacked direct connection to anti-imperialist political movements and writings of the time. While they challenged colonial hegemonic discourses, postcolonialism and postcolonial studies were often unmindful of and also blocked the anti-imperialist critiques created in the course of socialist and communist liberation struggles, especially in the 'third world'. Focused on discursivity, this was at once a radical and a restraining move, resulting in the displacement of a historical materialist or marxist approach by cultural critique connected to liberal thought. The problematic of colonialism was phrased in cultural terms, without accepting or even discerning a constitutive relation between colonial discourse and the expanding reproduction of capital from western metropoles, which resulted in colonial capitalist social formations and cultures. The issue of hegemony, mediated through everyday and official practices such as ideologies of gender, racialization and 'othering' practices of difference, was thus delinked from class. Internal differentiations within the colonized societies and their social repercussions were occluded in favour of decolonization of the mind rather than of the society as a whole. Performing 'decolonization' within this discursive approach amounted to creating a counter-discourse of cultural nationalism which relied on a rereading or an inventing of pre-colonial cultural forms and traditions.

As an alternative to a marxist, historical materialist approach, this culturalist understanding of postcolonialism tilted towards postmodernism, a coincidental and opportune ideological phenomenon arising in the 1970s in opposition to marxist theory.[3] Rejecting modernism, and treating both marxism and the enlightenment among its variants, postmodernism became the common sense understanding of postcolonialism. But this common sense association between postcolonialism and postmodernism is not dictated by any logic from within the idea of postcolonialism itself. Currently, then, there is a necessity to connect postcolonialism with modernism because of the relativism that deprives postmodernism of being the basis for a thorough anti-colonial/anti-imperialist critique, inclusive of culture. More particularly, it is important to assert the value of modernism for a proper assessment of the literature and social thought of the colonies in a pre-marxist time, when marxist ideas and practices had not been generalized. The constellation of ideas and practices coded by the notion of modernism has once more become important in challenging the various right-wing groups seeking political and related epistemological renewal today.[4]

For Tagore and other early Asian modernists,[5] decolonization enjoined universalist humanism and pedagogy understood, broadly, in socially transformative terms and accompanied by suitable institutions. This perspective simultaneously advocated agricultural and artisanal cooperatives as an alternative to industrial capitalism, within the purview of a universalist culture. Tagore sought decolonization of consciousness and civil society without resorting to nationalism. His anti-nationalist, universalist humanism was idealist, but not wholly abstract, because this world-view emerged from an extensive awareness of living conditions and power relations in the colonies and elsewhere. His critique of colonialism still has a global relevance.

Rabindranath's rejection of nationalism, especially through armed struggle and other modes of violence, dates back to the period 1905–08. From this time he elaborated the notion of 'constructive *swadeshi*' – in opposition to nationalism – for bringing about a genuine decolonization.[6] He synthesized socio-cultural resources from India, Europe and Asia for his project of a humanism which would provide a substantive social being and motives for thought and action without reference to the premises of colonialism. This new subjectivity and agency would not be reactive or reactionary, both responses Rabindranath associated with nationalism. His social thought is comparable to that of Frantz Fanon, who decades later developed his own critique of colonialism in similar ways. While Fanon, a combatant in the Algerian revolution, 'stretched' Marx to develop a variant of communism, Rabindranath leaned on the humanist values of the European enlightenment. However, over time and through his visits to Europe, the United States, Russia and other parts of the world, he became clearer about the relationship between capitalism and colonialism. He saw the workings of capitalism and its colonial imperative in the countries of their origin. His trips abroad between 1912 and 1930, and his continued reading of and correspondence with intellectuals and writers around the world up to his death in 1941, exposed him to the first world war, the rise of bolshevism, the Russian revolution, and the rise of fascism in Italy,

Germany and Japan. Throughout these decades, his idealist modernism conferred on his postcolonial world-view elements of a socialist critique.

In terms of Indian resources, we need to place Tagore's modernism in the projects of social reform that arose in nineteenth-century colonial Bengal. This period saw many social and ideological changes advocated by elite and middle-class sections of Bengali society in relation to religion, caste, the treatment of women and education.[7] The most noteworthy of these social reforms is the establishment by Raja Rammohan Roy, Dwarakanath Tagore and others of the Brahmo Samaj (1861), centred on a monotheistic interpretation of hinduism, the discarding of brahminical idolatry, ritualism and caste practices, and an introduction of progressive values to Bengali social life, especially to its members. Though this movement arose in the earlier phase of colonialism during the rule of the East India Company, christianity was not its main source of influence. Rejecting trinitarian christianity, it propagated universalism and humanism as found in the Upanishads[8] with a syncretic admixture of islamic rationalism and unitarianism.[9] Interpreted by many as a derivative form of colonial discourse (Chatterjee [1986] and Subaltern Studies theorists in general), on the contrary, these ideas and practices of Bengal's social reform and the tenets of Brahmo Samaj provided a basis for reception of the reformist values of the European enlightenment. They shared the principle of reason as a primary human attribute, as well as ideas of humanism, the individual, scepticism and belief in science. Enlightenment ideas of liberty, equality and fraternity, on which the political thought of the French revolution was erected, resonated powerfully with anti-colonial sentiments in Bengal and combined social reform with the idea of freedom. As a whole, social reform movements in Bengal involved an overall transformation of brahminical civil society, advocating the end of the caste system and questioning women's subordination. They moderated, or even outright rejected, religious and ethnic differences and introduced liberal values of secularism, criticizing orthodox family mores and male–female relations, insisting instead on women's education and social participation. This modernism also introduced demands for legislative changes such as abolition of the practice of *sati* (the burning of women on their husbands' funeral pyre), of polygamy and child marriage, the raising of the age of sexual consent, and the right to widow remarriage. These reforms were as much based on interpretation of hindu scriptures as on values of European modernism. This modernist trend was vigorously contested by hindu revivalism, which – contrary to the claim of current postcolonial studies – was neither anti-colonial nor unconnected to modernism. A form of reactionary modernism, often reliant on invention of tradition, hindu revivalists actually and opportunistically were supported by the colonial state as part of its divide and rule policy and internal hegemonic struggle. Subsequently, religious revivalism provided much of the content of cultural nationalism, gaining the upper hand in the anti-partition movement in Bengal in 1905. This unleashed communal riots with a loss of life and property, mainly of muslim traders and peasants. For the rest of his life, Tagore repeatedly engaged in debates and dialogue with both hindu cultural revivalism and colonial discourse.

Having said this, we need to note that Rabindranath's modernism and cultural anti-nationalist movements of Bengal do not have a simple linear relationship. The complex dimensions of modernity developed over a long period of time during the course of the development of capitalism. Its meaning is equivocal, and is marked by ambiguities and antinomies (Kaiwar and Mazumdar 2003; Berman 1988; Williams 1992). Historically speaking, it developed two main ideological strands. Philosophically, its main tenets, as mentioned above, consisted of universalism, humanism, freedom and the idea of the individual. Adapted through capitalism, these concepts are determined and modified through their practical usage for ruling and exploitation. In the rise of bourgeois society and social consciousness, the bourgeoisie claimed enlightenment for its own. Thus modernism provided the legitimization for the new anti-feudal development, and was used by the bourgeoisie in its claim of being a universal class and the rightful representative of the lower classes. And thus, in its compromised form, modernism devoid of its universalist humanism served as the ideological cover for the particularist interests of the bourgeoisie, both in their class exploitation and capital's colonial ventures. Secular and freedom-oriented humanist modernism, subjected to the cause of power, perverted the critical idea of reason, transforming it into the instrumental rationality of capitalism and its colonial expansion. This debased form of modernism was generalized throughout European societies as social and political common sense, and penetrated colonized countries in spite of the fact that capitalism proper could not develop there. The form of capitalism developed through colonialism in its monocultural plantations for the world market was modernist only in its anti-humanist sense.

This type of modernism gave rise to either essentialist or homogenizing, or particularist and fragmentary forms of consciousness, both in the colonizing and colonized societies. It brutally restricted the application of the categories of the human and the individual found in the European context.[10] We could label this form of modernity as bourgeois and colonial hegemony, which amounts to an apparatus of consent to capitalist modernization. Its principal conduits were the governing apparatus, a hyper-oppressive economic system and the use of the English language. The nationalist and imperialist state was indispensable for this system. On these bases Rabindranath rejected both the ideology of capitalist modernization and nationalist politics. In them he saw the primary sources of imperialism and fascism. In this regard, we cite Rabindranath's letter in 1926 to C.F. Andrews from Vienna. Here he refutes his earlier misled and confused pro-Mussolini views, upon coming to a better understanding of the connection between fascism, nationalism and dictatorship prevailing in Italy through the help of Romain Rolland, Albert Einstein and other European anti-fascist contemporaries. This helped him to understand clearly the situation prevailing in Italy, where he had been received with much fanfare. He wrote to Andrews:

> [T]he method and principles of Fascism concern all humanity, and it is absurd to imagine that I could ever support a movement which ruthlessly suppresses freedom of expression, enforces observances that are against individual conscience, and walks through a bloodstained path of violence and stealthy crime. I have said over and over again that the aggressive spirit of nationalism and imperialism, religiously cultivated by most of the nations of the West, is a menace to the whole world. The demoralization which it produces in European politics is sure to have disastrous effects, especially upon the peoples of the East who are helpless against the western methods of exploitation. (Dutta and Robinson 1997: 333)

He went on to say that Italy was taught its fascist principle by 'modern schoolmasters in America. This has suggested to my mind the possibility of the idea of fascism being actually an infection from across the Atlantic' (ibid: 334).

But it is not the case that Rabindranath rejected the entire project of modernism because some aspects of it were subjugated by capitalist colonialism/imperialism. He felt that on their own these enlightenment-derived ideas, when uncompromised, were in keeping with the creation of a just society for all resting on liberty, equality and democracy. In these two faces of modernity, we can make sense of his admiration and condemnation of Europe. He saw both the universalist humanist potential of modernism, of its project of critical reason, and the capitalist use of science and technology, its reduction of knowledge into power, and the creation of the state as the prime mover of a soul and imagination destroying force. This is why he could make an emblematic use of the idea of the 'good' and the 'bad' English (Europeans). The perspective enabled him to find lifelong friends such as C.F. Andrews, E.J. Thompson, Romain Rolland and many others. It is this perception of an antinomist modernism that helped Rabindranath to repudiate fascism in all its forms. American capitalism he saw as standing on the plinth of slavery and racialist culture, devoured by greed for money, material goods and the market. He was also massively disappointed with Japan, from which he once sought support for his world vision. His distrust of the politics and political parties of any country increased incrementally; instead, he turned for hope to the good sense of common people, artists, especially poets, and universalist philosophers.

Let us look now more closely at Tagore's views on nationalism, which allowed him no space to imagine humanity or sociality. They are most accessible to modern non-Bengali readers through his prose works – his translated novels, plays, essays and letters – and some of his own creative and critical writings in English. Especially useful are (with original dates of publication): his essay *Nationalism* (1916); his correspondence with Gandhi, C.F. Andrews, Elmhurst, E.J. Thompson, Romain Rolland and Yone Noguchi; four of his novels, *Gora* (1907–09), *Ghare Baire* (Home and the World) (1916), *Chaturanga* (Four Quartets) (1914–17), and *Char Adhyay* (Four Chapters) (1931); four plays, *Achalayatan* (The Immovable Edifice) (1911), *Muktadhara* (Free Waters) (1922), *Raktakarabi* (Red Oleanders) (1924) and *Dakghar* (The Post Office) (1912).

What Rabindranath meant by decolonization can be grasped from the following passages, the first from 1908 and the second from the 1921 inauguration of his university, Visva Bharati (World University). About Bengali/Indian nationalism, he says in '*Path o Patheyo*' (Ends and Means):

> Some of us are reported to be of the opinion that it is mass animosity against the British that will unify India. ... So this anti-British animus, they say must be our chief weapon. ... If that is true, then once the cause of animosity is gone, in other words, when the British leave this country, that artificial bond of unity will snap in a moment. Where then shall we find a second target for animosity? We shall not need to travel far. We shall find it here, in our country, where we shall mangle each other in mutual antagonism, a thirst for each other's blood. (Dutta and Robinson 1995: 152)

Here Rabindranath seems to speak as a prophet, but this is not really the case. His use of the future tense is actually born out of social-political experiences of the past and the present, out of the hindu–muslim riots that shook Bengal after Lord Curzon's 1905 partition and of others that followed – experiences based on the politics of 'two nations' popular with colonial rulers and Indian nationalists alike. The second statement provides Tagore's ideal of his new centre of higher learning as 'the centre of Indian culture':

> Let me state it clearly that I have no distrust of any culture because of its foreign character. On the contrary I believe that the shock of outside forces is necessary for maintaining the vitality of our intellect. … European culture has come to us not only with its knowledge but with its speed. Even when our assimilation is imperfect and aberrations follow, it is rousing our intellectual life from the inertia of formal habits. The contradiction it offers to our traditions makes our consciousness glow. (Ibid.: 221–22)

This openness to 'foreign', in this case European, cultures is followed in the same speech by a lucid observation on colonial relations that deform this knowledge both in terms of its content and reception: 'What I object to is the artificial arrangement by which this foreign education tends to occupy all the space of our national mind, and thus kills, or hampers, the great opportunity for the creation of new thought by a new combination of truths' (ibid.: 222). This obviously cannot be achieved by what postcolonial critics have called 'mimicry' or imitation.[11] Rabindranath calls for a different solution:

> It is this which makes me urge that all the elements in our own culture have to be strengthened, not to resist the culture of the West, but to accept it and assimilate it. It must become for us nourishment and not a burden. We must gain mastery over it and not live on sufferance as hewers of texts and drawers of book learning. (Ibid.)

Rabindranath seeks mutual and creative relations between cultures, which creates an ethos or syncretism in which a true humanism can be accomplished at moral and creative levels. But was he able to actualize this vision in his creative and critical opus, his pedagogic philosophy and his educational institutions? Or should we say that his success largely lies in articulating this complex proposal itself through his literary and artistic and critical articulations?

Crucially important sites of Rabindranath's critique of nationalism lie in his treatment of the themes of women, gender relations and motherhood.

Though motherhood was a central trope in the narratives of nationalism in India and elsewhere (Koonz 2013; Bagchi 2017), Rabindranath narrated the nation by introducing a critique of patriarchy through other emotional and social relations. Generally speaking, motherhood does not feature centrally in his national imaginary. Even when it does – in his novel *Gora* (1910), for example – he interprets it in non-patriarchal terms. The idea of the mother stands for India as well as universal qualities of compassion and nurturing. But he did not use the concept in a biological and familial sense (Bagchi 2017). As feminist critiques of nationalism show, this is an exceptional gesture, and especially so in South Asia, where hindu cultural nationalism excelled in this maternal and deified representational figure.[12] In other novels of Rabindranath freedom and bondage, the main motifs of colonial domination, are often imagined through sexual desires and male–female relationships. The ideas of the individual and individual choice are attached to the narrative of domination and liberation, and serve as the vehicle and the corollary for different understandings of freedom as the basis of this choice. Thus, the story of nationalism is a story of passion – which is figurated in terms of the passion of men and women for each other, passion for the freedom of the nation – both possibly leading to death or destruction. And thus, personal and political passions are transparently overlaid. The story of passion, however, is not just posited, but also critiqued. As Rabindranath sees it, passion should be contained within the frame of reason, which is ontologically paradoxical, and as such, the narrative poses a conflict between acquisitive individualism and humanist universalism.

The conflicts of passion and reason are further complicated by a perceived bifurcation between nature and culture. The idea of nature itself entails a duality in these novels. In *Ghare Baire* (1916b) or *Char Adhyay* (1934), for instance, nature is accorded two qualities: a hobbesian-cum-darwinian or survivalist aspect, as well as a nurturing, compassionate and creative one. While the former is expressed in nationalism and its socio-political variants, including emotional ones such as greed for wealth and domination of nature, the latter aspect of nature opens out to humanity in empathy and imagination. 'Freedom' in this context is tempered with, or not contradictory to, reason. It is this kind of freedom that provides Rabindranath with the basis for his idea of decolonization. This humanist assertion, however, is not expected by Rabindranath to be achieved without a struggle between a narrowly defined individuality and an empathic imaginative sense of the self and other, between a grasping, narcissistic aspect of human personality and that of the emancipated human. Given his own history with nationalism, his struggles to free himself from it, the presence of the trajectory in his novels and other writings seems inevitable. After all, as early as the 1850s, when nationalism had not yet congealed into clear political ideologies but was at the stage of cultural reactions and responses to colonialism, Rabindranath and his family actively participated in shaping the major aspects of Bengali 'nationalist' culture, with influence in other parts of India.[13] By the 1870s, ideological responses ranged from social reformism and hindu revivalism to liberal and economic nationalism, each sometimes affecting the other and providing the ground for future politics. For example, hindu revivalism politicized into cultural nationalism remained as a strand of the Indian National Congress (INC). Gandhi added a generous admixture of hindu culture, thus colouring bourgeois nationalism's liberal forms.

The problematic of nationalism and decolonization is perhaps best captured in *Ghare Baire*. In this parable of sexual and nationalist passion, an extravagant display of particularisms, the female character Bimala, the emblem of India, the country/nation and its peoples, has ultimately chosen the ethics of universality and so has chosen the good – *agape* over *eros*, and constructive social and cultural reconstruction or decolonization over a selfish, suicidal and murderous passion of nationalism. But this realization in Bimala does not come about until nature, in the shape of physical desire and violent politics, sweeps all before it, as a hurricane devastates a landscape which then awaits regeneration. The narrative indicates that for Rabindranath the road to decolonization is never a straight line. If his poet's psyche is the feminine Bimala, then it is through a wrenching struggle that she gives up the heady and heroic fervour of nationalism to choose the reasonability of the quiet and the relative obscurity of the good. But ultimately it is the last, hardest choice that she has to make, life-affirming though not spectacular – seeking reconciliation, not antagonism, between the self and the other. Rabindranath's decolonization, his stance of modernist 'post'-colonization, is not a mere rebuttal to or reversal or transvaluation of the values of colonialism. It stubbornly tries to posit ethical/cultural premises which are unconnected to either colonialism or what he sees as its child, nationalism. The project here is to create society anew on principles of emancipatory idealist modernism.

My assertion of a liberatory potential of modernism, even in its idealist variant, might be questionable for many scholars of postcolonial studies. This is true of the Bengal school of Subaltern Studies, who even many decades ago saw modernism as colonial discourse. Partha Chatterjee, Dipesh Chakrabarty and Ashis Nandy, considered to be major figures in postcolonial studies, considered postmodernism the fitting epistemology of postcolonial critique. Anti-modernism, in the shape of appeal to traditional culture, has been considered by them as the hallmark of decolonization. If the Subaltern Studies propositions are accepted, Rabindranath's modernist thought becomes derivative of colonial discourse. This essentialist understanding of modernity relies on the orientalist binary paradigm in which modernity and tradition, the west versus the east, confront each other. In this epistemological gesture of cultural essentialism notions such as 'east', 'west', 'tradition' and 'modernity' are interpreted in an ideological manner, and lead to the spatialization of cultures. They therefore occlude the presence of diverse and contradictory social relations and cultural forms existing within the same spaces. There is no recognition on the part of such postcolonialist thinkers that these terms are susceptible to socio-historical formations and contexts. They cannot see that the European enlightenment, with its modernist humanist philosophy, is not a univocal constellation of ideas; that they range from various liberatory notions, such as the human, the individual, equality, rights and democracy, and are mutated by their subjugation to the purpose of capitalist colonialism. Limited to Europe, from the rise of capitalism and slavery the idea of the human is restricted to Europeans and modernism becomes an ally of domination, hierarchy, authoritarianism and racism. Emancipatory characteristics of enlightenment thought are inverted in a conjuncture of colonialism and capitalism to become an oppressive force. However, this does not take away from the fact that, delinked from capitalist colonialism, enlightenment thought/modernism can be emancipatory and truly democratic. Thus humanism, when articulated through class oppression, slavery and colonialism, may have become a conduit for racism, ethnic supremacism and so on (Gilman 1985), but it still contains its liberationist qualities when articulated to the project of questioning all power relations. It should also be noted that a capitalist colonial turn of enlightenment ideas not only dehumanized non-Europeans, but also was a turn that became active among the Europeans themselves. Class and patriarchy created lesser human beings within the very heartland of Europe.

We have to recognize, therefore, that modernism has qualitatively different forms. There is a real distinction between utilitarian, techno- or instrumental rationalist modernity at the service of capitalism and imperialism, and the modernity of universalism, which refuses to compromise its idealist and anti-empiricist character. This stance, when integrated with Kantian imperatives of 'enlightenment' – of what an individual might know and live by, unaided by received traditions of conduct (Kant 1967) – introduces into the question of the self, self-making and the individual a completely different set of considerations than the ones posed by those who see modernity by definition as colonial. Rabindranath's idealist modernism cannot simply rest with the Hegelian master–slave parable so crucial to anti-modernist postcolonial critics. In his schema, the 'other' is not necessarily in an enslaved and antagonistic relationship to the self. Here sociality of a positive kind trumps the sociality of a sadomasochistic nature as projected by conventional postcolonialists. We should be mindful that modernity is a cluster of concepts and that it is actually sensitive both to relations of oppression and their negation.

During the eighteenth and nineteenth centuries in Europe and Bengal we hear much about humanist and universalist pedagogies for creating a new social consciousness. In this context, Bengal and Europe shared their modernist projects with each other. Particularly, the modernist idea of 'the individual' spurred the projects of European social transformation and political thought. It is only in such an environment that the complex, at times contradictory, project of the French revolution could be undertaken as the world's first attempt at consciously planning an anti-monarchic, anti-feudal revolution (Marx and Engels, *German Ideology* [1970]; *Communist Manifesto* [1985]). These European ventures in emancipatory ideas and politics in no way contradict the cultural resources and the moral philosophy of universalism that Rabindranath, the Brahmo Samaj and other reformers gleaned from Indian philosophy. Indian readiness for European modern ideas served as the shock absorber when colonialism, violently and suddenly, intruded upon Bengali/Indian society. In this openness to new ideas and forms of living, Rabindranath inherited the legacy of Rammohan Roy, Debendranath Tagore, Henry Vivian Derozio and Iswar Chandra Vidyasagar.[14] Contestation between modernist social reform and religious revivalism threw Bengal's upper class/caste elite (*bhadralok*) into fervent productivity along with their encounter with the west. Middle-class women, hitherto enclosed in the household, came to schools in large numbers, wrote, and became active in social reform and politics (Kumar 1993). Instead of subordination and paralysis of will attributed to the putative colonial subject by conventional postcolonial thinkers, projects of self-discovery and self-making were everywhere.

Rabindranath's two educational institutions provide good examples of an alternative decolonizing pedagogy. The first, Santiniketan (abode of peace), a children's school, was established on the family's estate in 1901 and evolved into a university in 1921 (Visva Bharati); and the second, Sriniketan (abode of grace), an agricultural and handicrafts institute, was established in 1923. Tagore wrote the following about Santiniketan in 1912:

> I have it in mind to make Santiniketan the connecting thread between India and the world. I have found a world centre for the study of humanity there. The days of petty nationalism are numbered – let the step towards universal union occur in the fields of Bolpur. I want to make that place somewhere beyond the limits of nation and geography. (Dutta and Robinson 1995: 205)[15]

Santiniketan's motto is still, 'Where the world finds itself within the same nest.' Here Rabindranath tried to practise his transformational pedagogy to create a microcosm of his vision of decolonization. Each participant was to aspire to a self-emancipation necessary for a humanist society. The presence of scholars and teachers from outside of India – for example, from Europe, the United States, China, Japan and Tibet, attracted by Rabindranath's reputation – gave substance to his universalist ideal. Departments of learning hitherto unknown in India, particularly related to Asia rather than to only Europe or England, were opened in Chinese, Japanese and Tibetan studies. Some European scholars who fled the hostile world of the second world war and the nazi holocaust waited out their time in Santiniketan (Aronson 1991).

Rabindranath's interest in young children and adolescents, an interest similar to that of Rousseau and other romantics, was essential in shaping subjects for his humanist vision. The trope of 'the child' (*shishu*) plays a central role in his literary and critical opus. For him, as among the European thinkers mentioned above, childhood is a time for complete receptivity, wonder and creativity. In symbolic clusters or metaphors in hundreds of poems, songs and drawings, in short stories, children's rhymes and textbooks, he celebrated the joy, play and sorrows of childhood as a quintessential moment of consciousness. Nor did he hide from children the destructive dimensions of colonialism and the perils of colonial imitation. As a critic of colonialist/racist humanism, he wrote the parable of the fox, Hou-Hou, in *Shey* (He) (Tagore 1937a), in which the fox deserts his own kind to be accepted as 'human'. To this end, he shaved off his dark fur, revealing the pink and white skin underneath, cut off his tail, tottered on two legs and spoke haltingly in an alien language. Needless to say, his fate was not enviable. This sad and amusing children's story has an uncanny echo of Tagore's 1921 letter to Edward Thompson about winning the Nobel prize in 1913 as a poet of the English language:

> You know I began to pay court in your language when I was fifty. … In my translations I timidly avoid all difficulties, which has the effect of making them smooth and thin. I know I am misrepresenting myself as a poet to the western readers. But when I began this career of falsifying my coins I did it in play. Now I am becoming frightened of its enormity and I am willing to make a confession of my misdeeds and withdraw into my original vocation as a mere Bengali poet. (Dutta and Robinson 1995: 264)

The universal – especially as imagined and expressed by a poet and an educator – obviously could not be reached by ignoring the concretely local and the personal. In this Tagore's creative transcendence was like that of a bird which is at home in both a nest and the sky. The line of his song from the collection, *The Gardener*, 'I am restless, thirsting for the afar', captures this mentality. His idea of being 'human' is one of a consciousness constantly moving outwards while also residing as a denizen of a local world. Thus the category 'human', as interpreted by Rabindranath, should be understood as a category of desire, always moving towards a simultaneous becoming and being, rather than one of an empirical achievement that colonial modernization arrogated only to Europeans. He exposed how the 'others' of Europe, the 'lesser' people of the colonies, the slaves and indentured workers, were portrayed as lagging behind or being consigned to an essentialism of savagery. However, the being of human identified with becoming is always incomplete and unfolding in time. This Rabindranath holds as the universal truth for all humanity. Nor does his dynamic modernist humanism allow the form and content of being human to absolutely coincide.[16] For him, the ideal towards which humanity moves always opens out to a receding horizon.

Speaking epistemologically, Rabindranath's modernism is idealist, but it is still a markedly different type of modernism than that of the idealist colonial or postmodernist varieties. It is definitely not colonial discourse. The difference between these two modernisms can be seen by comparing Rabindranath's ideas on the 'new man' with those of Nietzsche (1844–1900). Rabindranath articulated this concept within a universalist humanist perspective, while Nietzsche's superman (übermensch) was shaped within the ethos of capitalist colonialism, resting on class, slavery and other forms of unfreedom. Nietzsche's superman is an atomized, egotistical entity who lacks any positive connection with the rest of humanity. The übermensch 'surpasses' only to the extent that he negates any form of sociality. Though the idea of 'going beyond' is common to both, in Nietzsche it has a large measure of social darwinism that makes the übermensch vulnerable to an empiricist twist later on by nazis and other fascists.[17] This isolationist individualism is the content of the loneliness of Zarathustra, who despises the sociality of the 'herd'. Similarly, a colonial modernist understanding of 'civilization' implies that Europe has already achieved it, while the colonized societies were either decaying or are yet to attain this state. This is the meaning of the notion of human in colonial discourse, a racialized anthropology based on social darwinism. Evolution thus understood serves as an ideology of legitimization for capitalist colonization. It is a compendium of colonial power/knowledge (Foucault 1980; Gould 1996; Lewontin *et al.* 1984). Tagore's idealist modernism, on the contrary, does not compromise with empiricism. By virtue of that, it has the potential for providing a critique of the empirically existing here and now. Socially speaking, the 'self' and the 'other' are not in a dominating–dominated relation, but one of aspiring identification. The myth of the superman is replaced by 'Man' as everyman, and ideas such as 'purity of race' and ethnicity and 'race heroes' are unutterable within this framework. Thus Tagore rejected the ethnicism and civilizational/cultural supremacy inherent in nationalism.

Rabindranath's idea of freedom is compatible with that of a socially individualized self. He compares this self to a river which finds its way to the ocean of humanity. The metaphor is dramatized in his plays, *Muktadhara* (Tagore 1922a) and *Achalayatan* (Tagore 1922b). *Muktadhara* centres on a large dam project, based on a fetishistic attitude towards technology for the domination of nature and inspired by a mechanical or instrumental rationality. The common people, moved by their spontaneity and sociality and led by a visionary poet, unite against the machine-worshipping bureaucrats to stop their project of enslaving nature. Through their creative spirit and readiness of action, they succeed in breaking the dam and freeing the river. In this view, as opposed to the nietzschean one, nature is not a primitive force but rather a life-giving one, to be enjoyed and cooperated with. It is the colonizing of the river that turns it destructive, as life is deformed by processes of domination. Tagore makes a contrast here between the 'order' imposed by a wealth-driven modernization and the 'rhythm' of life and creativity invoking dance. In *Achalayatan*, this same message is played out with regard to students in a school which represses their creativity, curiosity and joy in learning. This repression is also considered by Rabindranath as anti-nature. The pupils, together with a poet, break down the walls of this sterile institution of dead learning. Once more, freedom is conjoined with emotion, imagination and sociality, and a concept of learning congenial to children's nature emerges. This learning is connected with an inner human need rather than an institutional one. In 1911, in *Jibansmriti* (My Reminiscences), Rabindranath expressed a similar sentiment:

> Only in a land where an animus of divisiveness reigns supreme, and innumerable petty barriers separate one from another, must this longing to express a larger life in one's own remain unsatisfied. I strained to reach humanity in my youth, as in my childhood I yearned for the outside world from within the chalk circle drawn around me by the servants. ... And yet, if we cannot get in touch with it, if no breeze can blow from it, no current flow out of it, no path be open to the free passage of travellers – then the dead things accumulating around us will never be removed, but continue to mount up until they smother all vestige of life. (Dutta and Robinson 1995: 431–32)

The play *Raktakarabi* (Tagore 1924) is most crucial in depicting the fundamental conflict between humanist modernity and greed-centred modernization, between the human and the machine. The action takes place in a gold mine, at the heart of which subterranean realm sits a king imprisoned by technology for exploitation of the earth by means of human labour. Here workers become mere numbers and their overseers a part of the machinery for extraction. In this space daily life, imagination, love and sociality are as absent as fresh air, greenery and the sky. Here, where the earth is merely its own skeleton composed of rock and minerals, enter imagination, spontaneity, and sexual and social desire. They are expressed through a poet/singer, a young woman, who is the principle of love and freedom, and a boy, the sign of innocence. Together they embody freedom, beauty and imagination, and they reject a machine-controlled civilization. They shift the movement of the play from darkness towards light, from the interior to the world outside, from a calculus of greed to poetry. They precipitate a turmoil of humane feelings and imagination into the ordered world of exploitation. Finally, the moment of freedom arises from a catastrophe, when the mine is flooded, as the workers rise up against the system. The king and the workers emerge from the dark chambers to join the humanity of the world outside in a celebration of life. The message is that nature, people and society are perverted into 'primitivity/savagery' by domination, mechanization, and a culture of rigidity, narrowness and acquisitiveness. Tagore's approach is reminiscent of Rousseau and romanticism, except that unlike Tagore, Rousseau has a unidimensional and negative view of culture. Rousseau's view of nature is equally unidimensional, except that it is all positive. For him, it is 'the chains' of culture that shackle humanity and destroy the impulse for the good and the social (Rousseau 1968; Coletti 1972). Rabindranath's humanist reading of both culture and nature redeems them from this attributive unidemensionality. Here imagination and empathy as capacities for apprehending the idea of the universal are the overdetermining faculties binding nature to culture.

To rescue Rabindranath from the accusation of a vulgar romanticism, we need to know that he was not anti-science or technology when they were used for serving humanity. He counted among his friends many scientists of note, such as Albert Einstein (1879–1955) and Jagadish Chandra Bose (1858–1937), and he created a school for agricultural science and technology. As his correspondence with Gandhi reveals, they thoroughly disagreed on these matters (Bhattacharya 1997a). A positive and non-instrumental view of science is found in Rabindranath's opinion on Gandhi's advocacy of the spinning wheel (*charkha*) as a challenge to English textile mills. He says:

> [We] fail to rise above the ideology of the *charkha*. The *charkha* does not require anyone to think: one simply turns the wheel of the antiquated invention, using the minimum of judgement and stamina. In a more industrious vital country than ours such a proposition would stand no chance of acceptance. (Dutta and Robinson 1995: 365)

As early as 1907–09 in the novel *Gora*, Tagore commented on the ugly reality of obscurantism and primitive agricultural implements oppressing rural India, and on the need for bringing to the countryside a scientific and humanist outlook, especially against caste and superstition:

> The ties of the samaj, the devotion to customs, do not give them any strength in practice. ... Gora realized that this samaj gives no help in times of need, no support in the face of danger, it can only harass people by enforcing a rigid conformity. ... In the immobility of the rural life Gora saw the real weakness of our country in an absolutely unadorned form. (Sarkar 1973: 62)

Last but not least, Rabindranath wrote a popular science textbook for his students, entitled *Visva Parichay* (Knowing the Universe) (Tagore 1937b).

The type of modernism that Rabindranath espoused did not endear him to the Indian, Japanese or European nationalists. He himself did not spare them in his furious condemnation of imperialism arising out of nationalism. An important example of this is to be found in his letter to the imperial Japanese poet Yone Noguchi, written in 1938:

> When you speak, therefore, of 'the inevitable means, terrible it is though, for establishing a new great world in the Asiatic continent' – signifying, I suppose, the bombing of Chinese women and children and the desecration of ancient temples and universities as a means of saving China for Asia – you are ascribing to humanity a way of life which is not even inevitable among the animals and would certainly not apply to the East, in spite of her occasional aberrations. You are building your conception of Asia which would be raised on a tower of skulls. (Dutta and Robinson 1995: 497)

Indian nationalists considered Tagore's unorthodox depiction of peasants and women in his creative and critical writings as a slur on hindu womanhood and social order. His secularism and universalist humanism were interpreted as collusion with colonial power. Though he rejected his knighthood after the 1919 massacre at Jallianwala Bagh perpetrated by the colonial rulers, hindu nationalists mockingly continued to refer to him as 'Sir' Rabindranath. They lacked the insight of Gandhi, who called him the 'Great Sentinel', the conscience of the nation. He was sustained by his stubborn belief in the possibilities inherent in human capacities and had a vision to convey, which he made many trips across the world to share. It is against this humanist vision that Rabindranath judged the hubris of both colonial modernity and imperialist nationalism. In the gathering darkness of the second world war and his own approaching death (1941), he expressed his pessimism in *Shabhyatar Shankat* (Crisis in Civilization) (Tagore 1941). In the two decades before he died he came to see, perhaps moved by Gandhi's moral suasion and the Indian National Congress's relatively non-violent mass mobilization, that there might be a necessity of a territorial independence and a nation state. A few lines from *The Crisis in Civilization* are worth quoting here; they are reminiscent of Romain Rolland speaking about 'pessimism of the intellect and optimism of the will', which Antonio Gramsci adopted as his own motto during his years in Mussolini's prisons (Gramsci 1971). Rabindranath wrote:

> The wheels of fate will some day compel the British to give up their Indian Empire. But what kind of India will they leave behind, what stark misery?

> When the stream of their two centuries' administration runs dry at last, what a waste of mud and filth will they leave behind them! I had at one time believed that the springs of civilization would issue out of the heart of Europe. But today, when I am about to quit the world, that faith has deserted me. (Dutta and Robinson 1995: 364)

But he continued in a vein of principled humanism and optimism: 'And yet I shall not commit the grievous sin of losing faith in man. I would rather look forward to the opening of a new chapter in his history after the cataclysm is over and the air rendered clean with the spirit of service and sacrifice' (ibid.).

Is there something still for us to learn from Rabindranath's vision of postcoloniality? The answer can only be in the affirmative. Rabindranath both dreamed and acted practically – creating institutions, making critical interventions, and taking advisory roles to Gandhi and the Indian National Congress as well as to European anti-fascist movements. The ideal character of his humanism notwithstanding, he learned that one could not fly to decolonization but had to walk through the mud and grime of actual history. His active intelligence, social awareness, moral responsiveness and profound imagination constantly grappled with existing enigmas and nightmares of history. The beauty of his vision remains compelling, as does his constant caution against particularism/narrowness, national chauvinism, and their horrific consequences. Though his humanism rested in idealism, he also made us feel that the future begins now, that this is worth striving for. Though Rabindranath himself was not a socialist, no socialist revolution could be imagined without these core values of humanist universalism. Especially now, in our present world, where ultra-nationalist politics in various disguises has emerged with a vengeance – in invasions, occupations, genocides, and the daily death of humanity in the name of democracy, freedom, god and ethnic belonging – Rabindranath's voice is as important to us as it was to generations before. The last radio broadcast in Paris in 1940, on the eve of the nazi entry into the city, was Rabindranath's play *Dakghar* (The Post Office) (Tagore 1912b) in André Gide's translation (Dutta and Robinson 1995: 351). It is about a dying child who awaits the king's messenger to bring him a letter from the king. Neither the boy nor we know what will be in that letter – a message of death or of hope? But we still need to wait, because in that act of waiting, which is not simply passive, we affirm our fight against violence and despair.

To conclude, we have to return to the concept of postcolonialism and point to the complexity of its meaning. In one sense it is no more than a simple descriptive category that signals to a historical period, but it does not offer any particular or definite content. Its epistemological stance depends on the politics that is connected with its deployment. Therefore, what passes as postcolonialism/postcoloniality does not have a fixed epistemological ground, nor a logical affiliation to either modernism or postmodernism. If postmodernism is the epistemological ground for postcolonialism, the project of decolonization could only be cultural and working at the level of consciousness. That would amount to saying that colonialism is no more than creating hegemonic consciousness among the subject population. Merely changing the discourse and leaving intact the socio-economic and practical dimensions of capitalist colonialism could not achieve a state of comprehensive postcoloniality. We need to ponder whether a postmodernist understanding and practice could even be meaningfully conceived when so much on the ground of capitalist colonialism remains unaddressed. To deepen the discussion, we need to remind ourselves of the distinction we make between critical idealist modernism and colonial modernism. Even though idealist modernism is not historical materialist, it still has the potential for questioning social life and consciousness as it exists in any point in time. It can help to negate what exists by holding up the idea of what could possibly be. Though this is not the most common way of interpreting idealism as a source for a critical perspective, it makes much sense to take this utopian use of idealism as a critical mode of thinking. In Rabindranath's case, idealism serves a critical purpose, particularly as he grounds his notion of universalist humanism in human capacities. This allows him to make truth-claims on the basis of humanism, connected to the desirability for a physically and socially encapacitated creative individual, justice and freedom. This composite figure of the human is based on commonality between individuals.

These ideas are non-negotiable in any project of transformation. As a hyper-subjectivist epistemology, idealist modernism cannot of course disclose the constitutive relationship between consciousness and the social, and accords them qualitatively distinct realms. Nonetheless, it can make claims of truth for the importance of imagination, for grand narratives of profound change of consciousness that involve fundamental social transformation. Postmodernism, in contrast, posits an epistemology, if we can call it that, of indecision. It challenges any truth-claim for ideas to be effective for change on a large scale. It cannot sustain a grand narrative of conscious making of history for humanity. It denies both subjective and objective truth-claims – any notion of real knowledge regarding the self and the world and their creative relations. As such, its world-view is fragmentary, relativist, and at best capable of bringing about change in local and culturally particular terms. Within the postmodernist framework, lacking space for history, colonialism takes on an episodic character, and resistance to it is manifested in terms of subversion, displacement and opposition of identities through cultural manoeuvres. Here the universal human is replaced by the particular individual without a sense of an irreducible interior self or sociality. With its narrow, barely possible formulation of anti-colonialism, postcolonialism gets into 'pitfalls of nationalism' – even when professing scepticism. Freedom, liberty, justice, equality and so on become the elements of an illusory narrative, and resistance is an issue-based piecemeal matter. The refusal of anything but a factual truth entrenched within this framework makes not only historical change but even critique untenable. It can only 'imagine' history or episodes of debates with an ineffable 'power'; its violences are only epistemic.

But unbeknownst to itself, the postmodernist postcolonial position does uphold a grand narrative, that of colonialism, its own point of birth and departure. Though it cannot explain the phenomenon of colonialism, it relies on that very notion to structure its own premises. Its end, therefore, cannot be going beyond colonialism, because its own epistemological validity lies in the colonial project. Unlike idealist modernism, it cannot provide an impetus for a larger vision of revolutionary social change. As the concept of the social cannot be accommodated by postmodernism, it can only speak in terms of atomistic individuals or, at best, in terms of fragments, each a bounded social/cultural group. If we contrast modernist idealism to postmodernist idealism, it becomes evident that the abstract generality of the former's universal ideas is matched by the latter's particularist ideas. The general identity of the human understood as a set of shared creative capacities, including that of empathy, is replaced in postmodernism by segments of cultural identities. The critical horizon of postmodernism is so narrow that it can only offer simple binaries to the existing colonial ones, thus continuing the project of colonialism in reverse. Postmodernism makes decolonization an inconceivable task.

Rabindranath's idealist vision of decolonization provides direction to a path to true decolonization. His humanism is more than a mere aesthetic trope of desire because it partially emerges from his awareness of the actual social deformation, economic deprivation and cultural degradation caused by colonialism and imperialism in India and elsewhere. His idealism made him think redemptively. Human redemption and decolonization became one in his thought. But as with all idealism, the path between the fallen present and the utopian future cannot be adequately charted to make a thoroughgoing social transformation possible. Rabindranath created pedagogy and processes of economic production to signal paths to be pursued. But his understanding of politics as something that exists only in the realm of state power, the frequent distinction he makes between political and civil society, made it difficult for him to entertain a framework for the role of transformative politics in human liberation. He could not conceive of how people might bring their consciousness to bear on the actual relations of power facing them. But from his modernist idealism the leap can be made to a struggle for a socialist human transformation. In fact, such a transformation without his humanist vision would not lead to decolonization.

Notes

[1] Fanon (1968) speaks to this in his chapter on 'The Pitfalls of National Consciousness.' See also Aijaz Ahmad (1996), where he speaks about the auxiliary classes of the bourgeoisie who become the ruling classes of the newly liberated countries, and aid and abet neocolonialism. See also Sekyi-Otu (1996), who, following Fanon's critique of the colonial bourgeoisie, establishes Fanon as a partially marxist left universalist in *Left Universalism, Africa Centric Essays* (2018).

[2] Ania Loomba, in *Colonialism/Postcolonialism* (2005: 7) rightly points out that postcolonialism entails two dimensions, one of temporality (history), the other ideological (politics).

[3] See Lyotard's *The Postmodern Condition* (1984), the primary text for postmodernism, inspired by his disappointment with communism and marxism in the context of failed communist and student uprisings in 1968 France.

[4] In this connection, left liberal secular modernist thinkers can come to the aid of anti-capitalist colonial critique. See, for example, Edward Said, *The Question of Palestine (*1979b); *Covering Islam* (1981); and *Peace and Its Discontents* (1995).

[5] This characterization could apply to other late nineteenth- and early twentieth-century Asian critics of colonialism, such as Zhou Shuren (Lu Hsün) of China (1881–1936) and Count Okakura Kazuko of Japan (1862–1913). See also the ideas of 'east' and 'west' with special reference to the art of Japan, published on the eve of the Russo-Japanese war. Pan-Asianism started as a political philosophy against imperialism and then mutated into Japanese imperialism in the late nineteenth and the first three decades of the twentieth century. See Pankaj Mohan (2010) and C. Stolte and H. Fischer-Tiné (2012).

[6] The word '*swadeshi*' means 'of one's own country', which came to be loosely translated as 'nationalism' for creating a political ideology. It could also mean 'patriotism', as no mention of a nation is made in Indian languages. Rabindranath's approach to the idea of *swadeshi*, dubbed by Sumit Sarkar (1973) as 'constructive *swadeshi*', is a version of political moderation, what he calls 'a moderate and broad'

social politics which, 'quieter and sometimes non-political in its tone, emphasized patient efforts at self-development, ignoring foreign rule rather than lauding an immediate attack on it' (ibid.: 48). This approach of Rabindranath's is in contrast to 'political extremism proper [which] tried to turn the boycott into a campaign of full-scale' political struggle, which 'set its sights on immediate independence rather than partial reforms or slow self-generation' (ibid.).

[7] See Susobhan Sarkar (1970b); see also Sumit Sarkar (1973, 1985) and Tapan Raychaudhuri (1988). The modernist values of the Bengali elite are comparable to the equally elite philosophy of the European renaissance and enlightenment.

[8] Late Vedic Sanskrit texts. They are philosophical ideas put forth in a poetic form of dialogues involving a quest for knowledge. They are also known as Vedantas and became the basis of philosophy. They mark a transition from Vedic ritualism to spiritual ideas.

[9] Most significant of these is the *mu'tazila* tradition, a school of islamic theology that denies the status of the qur'an as uncreated; it evolved between the eighth and tenth centuries. These strands of rationalist islam involve three principles: oneness of god, pursuit of justice and freedom of action that humans possess.

[10] See Raymond Williams' entry on the word 'human' in *Keywords* (1976); also see, in the same text, the entries on civilization, culture, modern and tradition.

[11] In his novels *A House for Mr Biswas* (1961) and *The Mimic Men* (1967), V.S. Naipaul elaborates the role of the coopted colonial middle class in continuing colonial hegemony. See also Wole Soyinka, *The Interpreters* (1972) and his other novels. The concept of 'hybridity' (see Homi Bhabha 1994) is not applicable to Rabindranath, just as 'cosmopolitan' is not (Collins 2012), the latter attribution implying aggregation.

[12] There is a vast literature on the topics of women and nationalism, and gender and nationalism. See, for example, Bannerji, Mojab and Whitehead (2001); Yuval-Davis (1997); Jasodhara Bagchi (1993a); and Kumari Jayawardena (1986).

[13] For western readers, the best source of information in English on this so far is Dutta and Robinson's biography, *Rabindranath Tagore: A Myriad-minded Man* (1995).

[14] Raja Rammohan Roy (1772–1833), Henry Louis Vivian Derozio (1809–1831), and Iswar Chandra Vidyasagar (1820–1891) were noted social reformers in nineteenth-century Bengal. For more details, see Joshi (1975) and Sumit Sarkar (1985). On Vidyasagar, see also Asok Sen (1977).

[15] For more on the foundation of Santiniketan and Sriniketan, see Dutta and Robinson (1995), chapters 20 and 21. See also Dutta and Robinson (1997), especially Rabindranath's letter to his son Rathindranath Tagore, dated 11 October 1917, and O'Connell (2002).

[16] As opposed to Hegel, for whom the ideal and the actual do coincide in his conceptualization of the fully formed state as an actualization of the Idea.

[17] Some aspects of this have been discussed in David McNally's *Bodies of Meaning* (2001, Introduction and chapter 1). Also, on Nietzsche's connection with Darwin, see Kaufman (1974). On self-making and the *übermensch*, see Norris (1993).

3

Always Towards

Human Development and Nationalism in Rabindranath Tagore

Introduction

> History reveals that institutions or artifacts produced by human beings can lead to the exploitation or the loss of freedom of other human beings. Thus the celebration of the good life of an Athenian citizen in Plato's time can hide the wretchedness of vast numbers of slaves whose labor made it possible for the few free citizens to enjoy that good life. Our criteria then must apply to all, or at least the vast majority of the vast human group concerned, if they are to lay claim to universality.
>
> – Amiya Kumar Bagchi, *Perilous Passage* (2006: 4)

At the end of Bertolt Brecht's *Three Penny Opera* (1973), the chorus laments the fate of those who sink, nameless, into the shadows under the glaring footlights of the stage or society. Narratives of both dramatic and economic development generally name as the 'successful', the 'heroic' ones, those captains of capital and class who know how to profit from the misery and poverty of others. Two Indian authors, Manik Bandyopadhyay and Mahasweta Devi, speak of this same darkness in the heart of light, the moral and social ethos of capitalist industrialism and its state. In his short story '*Sarisreep*' (The Reptiles) (2002), Manik Bandyopadhyay tells the story of human reptiles, the Bengali *bhadralok* (middle classes) of colonial Calcutta, who lure to his death a handicapped orphan child, sinking their claws into him to gain his inheritance. Manik ends his story by expanding this trope of deep penetration in search of property through the image of an airplane flying to the jungles of Sunderban, where animals cower in front of 'development' missions. Mahasweta Devi portrays the developmental predations of postcolonial capitalist India by the same class agents in her stories in *Nairite Megh* (Clouds in the Southwest) (1979). One story in particular tells us of the devastation of the *adivasi*s, the appropriation of their land and forest rights, through a description of their punishment for resisting forces of development. They are barred from buying salt. Attacked by the trinitarian forces of law, social order and capital, the *adivasi*s retreat deeper into the forest, blood coagulating in their veins. One dimly-lit forest night witnesses them crawling on all fours, sharing the salt lick with animals. This turn of the story is no more a trick of magic realism than the factual one performed on the *adivasi*s of Jajpur, Odisha, cursed by the presence of uranium under their soil. They were murdered by the forces of the state and capital and returned to their community from the police morgue with their hands chopped off, a mutilation for the ostensible purpose of identification reserved for the lowly and the nameless.

It is against this kind of 'development', of shadows under the proscenium lights of patriarchal, casteist and communalist capitalism, both national and international, that critiques have been made.[1] Mine is no exception, and it points out that there are other meanings of development unconnected to economic growth. This latter version, dominant in conventional understanding, largely originated from the modernization theories of the United States in the 1950s, which deeply influenced countries of the global south and provided the ground for present-day neo-liberal conceptions and forms of development. Critics of capitalism, however, have long insisted that another kind of development is possible, that 'another world is possible' – a long-standing demand given a slogan-like character by the Zapatista militants of Chiapas, Mexico.[2] But this refusal of the conventional idea of development with its corporate, anti-human connotations cannot be actualized without exposing and resisting the seductive and destructive paradigm of capitalist modernization, in both its ideologies and practices. The lure of 'India Shining', the glitter of hyper-shopping malls, miles of highways created through the destruction of villages and forests, the development of so-called 'vedic' villages with health spas as well as special economic zones (SEZs) among other examples of 'development', clearly indicate who the beneficiaries of this project are. Remembering the dire results of the once much-vaunted 'green revolution', we are continuing the eradication of any sustainable agriculture and facing food crises brought about by the extension of the capitalist premises of that revolution. Contrary to what Marx said, this tragedy did not become a farce, but rather a deeper and darker tragedy – with mind-numbing levels of dispossession including that of life itself for the majority in India.[3] Though such histories cannot and should not be replayed, as Walter Benjamin said in the dark days of the techno-fetishism of the nazis, history must be witnessed even as we move forward either towards resistance or the abyss (Benjamin 1969a). It is for this reason that Paul Klee's angel of history, driven forward by the winds of progress, looks back at the debris of burning cities piling up behind him.

This brings me to the sense of a paradox I regularly experience when teaching my seminar on the topic of 'women and development'. We, both teacher and students, are struck by the complexities and contestations encoded in this concept of development, and how differently it is understood by scholars and practitioners coming from divergent epistemologies, geopolitical locations and socio-economic relations.[4] The long-standing existence of this contestation about the meaning of development has receded in the now almost-forgotten debates and critiques of colonial capitalist modernization engaged in by Andre Gunder Frank, Samir Amin, Immanuel Wallerstein or Amiya Kumar Bagchi. We see expansions and modifications of their critiques in the works of Utsa Patnaik, Prabhat Patnaik, Jayati Ghosh and others, or in the global debates, reincarnating older ones, between neo-liberal globalizers, the market worshippers, and those who see through the mystifications and contortions of neo-liberalism, which is a fuller version of neo-colonialism/imperialism. Following their critiques, and others such as David Harvey, David McNally or James Petras, we can see that the expression 'development', standing by itself, is always slippery and needs an adjective denoting its characteristics and goals, and so at times has been accompanied by 'capitalist' and/or 'women's/human' development, also referring back to the dispossession of the majority in a society and enrichment of a few.[5] Thus there is an ongoing struggle between two types of development with radically opposed qualifiers: capitalist and human. Amiya Kumar Bagchi's book *Perilous Passage* (2006) provides an excellent exploration of the capitalist variant of this project of development. Bagchi shows that the pursuit of so-called development has betrayed the expectations denoted by the term and has been counter-productive for the popular good. A horrifying perilous journey has been the lot of most people as capital in the name of development has raised its way into a triumphal passage. As Iraq, Afghanistan, Sudan and Somalia indicate, this is how it is going to be for the time to come, until resistance in the name of the human and the recognition of an inherent value in that concept gather enough volume to challenge the ruthless principles of property and their related proprieties. It is amazing how this bland expression 'development', or its correlate 'growth', have come to hold so much menace. Was it always so? How did 'development' come to acquire such perversions? What were its earlier names?

Development: A Conceptual Composite and a Practical Contradiction

Let us begin by remembering that 'development' is an ambiguous notion. In order to make clear sense, it has to be specific in its social relations, intentions and procedures, in its subject–agents, those who perform 'development', and in its object–receivers, those for and by whom it is done. It operates in many registers, which include convergences of socio-economic, cultural and political forces, their coherence as well as contradictions. As such, any mention of 'development' should not only be adjectivized but also pluralized, though certain politics and practices have driven it in a singular direction. Inscribed in it are many definitions, objectives, and desires that have been brought to a particular meaning and incorporated within the grand narratives of industrial capitalism and imperialism. In this reduced and singular usage, development has lost its humane and ethical connotations. Its connections with equality and sharing have been erased, and it has become the instrument, the end and the legitimation of global capitalism. Historians of the concept who have traced its etymologies have shown us how the notion of development changed from its earlier incarnation as qualitative social 'improvement' of life to its present usage. Beginning in the 1700s and throughout the eighteenth and nineteenth centuries, the concept has changed in relation to the development of capitalism and the bourgeois state.[6] Undeniably, before the high noon of English industrial capitalism, it contained ethical and cultural dimensions. Emma Rothschild's *Economic Sentiments* (2002), for example, outlines a world of ideas where moral and economic concepts and their practices, such as development, evolved. But eventually 'development' has come to signify techno-centrism or industrialization in the service of capital.

In its earlier phase as 'improvement', this notion was secular, social and humanist. Though technology as the new horizon of capitalism already beckoned, neither it nor industry had become the driver of the notion of 'improvement'. The late eighteenth and early nineteenth century appropriated 'improvement' and the associated notion of development for the dual purpose of signalling individual or organic wholeness[7] and industrial revolution with its principles of utilitarianism and free trade, emphasizing skills training and accumulation of wealth. This dual ground was a forked road. As the nineteenth century rolled in, the idea of 'progress' also entered into the mix. This added a moral pedagogical dimension to that of economic acquisitiveness. These two elements of humanist education involving imagination, sentiments and sensibilities, and training for capitalist accumulation through a calculus of rationality, could be seen in their projects of education for children. It is in this context that Coleridge advocated the idea of 'educing the whole soul of man', while Bentham insisted on the teaching of rationalism and technology. That these two tendencies struggled with each other in the field of education is critically portrayed by Charles Dickens in his novel *Hard Times* (1854). Prior to Dickens, Mary Shelley had put forward her critique of scientificism or technologism in creating the modern myth of Dr Frankenstein and his creature (1818). She held up to view, the dangers of the utilitarian pedagogy of capitalist social engineering. Nor can the issue of class be left behind, as educational projects aimed at the children of lower-middle and working classes were generally technically oriented, with a smattering of christian morality, while only children of the elite could be indulged with humanist, child-centred education. However, the capitalist element of the notion of development or improvement entered in the education of the middle classes not as 'techne' of production but as statecraft, as strategies for ruling and disciplining the lower classes and colonial subjects. The education of moral and aesthetic pleasures became the preserve of the elite.

At this point we should also mention that in this period science education gained ground with increasing emphasis on sociobiology. Education resonated in many of its branches with the fallout effects of evolutionism, particularly of social darwinism.[8] This type of developmentalism in education reworked the concept of knowledge and methods of gaining knowledge, and was infused with power in all its dimensions. It helped to standardize social perception of development into 'normal' and 'abnormal', a distinction eagerly seized upon by those in control of knowledge apparatuses and their practicalization for the creation and maintenance of ruling (Foucault 2004). The horrific consequences of such normalization are found in many projects of science: an excruciating example is to be found in the extermination of physically and mentally disabled persons in nazi Germany and by colonial and enslaving powers elsewhere in the 'developed' world.[9] The terms 'developed' and 'underdeveloped', expressions of power/knowledge, became a hegemonic discourse providing legitimation for exploitation and elimination. Thus technologism, combined with a racially and biologistic culturalism/humanism, interpreted the idea of being 'human' only in relation to Europeans. In this sense, narratives of development are narratives of horror for those upon whom capitalist colonialism unleashed itself.

This dark side of development is reflected in what Karl Marx called 'the myth of primitive accumulation'. Though formulated in the context of capitalist development in Europe, Marx shows how an ideological reading of the development of the wealth of all nations obscures the real process of capitalist development by telling a story of ancestral hard labour and sacrifice which the rich can draw upon as the source of primitive accumulation.[10] Marx exposed the reality of so-called primitive accumulation as one of force, violence, and relentless extra-legal and 'legal' separation of most of humankind from their means of livelihood and their labour, and their eventual reduction to the permanent state of wage labour. This exploitive and competitive commoditization of labour power, as discussed by him in relation to alienation (Marx 1964), is accompanied by progressive elimination of the human capacity for creativity, self-development and individual freedom. The alienation and terror produced by 'primitive accumulation' has exponentially increased over centuries of capitalism – and those driven off land and away from productive resources, their habitations and cultural spaces have increasingly faced pauperization rather than proletarianization, especially in the current ex-colonized countries.[11] Scholars of critical political economy, critical geography, social sciences and other fields of knowledge have pointed out that the process of 'primitive accumulation' is far from over and will continue as long as capitalism exists.[12] The current 'globalization' with its financial/military compulsions should be understood in this perspective.[13] What Marx termed the 'genesis' of capital, with its history written in 'annals of blood and fire' (*Capital*, Vol. I), both within and outside of capitalist colonial nations, is a process that continues in predatory dispossessions from earliest to recent times. The same process of separating peoples and nations from their geographical socio-economic and cultural resources, of controlling and marginalizing them to the point of eliminating whole populations, is the hallmark of capitalist expansionism. These phenomena, as Ellen M. Wood (2003) shows, are the necessary syllogisms of the 'logic of capital'. This 'little matter of genocide', as Ward Churchill (1998) ironically calls it, can no longer be denied, and King Leopold's ghost (Hochschild 1998) still haunts us in the quagmires of the Democratic Republic of Congo, Mali and other African countries.

The current neo-liberal, corporate-driven 'development' conducted by expelling people from land and separating them from other natural resources in primarily agricultural countries, such as in India, is an ongoing part of this process. As Marx said, 'All that is solid melts into air' (Marx and Engels 1985; also see Berman 1988), carrying along with this dissolution all sustainable reproducibility, introducing large machinery for agriculture. Seed, pesticide and fertilizer packages, all from corporate monopolies such as Cargill and Monsanto, have led to thousands of farmer suicides, especially in India (Sainath 1996). Putting profit before people, erasing critical scientific knowledge that stands in its way, the market has become the only venue for exercising social relations, for meeting the most basic needs, and for fulfilling desires and creating pseudo-identities. Those who cannot buy the necessities for their lives, whose governments refuse to provide for them basic amenities after failing to protect them from predatory capitalism, are rendered into unnecessary lives, as so many mouths to fill. The project instead is to divert public revenues to subsidize local and foreign capital. Such people must get out of the way of the path of 'development' and die in the process of facilitating it. Modernization, with its anti-human approach, has been pitted against people and nature. People have been transformed into working hands and declared redundant irrespective of the size of the population.

It is obvious, then, that 'development' in the service of capital is against human welfare, liberal democracy notwithstanding. Such a democracy is only a ruse and an emanation of capital. A constant state of alienation, consisting of self and social objectification and commoditization, a depletion of people's sensuous human capacities, all converge in depicting the poor the world over as almost a separate and sub-human species. The power of capitalism for objective externalization of human capacities against the very producers themselves is breathtaking. The problem does not lie in technology, or even its products, but in the motivation of their invention and their use.[14] The social content and direction of scientific research are decided by corporations, prioritized and subsidized by so-called democratic governments at the cost of ordinary people. Thus, the production and sale of all items – such as armaments, agriculture, health and pharmaceuticals – is profit-driven. Such commodification extends to the conversion of objects of vital need, like water, into profit-making commodities.[15] Finally, the low price of labour in poor and formerly colonized countries, of poor women's labour in particular, contributes to the hyper-exploitation of this type of development, to which should be added the invisible labour of migrant, trafficked and refugee populations daily swelling by wars.[16]

As consciousness is socially grounded, this type of development generates a glittering, vacuous culture of techno-romanticism and consumption. It generates an aesthetics reaching from war to the mega-modernization of big dams, automobiles and blood diamonds, considered as a woman's best friend, forever. From this anti-human fountainhead of capitalist progress, a synonym for development, a vision of endless consumption springs forth. Since statistics and economics rest on averages, the discourse of 'development' can easily omit the question of whom development benefits, by whom it is undertaken, and with what means and real objective. A great deal of triumphalism went on in the past, and it has now reached a zenith in the domination of nature. An instrumental rationality bypassing the issue of the human good annihilates the possibility of the very existence of humans on earth and the planet itself, devastated and vanishing in a nuclear glow, while simultaneously trying to create human beings and immortality in laboratories.

What I am saying is, of course, not new. The cases of India's 'green revolution' and capital's fascination with big dam projects have come up for sustained and trenchant criticism. If things could improve through such modernizing undertakings, then lives would have changed for the better a long time ago, both for developed and underdeveloped countries. In the case of the 'green revolution', for example, hunger should have been eliminated. But instead, it culminated in giant agricultural corporations, farmers' suicides and expulsion from land.[17] Nor has the barrage of acute feminist critiques of such a development had any real impact;[18] lamentably, many of the critics were eventually coopted to serve a 'femocracy'[19] in the cause of globalization. National and international non-governmental projects, consciously or unconsciously, ended up applying band-aids to the violence of development. Yet there are many feminist activists and scholars still concerned with the fate of peasants and farmers, of environmental devastation and degradation, who through a trenchant critique of patriarchy continue to tear at the façade of 'development' and try to wrest from the state socio-economic justice for its victims. They engage in political struggles, social movements and public interest litigation, taking recourse to national and international human rights organizations. A few names will show how social research enriched by gender analysis has exposed the contradictions and the dualisms of masculinist dimensions of capitalist development, and how the domination of nature has resulted also in the domination of poor and indigenous people, particularly of women and children – Maria Mies, Geeta Sen, Arundhati Roy, Veronica Benholtz, Swasti Mitter, Sheila Rowbotham, Beena Agarwal, Vandana Shiva, Virginia Vargas, Domitila Barrios Chungara and Rigoberta Menchu are some of the notable political activists and social critics. They remind us of the horrendous price that poor women in particular pay for 'development' of the rich of all genders.[20] Criticism has ranged from sweatshop labour to the foraging activities of aboriginals or poor women living in the jungles of the cities or the countryside – in Bombay, Rio de Janeiro, or the Amazon. Victimization of poor women and children has been conducted through their bodies and unpaid labour. The reproductive capacities of women have been bonded to corporate enterprises and the ruling apparatuses. Susan George (1977, 1988) and many others have repeatedly exposed how the poor, especially women and children, pay the price of foreign debt and the so-called economic reforms of strategic adjustment programmes (SAPs). Authors such as Utsa Patnaik or Madhura Swaminathan and V.K. Ramachandran have also written in depth about the disorders and disasters of public distribution systems and food security in India (Patnaik 1999; Ramachandran and Swaminathan 2002). The list goes on.

Yet, after this litany of horrors, if we should still wish to use this notion of 'development', or its equivalents such as 'progress', 'improvement' and 'modernity', we need to switch to a radically different interpretation of these terms. In order to accomplish this reclaiming and refashioning, we would need to pay heed to the voices of the early romantics, with their insistence on a humanism that once inscribed these notions. The human-centric, socially motivated use of the concept of development needs to replace the capitalist version of it. This is what C.B. Macpherson said in his reconsideration of development in the context of participatory democracy, a system in which development would not be at the service of the rich and ruling classes. We need to get off John Stuart Mill's liberal 'see-saw' between human and market/capitalist development, and acknowledge the contradiction between capitalism and democracy (Macpherson 1962, 1973). Nurturing and celebrating human capacities for the creation of a good life for the society as a whole should be the goal of development.

Criticism of liberal thought shows how we need to read into 'development' a creative, humanist approach. But so far, liberalism, in its deep association with capitalism, has not given us a way of actualizing these ideas (Macpherson 1977). Capitalist liberal democracy cannot by its own logic create the necessary conditions against class and capitalist exploitation, nor make space for the full participation of ordinary people in their governing. To accomplish this social objective even marginally, even to think about it, the ideas and practices of universal citizenship, human rights and the right to imaginative productivity are indispensable. The exploitation and domination that is integral to capitalism, to corporate capitalism in particular, and the contradiction between social well-being and a political economy of profit constantly confront those who want to invent a capitalism with a human face. Universal citizenship contradicts 'corporate citizenship', and 'empowering' poor women is again a contradiction in terms. Some of those who work within the parameters of women and development end up acknowledging that to redeem 'development' for a human purpose, the very system that creates that need must be abandoned. We have long lived in a world where techno-fetishism in many guises has become hegemonic. Even for those who subscribe to left positions, sometimes 'development' and its perils have not been clear. Rather, the ruse of 'science' and 'progress' adopted by capitalism has blindsided them. This misguidedness is indicated by a part of the left's use of the discourse of 'backwardness' and the 'realist' paradigm in capitalist thought. From the now-defunct Soviet Union to present-day China, there are lessons for the left to learn.

It is not presumptuous to say that the end of all development should be the people themselves. The discourse of development cannot be an alibi for popular empowerment and well-being, for happiness for the short time allotted to humans on earth. We must expose the gap between the ideals of human development and its impediments brought about by existing socio-economic and political conditions that prevent their actualization. In order to do this, we should hear further of how Rabindranath Tagore conceptualized and practiced 'development.'

Rabindranath, Development and Decolonization

> Decolonization never takes place unnoticed for it has an effect on being, it changes being fundamentally. It transforms spectators crushed with their inessentiality into privileged actors, caught in a spectacular manner by the

> floodlights of History. It introduces into being a peculiar rhythm, heralded by new people, a new language, a new humanity. Decolonization is a veritable creation of new human beings.
>
> – Frantz Fanon, *The Wretched of the Earth* (1968: 2)

> One day while I stood watching at early dawn the sun sending out its rays from behind the trees, I suddenly felt as if some ancient mist had in a moment lifted from my sight. ... The invisible screen of the common place was removed from all things and all men, and their ultimate significance was intensified in my mind; and this is the definition of beauty. That which was memorable in this experience was its human message, the sudden expansion of my consciousness in the super-personal world of man.
>
> – Rabindranath Tagore, *The Religion of Man* (1966: 93–94)

Though the notion of 'decolonization' was most prominently articulated by Franz Fanon in the context of the Algerian and other North African revolutions, I have chosen to use this term in relation to Rabindranath's humanist developmental proposals for the achievement of a true postcolonial stage. The notion of decolonization is a more apt concept for what Rabindranath envisioned and practised than either anti-colonialism or its ideology, 'nationalism', for reasons that we will see below. Rabindranath's criticism and rejection of nationalism in general, and its Indian manifestation in particular, have been extensively remarked upon for a long time. The most important and early exploration of his critique of nationalism can be found in Sumit Sarkar's *The Swadeshi Movement in Bengal* (1973). Sarkar provides an examination of Rabindranath's untiring lifelong effort to shape culture and social subjectivity in such a way that these are substantive and independent of colonial discourse, administration and the idea of development. Rabindranath's vision of human development, termed by Sarkar (and following him, others) as 'constructive *swadeshi*' (constructive nationalism), seems to be best captured by the humanist idea of decolonization, in which social transformation is articulated along a humanist/universalist path and conducted within the space of civil society; his emphasis was on the development of complex and diverse aspects of Bengal's/India's civil society. It concentrated not only on the development of industry but on technological development for popular empowerment, at the heart of which lies a positive development of the self and of mutually enhancing self–other relations. In negating the perspective of capitalist colonialism, this self–other relation went far beyond the personal to a wider social sphere, beyond the local to extra-local, extra-national spaces. Rabindranath was especially critical of types of colonially inflected cultural identities and their accompanying political and moral subjectivities which shaped the Bengali middle classes, the classes themselves originating in the colonial terrain. The formative relation between colonial discourse and the templates for 'national' identity were exposed and critiqued by him. In his novel *Gora*, for example, written in response to the *swadeshi* movement, we notice how furiously he reacted to this ethnicist hindu national identity and its implied subjectivity and politics. In this novel, he narrated the process of formation of a decolonizing identity.

In his anti-colonial response, Rabindranath devised a pedagogy or a conscientizing praxis of decolonization rather than participating in conventional politics. His educational institutions – Santiniketan (established 1901), Visva Bharati (1921) and Sriniketan (1923) – evolved along the lines of his decolonizing humanist developmental vision, synthesized from values and practices of the west and the east. His intention may be surmised from the statement: 'I have no distrust of any culture because of its foreign character. On the contrary, I believe that the shock of the outside forces is necessary for maintaining the vitality of our intellect' (cited in Dutta and Robinson 1995: 221). Furthermore, he stated that 'all the elements of our culture have to be strengthened, not to resist the culture of the West, but to accept it and assimilate it. We must ... not live on sufferance as hewers of texts and drawers of book learning' (cited in ibid.: 222).

In his project of shaping an autonomous, creative and open social subjectivity, Rabindranath wanted to chart a path away from both national and colonial/imperialist outlooks, as he saw nationalism as a direct inversion of colonialism. His desire was to open up a larger space of creative self and self-individualization marked by mutuality and receptivity. The critical knowledge basis he relied on was the legacy of social reform, in the tradition in which he grew up. This legacy was comprised of the towering figure of Raja Rammohan Roy, the major founder of the Brahmo Samaj, and his own father, Debendranath Tagore, among others.[21] His intention was to go beyond these limited cultural and institutional reforms towards the construction of an aesthetic and moral philosophy, a typology for a 'new man' and a 'new society' that was, incidentally, aspired to in the west. His vision was not different from those of the European utopian romantics, whose proposals for a social pedagogy reverberated in his own time. The century in which he was born was a century of innovation in secular humanism.

Within his limited means, Rabindranath tried to practicalize his vision of humanist development, which required the redemption of the violated and violent spaces of capitalist colonialism/imperialism and nationalism. In his schools for children and adults, in arts and agriculture, he experimented with building models for a 'free' and creative society. The necessity for such an achievement which captures the dialectics of colonial experience and the struggle for freedom is noted by Amiya Kumar Bagchi in his charting of the 'perilous passage' of capitalism: 'Throughout the history of colonialism, there was a dialectical relationship between the civilization mission of the colonizers and the absorption of the learning of the Europeans; many of the new perspectives and knowledge were used by the colonized for resisting oppression and cultural imperialism' (Bagchi 2006: 48).

Thus, the violence of the conventional and colonial classrooms with rote learning of inert facts punctuated by various punishments, which Rabindranath had suffered and rejected since childhood, were never to be practised in his schools. In the parable *Tota Kahini* (The Parrot's Tale), he criticized the dire and enduring consequences of feeding children with facts and numbers in the name of knowledge and learning, much as Dickens exposed the ills of utilitarian schooling in *Hard Times* (1854). What Rabindranath sought to develop in and through his pedagogic philosophy, its spaces and practices, was a creative–ethical environment in which the mind and imagination of students have free play and thrive. His project of a universalist human development aspired at once to free the individual mind which would constitute culture and society.

Rabindranath's developmental philosophy and practices were romantic, but not in a traditional reactionary sense. They were liberal, with elements of the European and Indian enlightenment, but they were so in the teeth of colonialism and brahminical/casteist hinduism. Thus, he not only sought to unbind the liberatory and creative potentials of children and adults, but had to steer a fine course between the perils of colonialism and the reactionary impulses to which it gave rise. In fact, Rabindranath's developmental vision was itself radical, because for a colonized subject to aspire to a universalist humanism was indeed a project against the grain – a challenging gesture that could be, and was, misunderstood by both Bengali nationalists and European colonialists. Reversing the focus from the colonizer, this humanism aspired to a universalist understanding of the notion of 'human', and resisted the social background of a casteist and communalist society thoroughly provoked and manipulated by the social formation and class politics of colonialism. He declared an unqualified rejection of narrowness, chauvinism and binary epistemology, in fact, of all forms of particularism, all of which had become an easy reflex for the colonized peoples. But his was no vacuous transcendence, as it retained the lineaments of strong specificities of its socio-historical origins and the political bondage of India. His decolonizing developmental pedagogy marked a journey between what is and what ought to be.

It is obvious that this humanism demanded an end to the antagonism between the self and the other, between nature and culture, imagination and reality. It would appear that Rabindranath was largely successful, at least in educational, ethical and creative dimensions. A few words are needed here about his conception of the self, whose mutuality of recognition with the other and whose aesthetic–spiritual aspects lie at the base of his social thought regarding the personal and the individual. The achievement of an expressive individuality of a 'self' within himself and others, comprising his students, readers, interlocutors and audience, was his primary task for decolonization. This calls for a surpassing of the one-sided identity of a colonial subject. It goes with the notion of the self as personal and specific, on the one hand, and indivisible from 'life' and society, on the other. This life-oriented self is not static, but rather a self-directed *poiesis* or making, a constant becoming, in and through both imagination and reason. This self personally and experientially takes the form of a defined personality, but also follows 'the path of human evolution' which connects it with others and displays 'qualities of creativity' which embody and project an excess or surplus of affectivity and an evocation of form (O'Connell 2002: 106).[22] In this formulation, reason, for Rabindranath, is not inevitably utilitarian or instrumentally rationalist. Though reason is a faculty for abstraction or generalization, it can also serve as a reflexive and critical faculty. It is with this recognition of and the ability to bring together the particular and the general that Gora, the protagonist of the novel of the same name, grows from a narrow nationalist into a humanist, and Bimala or Nikhilesh, the dual protagonists in *Ghare Baire* (Home and the World), learn to venture beyond their initial reactive selves to become ethically and emotionally developed. This aspect of reason is not antithetical to nature, if nature itself can be comprehended, as Rabindranath seems to think, as having two aspects or levels. On one level nature is, for him, physical, primordial or instinctual, but on another, nature is equally nurturing and gifted with an inherent sociality. The duality between nature and reason is overcome or mediated by imagination and ethics or empathy, and a sense of beauty or aesthetics:

> I have expressed my belief that the first stage of my realization was through my feeling of intimacy with Nature ... not that Nature which has its channel of information for our mind and physical relationship with our living body, but that which satisfies our personality with manifestations that make our life rich and stimulate our imagination in their harmony of forms, colours, sounds and movements. It is not that world which vanishes into abstract symbols behind its own testimony to Science, but that which lavishly displays its wealth of reality to our personal self having its own perpetual reaction upon our nature. (Tagore 1966: 18)

This postulation of a constitutive relationship between nature and reason through the mediation of imagination and a sense of form is productive of subjectivities, self–other relations and cultural identities which are positively social and humane. This view, which sees nature and reason as components of the human and the social, is diametrically opposed to that of Hobbes's idea of nature or of social darwinism. Rabindranath's triad of reason, nature and imagination, implicitly aesthetic, together form the building blocks of sociality and culture and provide the basic ground for universalized identification. It is to this realization that characters in Rabindranath's novels arrive by the end of the narrative. In *Gora*, the protagonist expresses in his idea of 'India' this feeling of oneness with its millions of 'impure', nameless, poor people of all castes and creeds. For Rabindranath, the be-ing of a human self entails empathy and identification with others, that is, a universalist humanism. Humanism provides the way to a better world for all, unless ideologically distorted or deformed through the relations of power of colonialism, capitalism or ethnic nationalism. Colonial hegemony and nationalist ideology aspiring to such relations and incorporated in binaries of power become mirrors of each other. But this intimation of one's own and the other's humanity is not an automatic, unconscious or instinctive natural reflex. It requires changes in the existing particularities of consciousness. It involves a reflective, critical, gradual and constructive process. It entails not simply joy, but sorrow and sacrifice, painful learning. Even when the awareness or proclamation of the universal human cannot be stated and demanded, as for colonial subjects or any other dominated group, it still lives at the heart of desire, as what Ernst Bloch called 'the principle of hope'. In the novel *Ghare Baire*, a narrative of the tragic consequences of nationalism, Rabindranath did not celebrate the visceral nationalist passion of the anti-hero, Sandip. He could portray in the heroine, Bimala, the almost sexual seduction of such nationalism, but also through the same character, feel its repulsion. What prevails in the end is humanism.

This homology established by Rabindranath between social darwinist naturalism and nationalism, his rejection of passion without compassion, of a ruthlessly negative bond between the self and the other, as obtaining between the colonizer and the colonized, allowed him to construct all particularism through the trope of a struggle between aggression and yearning. Domination and subordination, which together create the problematic of freedom, the vicissitudes of self-making in a hostile world, the pedagogy of universalist humanism, are key thematic presences in all his works, both literary and critical. If we consider decolonization in these terms, the question of politics includes the immense realms of desire, affirmative social relations and their relationship to creativity/imagination, all of which constantly shape the self and provide content for subjectivity.

Rabindranath's humanist critique of nationalism, imperialism and instrumental rationalism points towards a holistic approach for decolonization. But these critiques also expose in this process the double-face of modernity. Although sharing the principle of secularism, belief in science and the idea of the individual, Rabindranath's humanism and modernity differ in important ways. A very important difference lies in the way they conceive the idea of the individual, one whose meaning is overdetermined by capitalist colonialism and imperialism. This factor compromises the humanist ethics of the enlightenment, which deprives the concept of the human of its universalist social and creative core. The individual in the capitalist colonial version is characterized by narcissism, possessive individualism, competition and active aggression towards the other, but in the humanist strand, the individual is animated by universalism and thus by a relation of empathy and mutual self-fulfilment with the other. Though both approaches are modernist in so far as they are not religious or traditionalist, one speaks to the holistic development of human capacities, and the other to the growth of wealth without regard to harm done to others in the process. This is the developmental approach that we call modernization. Here reason and imagination are sacrificed to instrumental rationality and to the fetishization of technocratic production and ruling relations. It is this colonial modernity or the goal of modernization that logically involves aggression and war, a situation that Rabindranath exposes and decries in his social thought. It is the reason for his condemnation of the developmental path of Japan that leads it to becoming an imperial power. His letter to the poet Yone Noguchi, who celebrated Japan's rise to imperial power, expressed his frustration and anger.[23] In thus directing us to recognize the paradox of modernity, radically opposed meanings of modernity in two different contexts and goals, Rabindranath teaches his readers to conceptualize decolonization beyond nationalism.

The main feature of modernity is its claim of distinction from the past. Nineteenth-century Europe in particular, and India from the middle of that century, resonated with a call for the 'new'. This call for a 'new man' and a 'new society', for transformation of the existing world and the way to achieve this, of course had different interpretations in different contexts, politics and epistemologies. Rabindranath's ideas regarding them were radically opposed to someone like Nietzsche (1844–1900), for instance, or the utilitarians. Nietzsche articulates his ideas of the self or the individual in anti-social, isolationist terms. The self and individuality are not formed and individuated in a collectivity. Though Rabindranath is equally concerned about the same issues, he does not define the self against the other; rather, for him, the individual needs society for the purpose of individuation. Nietzsche's individual, in spite of his seeming disdain for others, for the existing society, is only possible in a capitalist culture composed of competitiveness and possessive individualism. In fact the necessity of the emergence of an 'over-man/super-man' is not only postulated upon contemporary capitalism, but confuses it with an essential human condition. Here we can depend on David McNally's insight when he points to the social darwinist underpinnings of Zarathustra, Nietzsche's 'over' or 'super' man. McNally states:

> For millennia, claims Nietzsche, human history has been a story of the victory of the weak over the strong, herd-instinct over individualism, slave morality over aristocracy, the subjugation of the rare and the exceptional to the vulgar and the common. But today … the development of hard, courageous individuals ready to accept the challenge of thinking against truth and morality requires reversing this state of affairs … and establishing a new race of masters. And Nietzsche does not shrink from spelling out the politics of his attack on slave morality, socialism and democracy. 'We simply do not consider it desirable that a realm of justice and control should be established on earth …'. He continues: 'We count ourselves among conquerors; we think about the necessity for new orders, also for a new slavery…'. (McNally 2001: 23)

In contrast to Nietzsche, Rabindranath's idea of the individual is deeply social and identified in a congenial manner with all human beings who share the same human capacities. His philosophical stance, his praxis and aspirations, are all in opposition to this type of individual. Though his typology of the human is an idealization, as is Nietzsche's, it is positive and points to a shared basis among humans. His transcendent subject is not an apotheosis of social darwinism, a master among the master race. Rabindranath's humanism is a social humanism both in its epistemological inception and result. Based on his premises, the idea of development contains the idea of a 'good life' as espoused by Plato and Aristotle, who were sources for the European enlightenment. Rabindranath's 'new man' signals to a process of becoming. His universalist humanism, though a variety of idealism, had a social character to it. While mindful of the particularities of the present, it does not compromise by being conflated with the immediate and the empirical, and thus as a pure form of metaphysics it can have a critical dimension to it. Here idealism itself becomes the ground of measuring the empirical.

Nietzsche, on the other hand, compromised his idealist vision, and thus no less generalized or idealized its potential for critique with a particularly nineteenth-century European–colonial empiricism. His ideal man, the super-man, was a prototype of the capitalist ethic, the archetypal colonialist. This accomplished a switch in his position, which converted an emancipatory modernism to one of colonial modernity. The socially individualizing self was substituted by a rabid individualism and contained a racialized view of civilizations intrinsic to colonial discourse. This stance of disguised bourgeois colonialism projected as a human type made Nietzsche's philosophy of a surpassing self so vulnerable to nazi and generally fascistic appropriation. A peculiar form of empiricist idealism led to a compromise with an anti-social notion of the human individual – which, combined with scientifism and racist evolutionism, was a toxic mix. Instead of an empathetic and imaginative identification, the other became an inferior object, whom he called 'the herd'. This extraordinary individual turns out to be a posturing and personalized version of competitive capitalist ethos. Thus, the loneliness of Zarathustra is a sign of superiority, a proclaimed badge of pride (Nietzsche 1961). The evolution of Zarathustra consisted of his ascent to the top of the human heap, a singular, solitary space of being, to be radically different from ordinary mortals. His identity is fully fixed or reified, and it exemplified an ideal type whose persona could be that of an ideal white colonizer. This solipsistic man, a variant of the 'new' man, was the very opposite of Rabindranath's *mahamanab* (the great human). Though an ideal type, this 'new man' is not a reified typology because it is replete with the potential of becoming through an ongoing interaction of the self with the world/the other(s). He is incomplete and needs others for his completion. As a metaphor of constant becoming, his physiognomy is not fixed or fully defined. His transcendence consists in a constant unfolding and development of human capacities which moves beyond the immediate and the local. Unlike Zarathustra, the *manab* or the *mahamanab* is never an achieved state, and is not a disguised version of a present and actual social ethos. Considered thus, the idea of development is by nature 'human' development. Furthermore, it is by the logic of its epistemology an incomplete image to be drawn through time and social participation.

Conclusion

Rabindranath's vision of development is a fundamentally alternative one to that of economic growth for profit. Here the human factor is what counts. It is the other of techno-romanticism and accumulation of wealth. Its nature is sharing rather than acquisitive. I may be branded by diehard realists as a utopian whose approach is a spin-off from Rabindranath's own. I can only reply that utopianism is an essential aspect of social transformation and say, in Yeats' words, 'in dreams begin responsibility'. Ultimately this utopia, this humanist universalism, grows by having to come to terms with the embodied, social dimensions of the historically specific realization process of development. And that is where the test lies. The process of this humanist development will have to proceed by dismantling the existing structures and ideologies, cultures, and psychic reflexes of a profit- and property-oriented society. It would need to challenge the habitual rendering of others into objects of service, of their self-gratification. It will laugh at George W. Bush's advice to cheer up by going shopping in the face of the disaster of 2001. Rabindranath's idealist but modernist vision and practical experiments with cooperatives and schools will have to fuse with Marx's vision, with his analysis and politics against capitalist alienation. In many ways similar to Rabindranath, Marx, in the *Economic and Philosophic Manuscripts of 1844* (1964), critiqued social organizations and relations of accumulation of profit and power which produce a multifaceted alienation. This alienation impacts humanity as a whole, because it means an alienation from nature, from others and one's own self, and even from creations of one's own hands. This alienation, so deeply ingrained now, needs to be challenged by an anti-capitalist and anti-imperialist development based on a 'new humanist' vision, such as that of Tagore, and commensurate practices. For this 'new humanism' we also need to return to ideas of decolonization to be found in Frantz Fanon, Aimé Césaire, and many other anti-imperialist artists and thinkers. For our own time we have much to learn from Fanon, who forged the idea of a free human subject in the fire of the Algerian revolution. About this required 'new humanism', Ato Sekyi-Otu, in his *Fanon's Dialectic of Experience*, has something important to say, since it is both the way and the goal of a 'true' decolonization: 'Fanon ... tells us that it is from the vortex of lived political experience that a novel idea of humanity would be refashioned: "In the objectives and methods of the struggle ... is prefigured this new humanism"' (Sekyi-Otu 1996: 21).

Rabindranath never forgot the fact of India's colonized condition, nor the deformation introduced in its resistance through the ideology of nationalism. The struggle for decolonization that he undertook through his ethical and cultural pedagogy was political in its implication in highly nuanced and social ways. His humanist dream of development and Fanon's 'new humanism', his 'partisan universalism' (Fanon 1968: 118), coincide with each other, even though their paths were not the same.

Notes

[1] See, for a general critique, Amin (1976); A.K. Bagchi (1982). For feminist critiques, see A.K. Bagchi and Nirmala Banerjee (1981); Sen and Grown (1987); Mitter (1986); and Mies (1986).

[2] See McNally (2006); M. Bhattacharya (2004).

[3] On agricultural crisis and food (in)security in India, see Utsa Patnaik (2003, 2004); P. Sainath (1996).

[4] On the location and situation of knowledge production, see Sekyi-Otu (1996); on the standpoint of knowledge and issues of ideology, see D.E. Smith (1995).

[5] This has also been associated with 'primitive accumulation' in the era of neo-liberalism by Harvey (2005); see also Himani Bannerji (2016).

[6] For mutation in the concept of development, see Larrain (1989) and Williams (1976). This mutation indicates an ideological use of the concept, which allows for an occlusion or concealment of the actual social relations and politics on the ground. We may include in this ideological use the notions of 'modernity' and 'modernization' in connection with 'development'.

[7] For example, as in Samuel Taylor Coleridge's or William Wordsworth's writings.

[8] This is emphasized by Sandra Harding in her introduction to *The Racial Economy*

of Science (1993) and other authors in the volume, as well as Gilman in *Difference and Pathology* (1985) and Stephen J. Gould in *The Mismeasure of Man* (1996). The critical epistemology of these texts evokes Michel Foucault's critique of knowledge as power/knowledge and points to the ideological and governing dimensions of this type of positivist education.

[9] The connection between eugenicism and development is too extensive to require any listing. However, in the context of the United States and Canada, see Harding (1993) and Levine (2016), among others.

[10] For this, see Marx (1954), Part 8, on the concept of 'so-called "primitive accumulation"'.

[11] See also David Harvey's (2005) interpretation of the concept of 'primitive accumulation', connecting it with dispossession rather than growth and with pauperization rather than proletarianization. This situation was powerfully captured in the earlier phase of capitalism in the poems, prophesies and illustrations of the English poet and engraver William Blake. See, for example, his *Songs of Innocence* and other poetic and prophetic publications; see also E.P. Thompson (1993) with regard to these themes.

[12] For critical geography, see Harvey (1989, 2003) and Davis (2006). See also A.K. Bagchi (2006); Saul (2006); Saskia Sassen (2014); and Federici (2018).

[13] What Hardt and Negri (2000) call 'Empire' is the same entity, with the marxist emphasis on imperialism left out.

[14] See Walter Benjamin (1969b).

[15] For conversion of water into a profitable commodity and the dire consequences of this globally, see Barlow (2002).

[16] For useful studies of migrant and undocumented workers, see Sharma (2006); Walia (2021).

[17] See the excellent documentary film on the 'green revolution' in India by Manjira Datta, *Seeds of Plenty, Seeds of Sorrow*, British Film Institute, 1992; also found in Bullfrog Films.

[18] For a feminist critique of development and land-related issues, an important contribution is that of Agarwal (1994).

[19] 'Femocracy' is a term that originated in Australia from an unknown source to describe mainstream liberal feminists who have become administrators or bureaucrats of the state and other ruling institutions.

[20] See, for example, Stiglitz (2003).

[21] Raja Rammohan Roy (1772–1833), who co-founded *Brahma Sabha* in 1828, is seen as 'the father of Indian modernity'. Debendranath Tagore (1817–1905), a central figure of brahmoism, joined in 1842. For this period in Bengal, see Susobhan Sarkar (1970b).

[22] Though O'Connell does not speak in terms of a 'decolonizing' pedagogy, the book gives us an account of Rabindranath's pedagogical trajectory in a detailed and straightforward manner that speaks in terms of transcendence and humanism.

[23] See Cipris (2007) on Noguche debating the China–Japan war with Tagore.

4

Home and the World

Women and Nationalism in the Novels of Rabindranath Tagore

Introduction

The Indian school of Subaltern Studies, following the lead of Partha Chatterjee in *The Nation and Its Fragments* (1993a) and his essay on women and nationalism (1989), decided long ago that Bengali/Indian nationalism had arrived at a 'resolution of the women's question'. In fact, this school claimed that the measure of the success of that nationalism lay in its ability to produce this 'resolution'. The secret was to introduce, à *la* European bourgeois thought, a schism in Bengal's social space, dividing this into an interior 'home' and the world. As Chatterjee and his fellow Subalternists saw it, it was in this interior world of 'home' nestled into and even comprising the civil society that the nationalists were able to establish their social hegemony, for them an appropriate national culture. In this schema the idea of 'tradition' provided the conceptual device for mutating and subjugating 'modernity', considered as the essence of western/colonial hegemony. This ascribed autonomous national cultural space was the home, where family life, its daily social interchange and moral conduct, provided a constructive retreat (for men) from the pressures and perils of public life under colonial rule. In the public/political sphere, as Partha Chatterjee (1986), Dipesh Chakrabarty (1998) and Asish Nandy (1979) saw it, substantiveness of the national imaginary was compromised by the disciplinary measures and seductions of modernity and colonial discourse. That is, the cultural hegemony of nationalism as manifested in the private life or civil society did not achieve a commensurate and authentic form in the political society. But whatever the failure on the public/political front, the success at 'home' in the family felt secure, and women as the primary denizens of home became signifiers of this success. Through subtle and complex conceptual moves, this figure of the woman partially incorporated the mores of the existing world into its form. This new, nationalist woman icon could incorporate some aspects of modernity – such as a measure of formal education, public cultural participation, even a profession – into an overall format of traditionality required for an ideal home. It is this containment, the overdetermination of modernity, of the mores of the world in the feminine figure, that marked the 'resolution of the women's question' for Partha Chatterjee. Within this formulation the new woman never needed to leave 'home', and the bifurcation between the home and the world remained undisturbed. For this to happen, women were primarily signified as mothers and wives in the national imaginary rather than as sexual or intellectual beings.

This conservative, traditional 'resolution' championed by the Subalternists has been challenged by feminist scholars, who have shown why this is no 'resolution' at all but actually a project for the subjection of women in the cause of the casteist patriarchal nation.[1] This critique has been voiced not only regarding nationalism in India/South Asia, but is also the general substance of feminist critique of nationalism everywhere.[2] But it is important to note that this feminist critique has not effectively challenged the notion of nationalism's successful bifurcation of the home and the world, nor has it destabilized the trope of motherhood and nation, leaving it intact as supreme and iconic. This critique has also left unexplored alternative figurations of womanhood in nationalist discourse, or women's actual social relationship to or location in the home and the world. This has led to the oversight of not noticing the variances in women's social subjectivities and their relationships to nationalist politics, depending upon the character of nationalism proposed in the colonial project (see Radha Kumar 1993).

Though I myself do not dispute the truth of the general feminist critique regarding motherhood and nationalism, I would like to offer a more nuanced view, one that extends beyond both the Subaltern claim and conventional feminism. I propose to do so by discussing Rabindranath's portrayal of women's highly complex figurations and relationship to nationalism, especially in his novels and essays. Rabindranath, we should note, was no friend of nationalism, at least of the variety with which he was most familiar and which is considered to be 'resolutionary' by the Subalternists. In his essay 'Nationalism', he said: '[T]he idea of the Nation is the most powerful anaesthetic that man has invented. Under the influence of its fumes the whole people can carry out its systematic programme of the most virulent self-seeking without being in the least aware of moral perversion' (Tagore 1996a: 434). For an in-depth critical view of women and nationalism we can turn to Rabindranath, because he destabilizes the assumption of a comfortable bifurcation of the home and the world. He shows that when women exit into the world, they do so with more than the interests of home or tradition at heart, not as ultimately derivative subjects or agents at the behest of a conservative patriarchal vision of the nation (see Datta 2003). They are, in Tagore's works, striving to be autonomous socio-political subjects, not just tamers of modernity in the cause of tradition or national culture. Their emergence into the world breaks through the public–private divide and is marked through self-assertive actions, emotions and discourses of anti-traditionality fraught with risk, danger and devastation.[3] The narrative of their emergence, their public/political involvement, is one of transgression and full of jagged edges, rather than one of comfortable 'resolution'. It must be so since these women break the barriers between the home and the world rather than accept domesticity and the maternal familial roles prescribed by nationalist discourse. They do so with personal passion saturated with a rhetoric of freedom, sexual desire and individuality. Women in Rabindranath's novels embody a kind of modernity far from colonial, and born of a thorough questioning of tradition, with an unmitigated uncertainty regarding the outcome – rendering his portrayal of nationalism as a charged and contested terrain.

But before going on to discuss the particular novels, there are a few things to be noted as a preamble. To begin with, the rhetoric of individual freedom pertaining to women in the national imaginary contains ambiguity and ambivalence. As rhetoric it can signal something which ideally should be and is not, and thus has wide and contradictory connotations that exceed the boundaries of the stated or the intended. Thus, in the name of freedom, even when associated with conventional nationalism, it can arouse energies, hopes, subjectivities and agencies beyond the targeted and specific political scope. Through this emotional and conceptual arousal rhetoric can unleash forces which are antithetical to the proposed national imaginary and its practised and projected political institutions. Furthermore, what the notions of freedom and individuality mean at different levels of articulation also needs to be contextually unpacked. The expectations, reasons and expressions of those who seek them need to be carefully explored. Not the least aspect of this exploration involves inquiring into the connection of individual freedom to desire, to reason, social participation and politics.

This inquiry also needs to question the conventional conceptual opposition between feminism and nationalism. Scrutiny reveals that nationalism in the colonial context cannot be reduced to a simple ideological/political entity. Examined historically and specifically, ventures of nationalism turn out to be plural and complex. Their relationships to women vary accordingly, depending on the social analyses, political stances and objectives at work. There are projects of nationalism which call on women to 'come out' into the public sphere of politics instead of residing with ease in the privacy of home. Anti-colonial nationalism unleashes an outward propulsion – impulses and resonances that cannot be gainsaid or pulled back once released. Such a bid for freedom and individualism is modernist in character. As shown by Radha Kumar's *History of Doing* (1993) on women's movements in India, Kumari Jayawardena's *Feminism and Nationalism in the Third World* (1989), or Joanna Liddle and Rama Joshi's *Daughters of Independence* (1986), among other texts, the emergence of many of the core ideas of feminist social movement and politics is based on the same rhetoric of freedom, of liberation, spun off by all anti-oppression struggles including anti-colonial nationalism. Third world feminist thought and practices originated in the times and milieux of anti-colonial national liberation struggles. It can even be argued that whatever the specific *political* outcome of a particular anti-colonial nationalism, the very dynamic of women's participation generates an overall politicization of personal and cultural life. This change, in conjunction with social reform movements for women in the last quarter of the nineteenth century in Bengal, culminated in frameworks for various types of uncharted socio-political mentalities, moralities and practices among women.

It should also be noted that the rhetoric of freedom can only be meaningfully deployed by anti-colonial, anti-slavery, feminist and working class struggles. Unlike European nationalisms (with the exception of Ireland), which were annexationist, third world nationalisms in their colonized state are preoccupied with themes of resistance and the overthrowing of domination, subordination and colonization. As such, Indian nationalist movements radically differed from the imperialist nationalisms of capitalist colonial Britain or nazi Germany. Thus, anti-colonialism inspired a generalized desire of freedom not only from foreign hegemony, but also at the level of social subjectivity and individuation. The narratives provided by

Rabindranath show us that though anti-colonial nationalism initially opens up spaces for the participation of women and other suppressed groups, they may be eradicated as the broader anti-colonial impulse congeals into political parties defined by their ideological and class positions aspiring to a state formation. Depending on the explicitly political objectives of anti-colonial movements, participatory spaces for women might widen and branch off in uncharted directions or be closed within prescribed ideological precincts.

No assessment of nationalisms, and of Rabindranath's understanding of them, can be made without taking into consideration some material factors which determine their character.[4] Nationalist politics vary according to their relationship to: colonial occupation of lands, peoples and cultures; indigenous social organization and relations of class, caste, private property and patriarchy; and the ideologies of state formation and structures of governance in the spaces where capitalist colonialism enters (Fanon 1968).[5] Thus, a nationalism committed to the power relations of private property and class and susceptible to religious forces, in spite of its anti-colonial claims, could not but fall back on patriarchy, race or caste, which sustained colonialism. A nationalism aimed at bourgeois liberal democracy, secularism and individual citizenship and rights would hold a different agenda for women. Both would, of course, differ from a national liberationist politics that is anti-feudal, anti-capitalist and anti-imperialist with an agenda for social and economic equality. This kind of liberationist nationalism would have to address patriarchy or caste, for example, within the very logic of its own political premises for freedom.[6] Common sense dictates that when we consider women's relationship to nationalism, we should be particularly attentive to these specific terms.

Nationalism, Women and the Novels of Rabindranath Tagore

When we speak of women and nationalism in Tagore's novels, we only speak of India, especially of Bengal, and of the emergence and articulation of nationalism within that space and its inchoate beginnings as different responses to colonization. The fictional time–space conjuncture of Tagore's novels extends from the last decades of the nineteenth century to the first three of the twentieth. This period covers the time between demands made by the Bengali middle classes for constitutional and representative rule and the stage of mass political upheavals involving boycott and attempts at destruction of colonial economic and administrative institutions, such as of imported textile products and schools. This was accompanied by the emergence of small armed nationalist groups using 'terrorist' tactics, including assassinations of colonial officers and their native allies. The novels' narratives are placed in the time when the Indian National Congress (INC), established in 1885, is in its pre-Gandhian phase, and covers the time of struggles among the nationalist groups themselves with divergent agendas, tactics and ethically demarcated constituencies. The momentum especially increased during the 1905 division of the Bengal Presidency promulgated by Lord Curzon and influenced by colonially constructed religio-political identities which pitted muslims against hindus. The roots of the later religious communalist struggles lie in this time.[7] Overarching these indigenous political formations at every step is the ubiquitous presence of capitalist colonialism, ranging from the state and economy to civil society, aiming to draw in all of Bengali society into its sphere of domination.

Under these circumstances, a rhythm of struggle activated by the rhetoric of freedom reverberated in the social environment, and this rhetoric is not only that of negation with a single note of 'us' versus 'them', but of something larger. It mobilized the middle classes in particular to imagine the notion of freedom in very broad social and political terms. This led to imagining free subjectivities, agencies and social institutions in hopes and demands of self-rule. In these imaginaries, 'freedom from' and 'freedom to' are conjoined with quests for authentic and 'free selves'. This great change in the realm of consciousness resonated in acute awareness of daily and historical unfreedoms which are memorialized or even invented, for example, through orientalist revisionist history which arrived with the East India Company administrators.[8] In some cases, it enriched the cultural memory of mughal rule in India; in others, it amplified the glories of the ancient hindu past. Colonial domination thus became the mirror in which other ruling relations and oppressions saw their faces. This is how the rhetoric of freedom gained its complex individual and national psychic resonances, desires, different socialities and political ideologies.[9]

Both the projects of social reform and hindu revivalism involved Bengali hindu women through cultural forms which had emerged in the mid-nineteenth century. The new rhetoric of freedom contained typologies of different kinds of womanhood. By the last quarter of the nineteenth century, women writers such as Krishnabhabini Das had become active in expressing their opinions about both indigenous and colonial patriarchal oppression and the need for women's economic independence.[10] Around the same time, hindu middle-class women in particular become increasingly politically active, joining existing political organizations and creating others specifically for women. Since they are side-tracked by their opposition to patriarchy from their anti-colonial premise, their projections of social reform for women nonetheless blend into anti-colonialism. As happens in critical times, their everyday life becomes saturated with the need for change at multiple levels. Their household aesthetics, such as the embroideries on their walls and their sense of fashion and food, as well as their taste in literature, reflect this, as also their support for male family members and other men engaged in nationalist activities. Some women do not hang back from supporting armed militancy and the development of a martial culture among Bengal's (especially male) youth. In their writings in various magazines and books, women continue to speak about the tyranny of casteist patriarchy, especially describing family settings as 'gilded cages' for women. They also liken this patriarchal tyranny to colonialism and dare to imagine a women's utopia, as in Rokeya Sakhawat Hossain's *Sultana's Dream*, where male domination is fully abolished.[11]

It is against this backdrop that we need to read Rabindranath's novels. It should be noted that he wrote as a conscious participant in the shaping of the national cultural imaginary of 'India' as an insider of the culture of Bengal. He was frequently drawn into debates between the reformists and the revivalists about the status of women, which intensified from the last quarter of the nineteenth century. Given the extensive scope of his opus, and the national as well as international influences on and of his works, my effort to capture his views on women and nationalism through the study of a few novels cannot be considered as more than a mere sketch. But the novels examined here are today his most well-known ones, and therefore hold a representational status in capturing themes and concerns of his time. They are erected on a symbolic/iconic narrative apparatus which is also present in his works in other genres. The novels I have chosen to explore are *Gora*, *Ghare Baire*, *Chaturanga* and *Char Adhyay*.[12]

Contrary to much of the writing on women and nationalism, Rabindranath did not fictionalize or narrate the nation by primarily placing women and imagining India, the land and its peoples, within the trope of motherhood and domesticity. As the feminist critique of nationalism shows, this is exceptional, especially in the context of South Asia where cultural nationalism, particularly with its hindu overtones, has generally done just that. I need only mention the nationalist epic, Bankim Chandra Chattopadhyay's *Anandamath* (The Abbey of Bliss), in which motherhood, motherland and nationalism are archetypically co-constituted not only for Bengal or India, but as a necessary feature of nationalism.[13] Rabindranath, instead, offers us the woman–national figuration in a radically different way from Bankim's. The following quotation is from a monologue of his heroine Bimala:

> One night I … slipped out of my room onto the open terrace. Beyond our garden and walls are fields of ripening rice. Through the gaps of the village groves to the North glimpses of the river are seen. The whole scene slept in the darkness like the vague embryo of some future creation.
>
> In that future I saw my country, a woman like myself, standing expectant. She has been drawn forth from her home … by the sudden call of some Unknown. ... I know well how her very soul responds … how her breast rises and falls. … She is no mother. There is no call of her children in their hunger ... no household work to be done. ... So she hies to her tryst, for this is the land of the Vaisnava poets. She has left home, forgotten domestic duties; she has nothing but an unfathomable yearning which hurries her on. (Cited in Tanika Sarkar 2003: 34)

By rejecting the metaphor of motherhood and the familial domestic mode, Rabindranath introduced other affective aspects, recuperating the romance of Radha and Krishna through which to imagine simultaneously the nation and woman's role within it. With him the rhetoric of freedom shifts from that of freeing the mother nation from the bondage of servitude and dissociates the nation from icons of heroically protective or lamenting mothers.[14] Rather, in Rabindranath's iconography we are presented with an image in which freedom and bondage are imagined through personal and sexual desire, and the boundary between licit and illicit desire is swept away. Here, individual longing and choice dictate transgression and serve as a necessary corollary for freedom. As we see in the quotation, femininity and sexuality are fused in imagining the nation's emotional and political geography, which complicates the theme of woman's relationship to herself and nationalism. Thus, the narration of a nation in the making becomes a story of transgressive passions – of men and women (Radha and Krishna) for each other, for the nation itself which emerges through this freedom struggle, for possible death or martyrdom. These passions are transparently overlaid and framed within the story of the struggle between passion and reason, and eventually a dialectical relationship is sought between them in order to validate a humanist and universalist vision. Individual sexual and political choices and conceptions of freedom, of a social vision, are thus imaginatively projected beyond the binaries of nature and reason, familial and romantic love, action and contemplation, choice and compulsion. The complexity of this vision is such that in it, nature itself is not a unitary entity, nor is reason. Nature is presented differentially in a self-divided manner, as is reason. There is, on the one hand, a hobbesian or a social darwinist interpretation of nature, and on the other, nature fused with nurture, a non-narcissistic love and deeply social bonds. Needless to say, it is an ambitious project, and therefore to explore it even rudimentarily requires an open, nuanced form of reading.

At this point we confront a paradox. As I stated before, Rabindranath was the most powerful critic of nationalism that India produced outside of the communist movement, and probably one of the most significant internationally. And yet, a firm anti-nationalist as he became, he was also most profoundly committed to an ideal of decolonization. How to create decolonization without nationalism is the puzzle that we must solve if we are to do justice to his vision of social transformation. We have to delve into what he meant by nationalism and its shortcomings for decolonization, and why he came to consider nationalism as a pernicious and narrow ideology of chauvinism and hatred. There is more to it than his view of nationalism as a particularist cultural and political enterprise. We may be helped in this task by looking into how Rabindranath himself phrased his resolutionary problematic. On 22 December 1921, in the Visva Bharati inauguration speech on 'The Centre of Indian Culture', he showed us both sides of the ideological coin and their antithetical bases:

> Let me state clearly that I have no distrust of any culture because of its foreign character. On the contrary, I believe that the shock of outside forces is necessary for maintaining the vitality of our intellect. … European culture has come to us not only with its knowledge but with its speed. Even when our assimilation is imperfect and aberrations follow, it is rousing our intellectual life from the inertia of formal habits. The contradiction it offers to our traditions makes our consciousness glow.
>
> What I object to is the artificial arrangement by which this foreign education tends to occupy all the space of our national mind and thus kills, or hampers, the great opportunity for the creation of new thought by a new combination of truths. (Dutta and Robinson 1995: 222)

How is this synthesis or 'assimilation' necessary for decolonization to be achieved? In unravelling Rabindranath's idea of decolonization, we need to consider the type of nationalism he saw in his own lifetime, as outlined in Sumit Sarkar's *Swadeshi Movement in Bengal* (1973). The paradigm or paradox of decolonization as narrated in the novels, although morally on the side of the universality of decolonization, leaves us with questions. The idealism of the narration leaves the portrayal of decolonization wanting a sense of concreteness, an experiential quality. The depiction of the decolonized state of being lacks the vividness of the nationalism he experienced, and a feeling of arousal continues in the reader. It is as though a shadow of ambivalence were cast on the clarity of his critical formulation and the choice of his characters (see Sprinker 2003).

Exploring this shadow of nationalism, of ambivalence within the fictional space, calls for a fresh look at Rabindranath's own political trajectory. Chasing this shadow reveals that he went through a radical shift in his relationship to Bengal's nationalism, from personal involvement to rejection. As early as the 1870s, when nationalism had not yet congealed into clear political ideologies, Rabindranath and a great part of the Tagore family actively participated in shaping a cultural response to colonialism in Bengal, which eventually became not only Bengal's but to some extent Indian 'national culture'. In the early stages of its development and the everyday responses to colonial hegemony, he took part in an inchoate, turbulent cultural beginning that proliferated and congealed over time into different nationalist ideologies and organizations. By the first decades of the twentieth century the ideological strands ranged from ultra-conservative hindu revivalism to liberal economic nationalism, from religio-cultural identities to secular humanist ones.[15] These ideologies and their political and cultural practices existed side by side and at times affected each other through mutual influences. For example, a pre-existing hindu cultural nationalism influenced Gandhi's politics, but could also accommodate a liberal modernist nationalism resting on a secularism different from the conventional western one. Rabindranath was fully engaged in meetings, debates and interventions about India's freedom struggle. He sorted his way through his own involvement with a hindu cultural identity and belief in an invented Indian history that once overdetermined his universalist brahmoism. But then again, brahmoism itself could be taken as reformed hinduism, a hinduism adhering to the non-idolatrous monotheism of the Upanishads. To put it concisely, Rabindranath shaped Bengal's nationalist culture and his own growing critical view of nationalism in both creating and resisting the prevalent divergent ideological and political practices of his time.

Tagore scholars and historians of Bengal's nationalisms and counter-hegemonic anti-colonial cultural identities have noted these changes in Rabindranath's own views. It is generally agreed that he took a critical and circumspect stance towards nationalist armed struggles in 1907 after the Bengal partition. Though he supported the popular resistance against the mutilation of the province, he did not support the ethnicist bias of nationalist activists whose response often pitted hindus and muslims against each other, playing into the British divide-and-rule policy on which the partition itself was based. Nor did he approve of actions such as the burning of imported British textiles and the persecution of traders through extensive boycotts or armed militancy. Instead, he took the stance of economic nationalism and reformism of a 'constructive *swadeshi*' movement. This amounted to efforts for the reconstruction of Bengal's civil society by creating projects of collective social reform and moral self-development that shunned any quest for power, either over other Bengali/Indian social groups or through the formation of a national state – the hallmarks of political nationalism. His aim was to pursue quiet, in-depth social work in order to create a substantive cultural–mental universe, without any direct reference to or the reproduction of a society and state in the image of a colonial power. He also felt that the national imaginary and decolonizing ideals suitable for a new India with a new and truly free people were to be created through the process of a long struggle. The independent India could not simply be the obverse reflection of western imperialism. His ideal of 'India' was to encompass the diversity of its peoples and cultures, nuanced with its long history and infused with pluralism implying a secular humanism; it could be inclusive of western values and cultural/aesthetic forms if they were in keeping with humanist and universalist ideals.[16] As Rabindranath felt that not all western ideas or practices were 'colonial', so too did he not wish to uphold all things 'Indian' (for example, the caste system) as socially desirable. He could not accept any system of ideas from anywhere irrespective of their intrinsic moral and social implications. On this point, Sumit Sarkar says of the hero of the eponymous novel *Gora*: 'The young man whose burning patriotism had led him away from Brahmo sectarianism to seek contact with his motherland through the traditional religion realizes in the depths of rural India the ugly reality of obscurantism stifling human initiative, setting apart caste from caste, Hindus from Muslims.' Sarkar substantiates his point by quoting from the novel:

> The ties of the samaj, the devotion to customs, do not give them any strength in practice. ... Gora realized that this samaj gives no help in times of need,

> no support in face of danger – it can only harass men by enforcing a rigid conformity. ... In the immobility of rural life Gora saw real weakness of our country in an absolutely unadorned form. ... No longer could Gora delude himself with a romantic make-believe world of his own. (Sarkar 1973: 62)

Rabindranath's idea of decolonization was marked by an aspiration for a synthesis of ideas, both Indian and western, which were pro-emancipationist and enabling of individual and collective freedom, and transcended narrow chauvinistic particularism. Whatever he had written in his early youth in glowing hinduized terms about the war hero Shivaji as the icon of Maratha independence, or about sikh militancy against mughal (muslim) emperors and rajput–mughal (read hindu–muslim) conflicts,[17] were left behind by 1908. He began to conceptualize a freedom outside of the hindu/muslim communal divide and casteist patriarchal oppression. In the high noon of Bengal's and India's nationalist period, Rabindranath emerged as its critic, as the 'great sentinel' of Gandhi – upholding the universalist, humanist secular counterpoint – to keep the conscience of India's anti-colonial politics from falling prey to narrow chauvinism and violent communalism.[18] Communal strife and other forms of social oppression in India itself, the violent nationalism of the European colonizing powers and their inter-imperialist wars with millions dead, Japan's triumph over China, claims of western and Japanese 'civilization' constructed 'over a tower of skulls', all combined to mature and delineate Rabindranath's world-view.[19]

But Rabindranath's own journey from hindu cultural nationalism and the armed militancy of its martyrs to a universalist decolonization was not easy or linear, nor, as his novels show, without a visceral struggle. A holistic idea of decolonization did not come to him spontaneously and take on concreteness. In actuality, the lived experience of colonialism, as portrayed in *Gora* or *Ghare Baire*, could only partially support the distinction he made between the 'good' and the 'bad' British, with the hope of the 'good' overdetermining the 'bad'.[20] But in spite of the fact that the 'bad' British regularly prevailed over the 'good', Rabindranath still rejected nationalism as he saw it in action in Bengal, Japan or Europe. The struggle involved in getting beyond nationalism was enormous. This is evident in three of the four novels discussed here, in which the narratives are fraught with frequent ambivalences, reversals and a sense of loss. Though the universal principle is asserted at the end of the novels, the particulars of the characters' experiences – the death of daily loves, confused desires and errors in the relationship between men and women – continue to haunt us. The indigenous cultural and political consciousness, often figured through a feminine persona, which has suffered love and disappointment at the hands of patriarchal and narrow nationalism, is somewhat at a loss to know how to get to the utopia of decolonization. The rise to a state of freedom uncontaminated by lustful sexual desire and political power, and so to a purity from the 'fallen' world of colonialism marked by practices of overt and covert domination, is not easy to portray in novelistic terms. The novels lack concreteness in the narrative analogue or translation, and thus continue to search for a more evolved literary and aesthetic form. Yet decolonization, with its core of transcending the interests of a closed group or familial identification, remains central to the purpose of these novels, and they reject the nationalist idea of blood and belonging in favour of a humanist world culture, of positive coexistence. This meant championing the conception of the entire world as one's home – a movement in social identity from a gendered and ethnicist one to seeing a home in the world. But the nuances and deficiencies of the actual and lived world, of an immanent self, are so vividly depicted that the ideal of universalist humanism remains somewhat abstract and disembodied. The leap of faith that Rabindranath wants us to make, from the lived particular to the ideal universal, from eros to agape, from passion to compassion, from nation to the world, suffers from a danger of coming across as didactic. It seems that Rabindranath is still looking for a narrative content of the universal, leaving the reader often at the level of wish fulfilment.[21] In spite of this artistic failure of representation, the universalist register still continues to be the major motivation of the narrative. Without this ideal in view, these novels lack a reason for their existence. In the next section, we will discuss this dilemma of representation of the relationship between the particular and the universal, the ideal vision and its representation in a concrete form.

The Power, Passion and Ambivalence of Nationalism

In the four novels considered here, the problematic of nationalism is present in a complex narrative form. They situate the characters in a period of intense upheaval against British rule, including armed insurrection in Bengal, which provides a tension in all the texts. The themes of sexuality and desire, in the broadest sense, inter-constitute each other and unfold in all the stories as a trope of the quest for genuine freedom and affirmative subjective choice. This is structured into plots in a dualist manner involving body–mind, public–private, passion–reason and individualism–humanism.

Rabindranath's aim is to establish a dialectical relation between these opposites and arrive at some resolution. The structures of feelings, ideas and events unfold best in *Chaturanga*, in which the formulation of the dilemma of desire can be seen as a template for the other novels.

Chaturanga (Four Parts) expresses this dilemma of desire less through a story of events in time, but rather in terms of thematics of relations, emotions and ideologies within and among the characters, leading either to implosion or a tenuous catharsis. The character cast of these novels involves two or more men and an essential central woman figure to or through whom they relate. The men are galvanized by her physical presence into experiencing passions, taking actions and coming to realizations about themselves and each other. Making choice or acting according to compulsion are the core themes and propulsive narrative forces. These forces are lived subconsciously by the characters as well as consciously reflected upon through debates between and within monologues. We might call these novels of Tagore 'novels of ideas' or novelistic forms of morality plays. They do not follow patterns of conventional storytelling as an exercise in realism, and they only partially rely on descriptive depiction or depend upon plot. They contain long discussions between the characters on ideas and inner critical reflections, and have a poetic, almost allegorical quality. They are composite products of imagination and cerebration. The male characters are defined ideologically, in terms of the values or beliefs they embody and attendant emotional stances. Though endowed with a personal psychology, they can also be seen as ideal types. It is as though the main male characters each represent one aspect of a moral spectrum, and only when taken together can they constitute a whole person, a multidimensional, actual protagonist.

Chaturanga is laid out in first-person narrations by three major characters, one of whom sometimes functions as an omniscient observer and whose narrative encompasses those of the others. The men are initially presented as static character types, then are galvanized by their desire to act, by transgressive and conflicted sexual passion for the primary woman character. The plots of all four novels centre on two or even three men who desire the same woman. Through this passion, intense enough to be rhapsodic and almost mystical, they reach out to an intangible freedom at personal and social levels. Damini, the heroine in *Chaturanga*, is a beautiful, sexually thwarted young widow who is looking for her self-fulfilment while serving as an emotional catalyst for others. She breaks the boundaries of brahminical patriarchal moral regulation in order to act out her desire, but her passion ultimately undergoes a transformation towards a kind of love that exceeds both the physical and the personal. Named Damini (lightning), she illuminates in her emotional struggle the truth about herself and the others, and the prevalent dictates of the upper-caste middle-class society. She is the vehicle that projects to the reader the novel's problematic of freedom, desire and choice. Driven initially by the impulses of her natural sexual attraction for the narcissistic Sachish, mistaken by her as love, by the time of her untimely death she has come to love the social good represented by her self-chosen life with Sribilash, a man of moderation and reason. Introduced as Sachish's devoted companion, Sribilash, who evoked only friendship in Damini, ends up as her chosen life partner. All passions spent, at the end of the novel and her own life her last words to Sribilash are: 'I did not get enough of you in this life. I hope that in lives to come we will be together' (Tagore 1916a: 177).

Here, then, is that movement from individualism to the social good, from passion to reason, eros to agape, that Rabindranath aspired to, but this happens at the outermost boundary of Damini's life, in which nothing quotidian, no social enactment of this great humanist love for the good, is possible or even needed. Damini, nature incarnate in woman, attains her wisdom at the cost of her life, and Sribilash, finally chosen by her, is left without a personal object for his own love and daily life. The dynamism of the desire for freedom (with different meanings attributed to this notion in different novels), the journey of the protagonists from a reckless abandonment to physical, political and mystical passions to a choice coherent with a universal human love, marks *Chaturanga*'s narrative progression.

The same tonal and thematic structure and dynamism of *Chaturanga* underlies that of *Ghare Baire* (Home and the World), here serving as an explicit critique of nationalism and personal sexual passion and its contrast with a true humane love and freedom of decolonization. The novel's schema interpellates passionate heterosexual love and nationalist politics within the same existential space. Again, we find two men who are close friends, Sandip and Nikhilesh, representing antithetical political passions and moralities with respect to social transformation and introspection. Embodying binary principles of compulsion and choice, nationalism and decolonization, impulsiveness and moderation, they are in love with the same woman and involved with the same political question of freedom. Bimala, the 'queen bee' as Sandip calls her, is married to Nikhilesh, a benevolent, progressive and modernizing landlord who has experienced the destructive side of political *swadeshi* or nationalism, and now only espouses its 'constructive' aspect of local social upliftment.[22] Though Nikilesh and Bimala are happily living in an arranged marriage, and he and an English governess have educated Bimala in social, political and literary matters, Nikhilesh is not content. He is a modernist man of reason who is seeking a companionate conjugality, the equal participation of wife and husband within marriage, and wants to introduce Bimala to freedom, to personal choice.[23] He wants to be individually 'chosen' by her outside of patriarchal, prescriptive caste/class familial conventions, and for her to do so with an active knowledge of the world that she inhabits. In order to accomplish this, both in her and for himself, Nikilesh introduces into their home a force from the outside, a daring nationalist figure illuminated by the light of blazing fires of the Bengal partition riots of 1905. This guest/outsider is his old college friend Sandip, a hero of political (read 'destructive') nationalism current at the time. Bimala now oversteps the seclusion of the *andarmahal* (the interior quarters), enters 'the world' (symbolized here by the outer quarters of their house or *bahir*, generally inhabited by men), and is swept away by its forces. A sexually charged passion of a chaotic freedom that knows no social or moral boundaries overtakes her, kindled by the passion of Sandip. Through her desire and admiration for him, Bimala is drawn into the nationalist violence that rages around them – the violence of mob lynching, of arson and armed robberies, of looting and hindu–muslim riots.

But Bimala, like Damini, is not blinded by her passion forever. As she watches herself hurtling into the hell of sexual compulsion and a disorderly and destructive experience which parallels her involvement with Sandip's nationalism, the difference between nationalist and humanist freedom becomes clear to her. She recognizes Sandip for who he is – an ego-driven, violent and amoral man, a greedy seducer who worships an animalistic freedom.[24] Through this relationship to him the conflagration of her home, her own ruin, is complete, but in that process of being stripped to the bare bones of her being, she does make her final and true choice – for Nikhilesh, not Sandip. But as with *Chaturanga*, it may be a little too late for this life, as Nikhilesh has been seriously wounded in trying to protect his muslim tenants from the predations of the hindu nationalists, the followers of Sandip and of *swadeshi* terror. As a fire ordeal for the genuineness of his modernity, questioning the very tenets of traditional masculinity, he has stood by watching the terrible results that his orchestration of freedom and choice has precipitated in his personal and social environment. In this parable of sexual and nationalist passion, Bimala has ultimately chosen the good. Furthermore, as the embodiment or emblem of the nation (which is frequently conflated by Tagore), the nation itself has chosen through her a constructive nationalism and decolonization over destructive political nationalism. But this wisdom does not come about before one aspect of nature in the shape of physical desire and its political correlate, power-driven nationalism, has swept all before it, as a hurricane devastates a landscape which now awaits regeneration.

This same allegory of passion/nature versus reason/humanism, political nationalism opposed to universal humanism, animates *Char Adhyay* (Four Chapters), a novella which might also be called a prose-poem. Nationalists here, characterized by the anti-hero Indranath as by Sandip in *Ghare Baire*, embody unbridled ego-driven particularism, and are the antithesis of transcendence from personal and chauvinistic nationalism to the ideal of humanism. Their motive force or ethics are similar in that the urge for power and domination which animates their politics also characterizes colonialism and their emotional sexual lives. The leading male figures of nationalism thus are driven by hunger for power and narcissism, and the young and innocent among them who are their victims are inspired by a passion for martyrdom and are misled, as is Atin, into an inverted morality. Ela, the central and animating woman figure here, is both an image of innocence and of the quest for power as a distorted expression of the self. *Char Adhyay* shows us a world in disarray, where an organized nationalist movement has not yet emerged and small bands of desperate armed men, after the defeat of 1905, fantasize their freedom in acts of random violence. Hiding among the dilapidated ruins of a landlord's country house, Atin and Ela, whose flame-like beauty draws young men to freedom's cause without sexually gratifying them, meet their nemesis, because at the last moment, at the edge of the narrative, Ela falls prey to her own woman's heart and Atin to a dead-end nationalism. Previously she had urged her lover Atin to sacrifice himself for the cause of the nation, but now she yields to save him for love, for a greater good. Like Damini or Bimala, Ela's realization of the good, of the love within her that directs her to the social, to a nurturing stance towards the other, comes at the ultimate moment – in a state of desperation at the boundaries of society and her death.

Ambivalence: Nationalism or Decolonization?

For Rabindranath decolonization is the ideal before mankind, for which the boundaries between homes, nations and passions have to be broken and the home-and-the-world antithesis transcended by a universal humanism. He sought to actualize this ideal of decolonization in Santiniketan, his educational institution, established in 1901. And yet, paradoxically, the novels of Tagore are haunted by the power of particularism. The ghosts of personal passions, of a self-centred nationalism and for a chaotic freedom, are never thoroughly exorcised in them. The rhetoric of freedom, even of false, unhallowed natural freedom fraught with exultations of power and pain, is branded on to the reader's consciousness. A vulnerability to the kind of power that Rabindranath repudiates, to a ruthless masculinity as much at the core of industrial capitalism as of nationalism, is portrayed in his play *Raktakarabi* by the heroine Nandini in her attraction to the king who sits self-imprisoned in the heart of his technological empire, in the bowels of a gold mine:

> BISHU: What was he like?
>
> NANDINI: Like a man from the epics – his forehead like the gateway to a tower, his arms the iron bolts of some inaccessible fortress.
>
> BISHU: What did you see when you went inside?
>
> NANDINI: A falcon was sitting on his left wrist. He put it on its perch and gazed at my face. Then, just as he had been stroking the falcon's wings, he began to stroke my hand gently. … Then he buried his fingers in my unbound hair and sat long with closed eyes. … I liked it. … It was as if he were a thousand-year-old banyan tree, and I a tiny little bird; when I alit on a branch of his and had my little swing, he needs must have felt a thrill of delight to his very marrow. I loved to give that bit of joy to that lonely soul. (Tagore 1925: 70–72)

It seems a great ironic reversal when, even inadvertently, Rabindranath's very criticism animates that which he seeks to eliminate. When Ela, Bimala or Damini leap across age-old social mores and find themselves in a nameless zone of desire at the end of the world as they know it, they also encounter a kind of universal, a freedom that is of devastation. Even if Tagore seeks to give them and his narratives other denouements, what emerges simultaneously is an ambiguity. The characters stand at the cusp of an end and a beginning of life. These turbulent chaotic moments await their fate and form – of extinction or a new life. The questions that face them as women, as embodiments of the nation, as ravaged nature, are of personal and political selfhood or identity. At the close of the novels, we wonder with them about their identities, about who they are now at the end of the story. What will they do from now on? What will be the new form of social definition and engagement in which they can participate? Somehow, choosing good, reasonable husbands, or regretting the loss of opportunity to build a personal life and a home together, does not offer a convincing representation or a vehicle for the notion of the universal, a good for all. As readers it is not Rabindranath's idea of the universal, social good, the need for a reasonable choice in life and politics, that we dispute, but narratively speaking, we do not see this end embodied, expressed and socialized within the fictional space. Even if we deplore the sadomasochism of the patriarchal sexual and nationalist passions, we still look for an embodied intensity and concreteness of experience and action, the presence of a subject agent in the realm of the advocated greater good. But a mood of melancholic ambivalence descends upon us as we close the books.

The great difficulty in representing the universal in narrative terms becomes evident upon reading *Gora*, the most social and the least sexually charged of these novels. Inverting the story of Kipling's *Kim*, here a white orphaned child is adopted by a Bengali family after the 1856 anti-British uprising, and, ignorant of his origins, he becomes an ultra-hindu nationalist. As he leaps to the most particularist of nationalist chauvinisms, even of glorifying the caste system or communalism in spite of his instinct to reject them, we, readers in the know, wait for hubris to strike. As the prevalent nationalism of the time rests on the myth of origin, on notions of blood and belonging, we wonder what will happen when Gora encounters the originary truth about himself. And when he does, we find him dropping with surprising alacrity the burden of hindu nationalism and embracing brahmoism, whose key notions of the world soul, universal brotherhood and love of contemplation provide him with tender refuge. Daily piety and social reform, good deeds of the everyday, a brahmo version of liberal ethics, are to occupy him from now on, practices in which he will be aided by Sucharita, a like-minded woman and the daughter of his preceptor into the conduct of universalism. This resolution seems rather pious, though entirely commendable, and the issue of national political freedom which earlier preoccupied Gora disappears.

But then this novel, compared to the others, is the least invested in passionate sexuality. Women feature here as social types of modernity – girls under the tutelage of a mother in a Jane Austen-like constellation

(Baradasundari with her poor, unmarried daughter could have easily descended from *Pride and Prejudice*), and another woman figure (Anandamoyee, Gora's mother) who has attained a universal morality through her motherly love. Though some sexual attraction is at work, it is muted by appropriate middle-class progressive mores and piety. Neither the two heroines, Sucharita and Lalita, nor Gora and his friend Binoy, are devastated by the impact of a passionate transgressive love, though some superficial social mores are contravened by Lalita in particular. These women, as members of the Brahmo Samaj, do not live as conservative high-caste hindus, as do women in the other novels discussed here, and they are formally western-educated. They are 'free mixing' unmarried women who undergo no radical break with family tradition when they choose their life partners. They have already had their sentimental education in their familial environment, and the modernity of their self-chosen love and marriage does not come as an apocalyptic surprise, as in the other novels. Nor are they swept away from the world of modernist social reform to that of chauvinistic armed nationalism in pursuit of the men they love. Marriage, actualized and promised, resolves the small upheavals of social transgression of hindu men falling in love with brahmo women, in fact with parental blessings.

Gora, then, is what things could look like in this life, in the daily world, if the good, the reasonable, the agape version of love would be pursued, and the politics it advocates signals Rabindranath's ideal of constructive *swadeshi*. Sucharita and Lalita do not stand alone under a darkening sky, as do the other heroines. Instead, we find two parental counterparts, a father and a mother, who hold the children (young adults, couples) by the hand so they will not be lost in the labyrinth of the world. The iconic figure of reason and contemplation is an old brahmo gentleman, the preacher of Brahmo Samaj, Paresh Babu. His complementary figure is Anandamoyee, Gora's mother, with wisdom of the heart, a pure maternal love. This she has shown in adopting a white child, an act that has propelled her forever out of the hindu caste system. It is to her that Gora returns after he has taken the vow of serving the universal ideal of 'India'. This novel brings in the themes of motherhood and nation otherwise absent in Tagore. Anandamoyee stands for his ideal construct of 'India' – an India that is a unity in diversity, an ideal of love and acceptance, an 'India' to be given as a gift to the world. We have moved from the heady mixture of eroticism and nationalism, or of motherhood as found in Bankim Chandra's goddess of power, Durga, the incarnation of the nation, to the love of the good and a humanist decolonization as a universal parental, especially maternal, love. Freedom has moved from the stage of 'free from' to 'free to', with a constructive future ahead, and to exit from the dark caves of natural passion into social kinship with others. A noble, utopian vision – but in practice and in narrative terms, it amounts to a domestic life of the Brahmo Samaj of Bengal espousing reformist, liberal values. Protest against destruction wrought by sexual and political passion has returned us to a conservative ideal of marriage and home, albeit dressed in the modern clothes of social reform in which the individual is significant within the social collective.

Conclusion

Perhaps the problem of ambivalence comes from a place that lies outside the scope of the novels themselves – from the epistemological and political standpoints from which Rabindranath projects his politics and social criticism, that of metaphysics and liberal values. To begin with, the notion of the 'universal' as an idealist concept is by definition best suited to being a spiritual frame of moral reference. It can only be a state of mind, an awareness, a feeling of unbounded space, rather than a social and material set of relations and practices that can be actualized as actions or lived daily. At an aesthetic level of poetry or music it relies on tonalities and metaphors, but one doubts whether this metaphysical vision can be narrativized as a piece of fiction. Socio-politically it translates into a quiescent attitude to all forms of conflict. The transcendence itself required for this kind of universality is after all from the very social ground created through actual relations of power. Thus, it is not surprising that Tagore's novels should portray a colonized world and nationalist resistance without almost ever portraying in any great detail foreign cultural or social domination. Nor do British characters feature in the novels except in the shape of a glimpse of Miss Digby pursued by local boys in *Ghare Baire*, a deracinated Gora and some incidents involving a cricket game in the same novel. Whenever they are spoken about, a distinction is maintained between 'good' and 'bad' Europeans. Thus, nationalism is critiqued in the novels mostly in terms of Indians (the colonized) oppressing each other, of their power-ridden society, without exploring how the local social formations on the colonial terrain are shaped by or exert pressures on people's political identities as hindus and muslims. Tagore does not pose the question in these novels, as he does elsewhere, about how an open world culture or constructive *swadeshi* could develop in an environment of active colonial domination. His novels leave us with the impression that colonial domination can be left to the Bengali/Indian society as an extraneous matter, just as he considers nationalism to be an alien political ideology for India. An ideal imaginary of 'India', it seems, could flourish under a colonial state at a socio-cultural level. It also leads us to believe that armed anti-colonial resistance could have no other politics except that of small cells of desperate assassins. This approach is not consistent with Tagore's disappointment with British rule expressed elsewhere in his writings, and often in the deepest terms of moral judgement and condemnation. The rejection of his knighthood following the massacre perpetrated by the British in Jallianwala Bagh (1919) expresses this disappointment:

> Your Excellency [Lord Chelmsford],
> The enormity of the measures taken by the Government in the Punjab for quelling some local disturbances has, with a rude shock, revealed to our minds the helplessness of our position as British subjects in India. The disproportionate severity of the punishments inflicted upon the unfortunate people and the methods of carrying them out, we are convinced, are without parallel in the history of civilised governments, barring some conspicuous exceptions, recent and remote. Considering that such treatment has been meted out to a population, disarmed and resourceless, by a power which has the most terribly efficient organization for destruction of human lives, we must strongly assert that it can claim no political expediency, far less moral justification. The accounts of insults and sufferings undergone by our brothers in the Punjab have trickled through the gagged silence, reaching every corner of India, and the universal agony of indignation roused in the hearts of our people has been ignored by our rulers – possibly congratulating themselves for what they imagine as salutary lessons. This callousness has been praised by most of the Anglo-Indian papers. … The time has come when badges of honour make our shame glaring in their incongruous context of humiliation, and I for my part wish to stand, shorn of all special distinctions, by the side of those of my countrymen, who, for their so-called insignificance, are liable to suffer a degradation not fit for human beings. (Cited in Dutta and Robinson 1997: 223)

In a letter to the English poet Sturge Moore, the same condemnation is heard in his rejection of colonial education or cultural mimicry, extending to the translations of his own works:

> Translations, however clever, can only transfigure dancing into acrobatic tricks, in most cases playing treason against the majesty of the original. I often imagine apes to be an attempt by the devil of a translator to render human form in the mould of his outlandish idiom. The case may be to some extent different in European languages which, in spite of their respective individual characteristics, have closely similar temperaments and atmospheres, the Western culture being truly a common culture.
>
> As for myself, I ought never to have intruded into your realm of glory with my offerings hastily giving them a foreign shine and certain assumed gestures familiar to you. I have done thereby injustice to myself and the shrine of Muse which proudly claims flowers from its own climate and culture. (Cited in Dutta and Robinson 1997: 451)

Rabindranath's proposal for decolonization as presented in these novels, due to its lack of a materialist and historical critique, cannot present us with an anti-colonial struggle, which needs to be both against imperialism and against the semi-feudal capitalism of Indians themselves. It lacks, because of its metaphysical or idealist and purely liberal standpoint, an ability to cope with actual relations of power, an exploration of connections between consciousness and social and historical materiality. The formulation of his criticism in moralistic-idealist terms strips the problematic of anti-nationalism of its social and quotidian complexity. To the degree that he wants to address a current and pressing actual situation, his novels pose it through stories of personal interactions of sexuality and desire. This device works well for portraying only some aspects of problems with nationalism. But even here the primality of this unto-death struggle of nature and reason simultaneously opens and closes the ground for critique. Consequently, the image of a universal humanity floats over a fallen world, missing the step of transition which would show us how to get there from where we are. In narratives which leave us with a generous modernist landlord, a deracinated Irishman, a Bengali middle-class man and a woman with liberal values as protagonists of decolonization and a moral imperative of being 'good', one cannot find much social or cultural direction. Under these circumstances 'freedom', an essentially political concept, seems to be a feel-good state of the mind, with the bars of the social and colonial prison mostly intact. The poetry of his prose sweeps the reader away through the transmission of the splendour and violence of passion, the ambiguity of desire, rather than the calm of resolution and transcendence.

Yet, outside the scope of the novels, as Gandhi leads India in a mass movement, as the first world war ravages Europe, the second world war begins to take shape as nazis and fascists, both western and eastern, become bearers of 'civilization', and as Rabindranath visits the Soviet Union, returning with admiration for the transformation of peasants and workers there, his view of decolonization grows richer, more complex. The problematic of decolonization shifts from the metaphoric and the rhetorical level of freedom to other possibilities of organizing resistance. But that is another story, to be told another time.

Notes

[1] For gender critiques of nationalism by feminist scholars, see Jasodhara Bagchi (1985), Himani Bannerji (2001a, 2001d), Uma Chakravarti (1998) and Tanika Sarkar (2001b).

[2] For more general critiques of women's roles and relationships to nationalism, see Yuval-Davis (1997).

[3] Himani Bannerji, 'Women, Gender and the Family in Tagore', in Sukanta Chaudhuri (2020). Here the issues of a woman's search for her 'self' and emancipation have been figurated in terms of nationalism and modernity.

[4] For some highly influential texts on nationalism, see Hobsbawm (1990), Anderson (1983), Gellner (1983), A.D. Smith (1983).

[5] The first chapters are especially relevant for this topic in understanding nationalism in the colonial context.

[6] See Ahmad (1992, 1996).

[7] For an excellent history and analysis of the development of nationalism in Bengal, see Sumit Sarkar (1973); see also Raychaudhuri (1988).

[8] For orientalist revisionist history and invention as well as reconstruction of cultural memory of muslim rule and hindu–muslim relations, see James Mill (1968); R.C. Majumdar (1962–63, volumes 1 and 2). For an unconscious diffusion of this mythic communal history among children, see Abanindranath Tagore's beautifully written and illustrated *Raj Kahini* (2004).

[9] Much has been written on this theme of desire and its sexual and political interpellation; see, for example, P.K. Datta (2003), 'Introduction', as well as, in the same volume, the contribution of Tanika Sarkar (2003). See also P.K. Datta (1999).

[10] On the kind of 'feminism' espoused by Krishnabhabini Das, see, for example, Himani Bannerji (2001b).

[11] On Rokeya Sakhawat Hossain, see Barnita Bagchi's introduction to her translation of Hossain (2005); see also Tharu and Lalita (1993).

[12] Most were first published in serialized form: *Gora* (1907–09); *Chaturanga* (1915); *Ghare Baire* (1915–16); *Char Adhyay* (1934).

[13] Bankim Chandra Chattopadhyay's *Anandamath* was published in 1882. '*Bande Mataram*' ('Homage to the Mother'), a song in this novel, even today – and

especially now favoured by the hindu right wing – competes successfully with the national anthem, which is a poem by Rabindranath. When consulted by the Indian National Congress, Tagore did not approve of '*Bande Mataram*' as an anthem for the Congress on the grounds of its distinct hindu, i.e. religious and culturally chauvinistic, markers. The guiding spirit of the diverse nation that is India, he felt, could not be represented as a sectarian deity.

[14] Regarding icons of heroic and lamenting mothers, see Jasodhara Bagchi (1993a).

[15] See Sumit Sarkar (1983).

[16] The best description of this construct of 'India' is embodied in *Gora* by the character of Anandamoyee with her quality of maternal humanism. This, however, needs to be complemented by a male abstract form of positive reason as found in Paresh Babu.

[17] See Tagore's *Katha o Kahini* (1908).

[18] For a nuanced and in-depth reading of relations between Rabindranath and Gandhi, see Sabyasachi Bhattacharya (1997b).

[19] See Tagore's letter to the imperial Japanese poet Yone Naguchi, in Dutta and Robinson (1997): 497.

[20] The distinction that Rabindranath rightly made between colonially minded, 'bad' British, and the 'good' ones as exemplified by C.F. Andrews, L. Elmhirst and others showing critical specificity, is presented in the tragic hope he offered in his essay, 'The Crisis of Civilization'. For a detailed reading of this text, see Dutta and Robinson (1995), Chapter 36.

[21] An interesting speculation as to why this might be so is to be found in Sprinker (2003): 122–23, where he considers the shortcomings of the nationalist project as conducted by the Indian National Congress.

[22] The type of landlord usually found at this time in Bengal and his relationship to the *ryot* (peasant) is well outlined in Sumit Sarkar (1983), Chapter 4. It is to this type that Nikhilesh proves to be a solid exception.

[23] On this, see Tanika Sarkar (2001b), Chapters 1 and 6.

[24] Sprinker (2003): 116 makes an interesting observation on Sandip; he characterizes him as a sort of 'Nietzschean superman' rather than 'an ordinary sinner, or criminal'.

5

A Transformational Pedagogy

Reflections on Rabindranath's Ideas and Practices of Decolonization

> Swadeshi, Swarajism,[1] ordinarily produce intense excitement in the minds of my countrymen, because they carry in them some fervour of passion generated by the exclusiveness of their range. It cannot be said that I am untouched by this heat and movement. But somehow, by my temperament as a poet, I am incapable of accepting these objects as final. They claim from us a great deal more than is their due. After a certain point is reached, I find myself obliged to separate myself from my own people, with whom I have been working, and my soul cries out: 'The complete man must never be sacrificed to the patriotic man, or even to the merely moral man.' To me humanity is rich and large and many-sided.
>
> – Tagore (2009b: 202)

Anyone writing on Rabindranath Tagore faces a daunting task because of his decades-long multi-genre creative, critical and philosophical opus, as well as the educational projects he undertook to implement some of his major ideas. These projects encompassed humanist studies, fine arts and crafts, and studies in agriculture inclusive of science and technology. His commitment to education led to the foundation of two institutions: Santiniketan (1921), which was expanded to Visva Bharati, and Sriniketan (1923), imbued with the aim of shaping a 'complete man' expressing the 'rich and large and many-sided' nature of humanity. This chapter is an exploration of Rabindranath's educational ideas concerning his overall vision of a new society and a new man, implying a formative relationship between consciousness/culture and social transformation. Understood thus, education takes on an extra-institutional, holistic character. His reflections explore this relationship in terms of challenging colonial hegemony through elite and daily cultural beliefs and practices. Our inquiry is directed to the ways and the extent to which his ideas contribute to a better understanding of *swaraj* and *swadeshi*, and to the necessary subject–agent for the achievement of decolonization.

Our inquiry reveals a radical difference between the conventional ideas and practices of *swaraj*/*swadeshi* prevalent at the time and those of Rabindranath, who frames the problematic of individual and anti-colonial freedom within the perspective of universalist humanism. It is this problematic that is present in the above quotation. Without rejecting the primary necessity of the goal of the *swadeshi* movement to end colonial subordination, he added another dimension to the meaning of the idea of freedom. He says that he is 'incapable of accepting them [the goals of *swadeshi*] as final.' He further explains his position when he says, 'I find myself obliged to separate myself from my own people, with whom I have been working, and my soul cries out: the complete man must never be sacrificed to the patriotic man, or even to the merely moral man.' Rabindranath's position thereby confronts us with a paradox. We ask: How is it possible to be free of colonialism while rejecting nationalism, the conventional ideology and politics of anti-colonialism? Is not the 'nation' rather than the individual the collective subject–agent of freedom? An answer to these questions requires a clarification of what Rabindranath means by colonialism and its end, such that decolonization might be achieved outside of the framework of nationalism.

Here it is necessary to comment on the term 'decolonization', since Rabindranath himself did not use it, nor is there evidence of its coinage in his time. By interpreting his ideas and practices against colonialism, which he articulated outside of nationalism, he arrived at something like the concept of decolonization as used by Frantz Fanon in *The Wretched of the Earth* (1961). Formulated in the context of the Algerian liberation struggle against French colonialism, Fanon also offers a critique of nationalism with regard to its potential for a 'true' decolonization encompassing all aspects of individual life and society as a whole. For Rabindranath, who wrote earlier, ending colonialism entailed theoretical premises, similar to those of Fanon, which were qualitatively different from a simple reversal of the premises of colonialism. This requirement for substantiveness in the oppositional theoretical premises sets Rabindranath apart from the *swaraj*-ists/nationalists, whose ideological position he saw as an inversion of colonial discourse/projects. He identified in nationalism the same fetishization of power over people through directly violent property relations and accumulation of wealth. This nationalist inversion would result in no real decolonization; only the caste/colour of the rulers or extortionists would change. Rabindranath saw here no challenge to the values of colonialism, nor a disarticulation of the notion of freedom associated with fetishized state power. His critique is echoed by the later distinction that Fanon drew between 'true' and 'false' decolonization.

For Rabindranath, exorcising India of colonialism meant undertaking a socio-historical process without reference to power-based values. His aim was to create a social culture in which a 'free' individual, that is, an individual unconnected with property related ideas, would be possible. The free 'new man' who would inaugurate the 'new society' would not be an atomized possessive individual. This indicates that Rabindranath held two interpretations of the notion of freedom: first, a negative freedom which refers to freedom from domination, without clarifying what that freedom would entail beyond its contextual reference to domination; secondly, a positive freedom which is substantive and moves towards a future humanist society. While the first view of freedom is shaped by response to colonial hegemony, the second relies on the idea of a self or an individuality substantively articulated beyond oppressive values and practices. For Rabindranath, without an insistence on substantive premises of humanity any attempt at freedom is in danger of sinking back into a world of unfreedom. For these reasons he critiqued both nationalism and colonialism, imagining decolonization outside the orbit of power.

In the context of his aspiration to decolonization, Rabindranath's ideas on education are primarily non-institutional and based on social and ethical aspects of pedagogy. Disarticulating the idea of pedagogy from a commonly held association with a formal and institutional one, he redefined the idea of education as ethical and aesthetic ways of seeing and being, rather than accumulation of facts and curricular content. His idea of 'pedagogy' is actually a mode of social critique, an earlier version of critical pedagogy which we later find in the educational philosophy of Paulo Freire, the central text being his *The Pedagogy of the Oppressed* (1970). This view confers upon education philosophical and socially participatory dimensions which signal to both relations of domination and resistance. For Freire, pedagogy is far beyond just literacy and factual content in aiming to raise consciousness about the relationship between the individual and society. This is an active process of learning which he calls 'social conscientization', augmenting human capacity for knowledge in its application to power relations. Education includes an act of critique and becomes a mode for social analysis, which includes in its purview the institution of education itself. In this pedagogy all the members are equally engaged in the learning process. This active version of education opposes the passive one, which amounts to the banking of facts in the mind of the student. For Rabindranath also, education connotes a broader consciousness-raising, going beyond literacy, facts and skills which prepare students for careers. This process confers upon education the power for social transformation, and thus enhances self-awareness, critical reflexivity and imaginative expressivity, linking the individual self with the other. His approach is reflected in the following quotation:

> We cannot remove the causes of our suffering from the outside, they have to be eradicated from within. If we wish to do that there are two tasks. First, to educate the common people of the country and connect their consciousness with all peoples of the world – detachment from the world has made their consciousness rustic and insular. They have to be lifted into the proud sphere of the humanity as a whole. ... The other [task] is in the area of livelihood. They will have to be united with the world's humanity [in this task] and their labour connected with that of others. (Tagore 1929a: 419; my translation)

Rabindranath aspires to a pedagogical method necessary not only for Indian individuals in the colonial context, but also for any society. It transcends national boundaries. Though he claims that his pedagogy is not 'political' – and it is not so in the conventional sense of politics and is certainly not geared towards state formation – its transformational ambition implies a thorough social critique, and as such has profound political implications. In this respect his pedagogic project is reminiscent of Antonio Gramsci's understanding of the concept of hegemony, which he grounds in what he calls 'civil society', the realm of culture/consciousness of everyday life. These issues are particularly well explored in Gramsci's essays in *Selections from the Prison Notebooks* (1971) on the roles of intellectuals and education, namely, 'State and Civil Society' and 'Notes on Italian History'. Gramsci's interpretation of 'hegemony', which ascribes a vital importance to popular consciousness/culture, is particularly helpful, as he extends the idea of hegemony beyond the direct force or coercion of the state. Rabindranath would have shared Gramsci's view that any fundamental transformation in society depends on the wide diffusion of an alternative and oppositional consciousness. His interest in the arrival of a 'new man', a 'new age', implies the creation of new ideas, images, symbols and practices, assuming the status of a general cultural common sense. Rabindranath and Gramsci both inform their ideas of education not only with the learning of facts and texts, but with the cultivation of sensibilities, ethics and aesthetics, thus altering the existing 'structures of feeling'.[2] Without going into details here, we can see that the project of 'pedagogy' in its deepest sense is a hegemonic project.[3]

Both Rabindranath and Gramsci were deeply concerned with matters of daily life, religious and moral beliefs, and aesthetic and imaginative expression. For them, change in basic forms of social consciousness involved not only intellectuals, writers, politicians and priests, but also and mainly, ordinary people as producers and carriers of complex, even contradictory world-views or philosophies, and thus of hegemony.[4] The location of this hegemony lay in the liminal space between the state and civil society, the space of life activity, experience and cultural expression. Gramsci's idea of hegemony differs from Rabindranath's in bringing into its composition the economy and the state, and in this he extends the notion of hegemony into the sphere of class relations. This is understandable as Gramsci was a communist politically active in the context of rising fascism in Italy. Rabindranath's efforts at decolonization centrally depended on the creation of new cultural values and practices of humanist universalism in the context of overcoming colonialism. Nonetheless, in rejecting and re-forming the so-called normal culture, the ways of being and seeing in brahminical and colonial terms, Rabindranath's vision and practice of education becomes cultural in the deepest social sense and thus 'political'; they simultaneously challenge the existing casteist hindu and British colonial hegemonies. His essays in *Kalantar* (1933a) or a novel like *Gora* (1910) bear testimony to this.

Rabindranath, Gramsci and Freire all concur that liberationist pedagogy rests on cultural and practical ideas and processes that are at once subjective and social, and the common people are central protagonists in this. They emphasize that the people should preside over the birth of their own emancipatory consciousness and fashion their own culture,[5] and, by implication, their political subjectivities and agencies. They reject any idea of a piecemeal transformation of society and the division of the social whole into its components and fragments, such as the discourse of the public and the private. Education ceases to be a pragmatic moment of intersection between perceived separated social strands. All aspects of Rabindranath's life-work deny this fragmentary approach and refuse a mere aggregation of the parts in the name of the whole. In that spirit, he eschews binary formulations such as tradition versus modernity, home and the world, individual and the social, and the personal and the universal.[6] This project of liberatory hegemonic transformation in the colonial context provides the content and form of Rabindranath's pedagogy of decolonization.

At this point we need to explore the concept of decolonization, both in its general meaning and as used here in assessing Rabindranath; otherwise, there is a chance of misunderstanding his pedagogy of decolonization as being a nuanced variant of nationalism. There have indeed been attempts to turn him into a better or a higher-minded nationalist than his contemporaries, a nationalist who is a cosmopolitanist.[7] A good example can be found in Uma Dasgupta's introduction to *Tagore: Selected Writings on Education and Nationalism*, where she clearly situates Rabindranath within the Indian nationalist tradition, albeit of a modernist variety.[8] Das Gupta insists:

> Tagore did not reject nationalism as is commonly said or assumed. It is that he formed his own understanding of it by studying what was 'authentic' in his country's history, and by applying it to an education that would relate to the past and be receptive of the present. That is how *his thought on nationalism and education became one.* (Das Gupta 2009: xxvi; emphasis added)

Setting aside the red-herring issue of 'authenticity', I claim that Das Gupta misrepresents what Rabindranath means by decolonization, a real or human emancipation, by converting him into a better nationalist as opposed to other 'narrow' ones. Read thus, Rabindranath's decolonizing vision becomes one of 'better' citizenship in a modernist national state rather than one of universal humanism. The fact that he not only rejected nationalism but also set little store by the state is unacknowledged. This flies in the face of a comprehensive reading of his works by all those who claim otherwise, including Rabindranath himself. One need only read his lecture on 'Nationalism' delivered in 1917 (Tagore 1996a) and *Sabhyatar Sankat* (Crisis in Civilization), published in 1940 (Tagore 1996b), to see that once he turned away from nationalism, Rabindranath remained a lifelong critic both of it and its ultimate political institution, the state. In 'Nationalism', he excoriates the very idea of the nation:

> And the idea of the Nation is one of the most powerful anaesthetics that man has invented. Under the influence of its fumes the whole people can carry out its systematic programme of the most virulent self-seeking without being in the least aware of its moral perversion – in fact feeling dangerously resentful if it is pointed out. (Tagore 1996a: 434)

He presents the first world war as an inevitable consequence of nationalism: 'This European war of Nations is the war of retribution. ... The time has come when for the sake of the whole outraged world, Europe should fully know in her own person the terrible absurdity of the thing called Nation' (ibid.). And in 1940, in the midst of the second world war, he wrote in 'Crisis in Civilization':

> In the meanwhile the demon of barbarity has given up all pretence and has emerged with unconcealed fangs, ready to tear up humanity in an orgy of devastation. From one end of the world to the other the poisonous fumes of hatred darken the atmosphere. The spirit of violence which perhaps lay dormant in the psychology of the West, has at last roused itself and desecrates the spirit of Man. (Tagore 1996b: 726)[9]

In his introduction to the third volume of *The English Writings of Rabindranath Tagore*, Sisir Kumar Das points out that Rabindranath was interested in politics in the deepest sense, as all relations of power, but not in its expression as 'nationalism'. He comments that 'many of the essays included here will come as a shock and embarrassment because of their unabashed political association' (Das 1996a: 20). Without discussing here the details of Rabindranath's idea of 'the political', we should note that for him, antagonism towards colonialism or its overthrowing does not automatically require a nationalist orientation. Nor does the idea of the 'political' only and necessarily lead to the construction of a nation state and its overall political apparatus (ibid.). Rabindranath's idea of decolonization, that is, freedom from colonialism, includes in the notion of freedom the obliteration of all power relations. His writings provide clues to another type of anti-colonial, that is, anti-oppression, politics which go far beyond the scope of the nation. His decolonizing philosophy, his project of an emancipatory pedagogy, was elaborated with the personally experienced failings of nationalism in mind. This holds true in spite of the strong temptations or ambivalence that Rabindranath sometimes felt in belonging to the great upsurge to shake off British domination, in participating in the major nationalist trends and in interacting with figures of his time. To this end, Sisir Kumar Das quotes a few lines from Rabindranath to William Rothenstein:

> I have nothing to do *directly* with politics: I am not a Nationalist, moderate or immoderate in my political aspirations. But politics is not a mere abstraction. It has its personality and it does intrude into my life when I am human. It kills and maims individuals, it tells lies, it uses its sacred sword of justice for the

> purpose of massacre, it spreads misery broadcast over centuries of exploitation and I cannot say to myself, 'Poet, you have nothing to do with these facts for they belong to politics.' (Das 1996a: 20)

In fact, it is because Rabindranath was a social and political *anti*-nationalist that he struggled throughout his life to maintain a praxis of decolonization, of universalist humanism, and he did so at considerable cost to himself. Das points out that he was 'often condemned as unpatriotic because of his uncompromising denouncement of nationalism, which he considered to be an instrument of political hegemony and an ideology to legitimize the oppression of one nation over the other' (ibid.: 21). Becoming 'the sentinel', serving as the conscience of Indian nationalism (see Sabyasachi Bhattacharya 1997b), extracted a heavy toll on him, particularly as his pedagogy of decolonization was often misunderstood as complicity with British rule.

Rabindranath's critique of nationalism in all its complexity requires a deeper scrutiny. An attempt is made in this direction by Tanika Sarkar in 'Questioning Nationalism: The Difficult Writings of Rabindranath Tagore' (2009); drawing mainly on the writings of Susobhan Sarkar (1970b), Sumit Sarkar (1973) and Chinmohan Sehanabis (1983),[10] she identifies a break in Rabindranath's thought on nationalism and in his proposal for overcoming colonialism from a non-nationalist standpoint. She situates the turning point between 1905 and 1908, and introduces the possibility of a new critical assessment by distinguishing between 'country' (*desh*) and 'nation' (*jati*). Loving one's country, she says, has an affective and non-ideological quality, an emotion or aspect which is absent from the state-oriented politics of 'nationalism'. When the idea of motherland replaces *desh*/country in the Bengali nationalist ideology, though it becomes more tethered to the public sphere and political organization, it still retains an emotional power from the discourse of *desh*. She writes:

> Rather the valences of intimate familiarity and concrete knowledge, as well as ties of inheritance, residence and familial connections that belonged to a personal birthplace were transposed onto the increasingly larger, mostly unseen and abstract, space of a province or subcontinent. The consequence of this was to cover over the distant and imagined with emotions that, in the first instance, derived from an active and sensuous relationship with an actual home. The affective power of the nation became all the stronger as a result. (Tanika Sarkar 2009: 230–31)

One might then see Rabindranath as a lover of the country/*desh* rather than a devotee of a state-oriented nationalist politics or a warrior son of the motherland. Tanika Sarkar's approach may dispel some of the speculations regarding Rabindranath's complicity with an adapted colonial state. Upon scrutiny, the kind of decolonization envisioned by him remains a valid alternative for a foundational individual and social transformation, and for a praxis of simultaneously creating an anti-colonial and generally anti-oppression project.[11]

Rabindranath's idea of decolonization resonates with that of Frantz Fanon, which was formulated during Fanon's participation in the Algerian revolution (1954–62). In a similarly critical tone, Fanon also spoke of the 'pitfalls' of national consciousness and, as indicated above, made a distinction between 'true' and 'false' decolonization. In the latter version, the falseness is associated with a particularist nationalism in which the rulers of the nation are merely substituted local ruling classes for foreigners, blacks for whites, and a new neo-colonial state is created. Though new anthems are sung and new flags flown, the actual social relations of power and exploitation are continued. Socio-economic practices and cultural values overdetermine the so-called independent state. The majority of the people of the new nation submit to a powerful capitalist minority and face violence as they did prior to decolonization (Fanon 1968: Chapter III). Injustices and deprivations of all kinds, inclusive of education and access to cultural production, emerge from this particularist national state, and essentially the old system continues with new cultural guises legitimizing the ruling relations. Fanon rejects a nationalism that relies on cultural identities without reference to class. Though culture and consciousness are central to his project of decolonization, the absence of attention to class makes it a 'false' one.[12] Fanon is similar to Gramsci in emphasizing a new cultural hegemony for resistance, in which cultural consciousness and class are implicated in each other. Rabindranath's ideas of decolonization, which are intensely sensitive to socio-economic injustices, are not at odds with those of Fanon. Not being a socialist, the role of inequality based on status more than a marxist sense of class pervades his social thought. While Rabindranath lacked a systemic analysis of the relationship between wealth and poverty, he could see them as impediments to the full development of the individual and of genuine freedom.

In their emphasis on universalist humanism, Rabindranath and Fanon overlap. They share an emphasis on humanism as a means and a goal of social transformation. For both, the epistemological stances and practical social premises necessary for decolonization must originate outside of the constellation of a totalizing relation of power which reduces humanity into absolute constructs such as of the native and the master. According to the renowned Fanon scholar Ato Sekyi-Otu (1996), Fanon demands that for true decolonization the identity of the resistant colonial subject must shift from that of the 'native' to one of 'man' or 'human', an identity articulated outside of the immediate moment of history. Thus the categories 'man' and 'human' are not mere abstractions but rather concrete ones distilled from long-term socio-historical relations and the development of human capacities, inclusive of consciousness. Fanon's humanism as a practical mode of decolonization, described by Sekyi-Otu, could also be used as a way of understanding Rabindranath. Sekyi-Otu writes:

> [This will be a] Fanon who did indeed frame his account of the colonial condition and its aftermath in the language of human possibilities; a Fanon in whom this humanist vocabulary was by no means an occasional lapse from the sturdy posture of a sophisticated nihilism; a Fanon for whom the *raison d'*être of racial and national liberation was that it would give back their dignity to all citizens, fill their minds and feast their eyes with *human things*, and create a prospect that is human because conscious and sovereign persons dwell therein. (Ibid.: 46)

What I have suggested so far justifies how the expression 'decolonization' can characterize Rabindranath's philosophy of pedagogy for individual and social freedom. His emphasis on humanism is not a derivative of colonial discourse but instead addresses basic issues of fundamental social transformation, indicating a long process rather than a series of events. Fanon's chapter 'Concerning Violence' supports my position when he tells us: 'Decolonization, as we know, is *a historical process*, that is to say, that it cannot be comprehended, it cannot disclose its intelligibility nor become transparent to itself except in the exact measure that we discern *the movement of historical becoming* ... which gives it form and content.'[13] There is certainly an affinity between Rabindranath's and Fanon's world-views, and the notion of decolonization, a term that Rabindranath did not use, suits universalist pedagogical goals. The vision and intention of his expressive, critical and practical undertakings move from the reactive posture of nationalism to a substantive and redemptive one of decolonization. Rabindranath, like Fanon, is mindful of the difference between being free *from* and being free *to*, and explicitly rejects the fetishization of the state as a goal of freedom. For him the goal of freedom is decoupled from state power or economic growth, and this is meant to foster a society without competition and possessive individualism, thus dispensing with greed and egoism – the core of the capitalist ethic. Furthermore, Rabindranath eschews not only cultural but also political nationalism. Thus, he jettisons nationalism as a means of 'freedom' for India, and focuses instead on the civilizational, historical and social reality of the country. Aware of the particularist and chauvinist character of nationalism, he tries to devise a universalist and humanist social pedagogy.

And so for Rabindranath the idea of a free individual has no contradiction with humanism. His life's work is to develop a social philosophy and its pedagogic praxis which sustain the possibility of a non-antagonistic and formative relation between self and 'other', the particular and the universal. This mediatory approach opens the possibility of a world society and a world subject. Rabindranath is therefore not content with only social and legislative reforms, though he supports them because they are immediately beneficial for oppressed groups such as women, lower castes and others caught up in relations of power. In so far as these reforms are in keeping with universalist ethics and are not merely pragmatic manoeuvres, Rabindranath is wholeheartedly involved in them. His decolonizing principles are thus not only meant for India but are applicable beyond that context to all societies experiencing social inequality, creative retardation and deformity. The ideal of decolonization integrates self and social emancipation. Here the end and the means coincide, altering the liberal meaning of being an individual. This is the subjectivity which has the agency and consciousness of leaving behind the 'native' identity for a 'human' one. Through Rabindranath's works a free, personified, individual subject-self gradually emerges from a faceless mass or an aggregation of particular beings. This individual human subject is incomprehensible or unutterable in any merely nationalist ideology. The self–other relation in Rabindranath, and latterly in Fanon, challenges a manichean one, positing a radically different relation based on other premises, making a non-antagonistic relation possible between them. Another relational possibility is present in which self–other relations are enunciated on the grounds of identification and empathy between individuals.

The key question regarding how this positively formative relation is to be arrived at, a journey from antagonism to agonism, remains a biding concern for both Rabindranath and Fanon. But as far as Rabindranath is concerned, he made a choice, contrary to all the evidence of violence that surrounded him. He had experienced the first world war and the dark days leading up to the second. But in the short piece 'Crisis of Civilization' (Tagore 1996b), written in 1941, the year he died, he continued to invoke the redemptive possibility of human history and humanity. This principle of hope is to be found early in his life at a time when he largely rejected nationalism and resisted homogenization of both the east and the west. Rabindranath's friendships with and positive memories of western intellectuals and artists display his ultimate humanism, his principled hope (see Das 1996b: 725).

Rabindranath's belief in universalist humanism and the possibility of a fulfilling relation between the self and the other did not occlude general cultural differences he perceived among societies produced by their historical and cultural developments. When considering world culture in particular, he made a distinction between the European capitalist colonial powers and non-European societies subject to them regarding their understanding of the state, the nation and civil society. He considered European cultures of his time as lacking in plurality and overly state-oriented, and Indian culture as being community/socially based. On numerous occasions he discussed the village-centred nature of Indian society.[14] Clarifying the difference between 'nation' and 'society', he says: 'A nation, in the sense of the political and economic union of a people, is that aspect which a whole population assumes when organized for a mechanical purpose. A society has no ulterior purpose. It is an end in itself. It is a spontaneous self-expression of man as a social being' (Tagore 1996b: 426). Contemporary western society Rabindranath considers to be 'on the side of power', and 'with the help of science' grows into an organization for domination, culminating in the nation state, a combination of power, greed and competition: 'The time comes when it can stop no longer, for the competition grows keener, organization grows vaster, and selfishness obtains supremacy. Trading upon the greed and fear of man, it occupies more and more space in society, and at last becomes its ruling force' (ibid.). Given this view, Rabindranath concentrated on civil society as the locus of redemptive change. The actual habitus of people is the source and goal of transformation. The nation state for him becomes a secondary formation for restraint, the over-emphasizing of which would lead to social rigidification and dehumanization of its inhabitants, the individual subjects. At best, he tolerated the state as a necessary administrative arrangement for a large and complex society.

By rejecting the state as the main source of social good, Rabindranath indicates that the problem of the contemporary Indian state lies not only in its colonial condition, but also in seeking the correctives from that very modern nation state from which colonialism emanates, and whose existential character it is to usurp individual and creative sociality. He saw this state form as a relatively new European invention, and anti-colonialism would find it counter-productive for its goal. He thought it ironical that Indian nationalists were striving to create the same nation state which served as the organizing tool for colonization. Furthermore, he felt that the state, a bureaucratic machinery, neither could nor should serve genuine human needs and aspirations (see Das 1996b: 372–74).[15] He thought that nationalism with its particularist ideology, its chauvinistic bent, could not possibly transcend its self-enclosed and reified identitarian culture. Nationalism merely demanded a binary and inverted mode of collective self-representation and rule in the name of freedom.

As well, behind the phenomenal forms of colonial hegemony Rabindranath saw other pre-existing indigenous sources of social and moral deformation, particularly in India's own religious history of institutionalization, ritualization and sectarianism. Age-old regressive feudal customs and ideas had seeped into the depth of the society.[16] Thus, the objectives of transformation consisted of the Indian *samaj* (society) itself and its modifications in response to colonial capitalism. As Jasodhara Bagchi points out, the ideal for the novel *Gora* rests on the protagonist's gradual realization that the primary object of transformation should be the Bengali *samaj* itself, and this would entail the creation of a secular, universal and empathetic world-view and the independence of the individual (Jasodhara Bagchi 1996). She shows that Rabindranath's idea of identity is an evolving one in which the self breaks out of its narrow confines and creates a new relation between the self and the world. She notes that Gora's evolving maturity depends on the disarticulation of his identity from a casteist hindu political one, which is an ideological compound made of religion and superstitions of ethnicity, birth, blood and caste belonging. Gora ultimately arrives at an identity which is not a fixed ideological type, one that is an achieved humanism animated by a secular fusion of reason, emotion and a spiritual world-awareness. The idea of the secular here is not aesthetic or positivist but rather one that is inclusive of the world, involving an active imagination and an awareness of the sublime. Jasodhara Bagchi writes:

> The secular outlook that *Gora* regains at the end of the novel is not just a narrative ploy, a happy ending that rounds things up in a spirit of reconciliation. Taking *Gora* and his discursive prose written through the first and second

> decades of this century, we see Tagore fighting religion as a basis of political life. While not denying the search for self identity, he searches for a secularism that is inclusive and indigenous at the same time. (Ibid.: 57)

Rabindranath's decolonizing pedagogy is characterized by a search for this humanist identity. Human rather than economic development charts the path of this search. His creative, critical and educational works all testify to this process, and his educational institutions, Santiniketan, Sriniketan and Visva Bharati, are concrete manifestations of his belief in this world-view. The institutional logic or instrumental rationality of formal career-oriented schooling cannot form this humanist–liberationist pedagogical complex. Humanist conscientization is the true path to this identity, which is to say, a part of this identity.

Rabindranath's conscientization project is not a *sui generis* enterprise. Its genealogical traces lie in the social reform movements of the nineteenth and early twentieth centuries in both Bengal/India and Europe.[17] But it would be misleading to see Rabindranath's transformative pedagogy as only an extension of these reform movements. His ambition and practices go beyond 'reform', a social adjustment, and seek foundational changes in existing consciousness and practices. Not only his writings on education, but also his reflections on the self, development of personality, on the individual as well as on identity and creativity, expose this. To understand his idea of *samaj* or society adequately, we need to be conversant with these reflections. His pedagogical critique also involves an exploration of the distinctions and relations he posits between the country and the city, between the socio-cultural and the political. Thus, he considers industry's relationship with agriculture and their relationship to profit-making and greed for wealth and power, which inflect the character of the contemporary society. A typological contrast is established for this purpose between actually existing Bengal/India and an ideal of India derived from the ancient past. The contemporary ethos of power which engrossed life in Bengal/India needed to be rectified as well as reconstructed with institutions of socio-economic cooperation and sustainable family farming imbued with a sense of responsibility to the community. Here science and technology are neither rejected nor fetishized but used for the common good, and humanist education and creativity are indispensable.

Pedagogy for a New Hegemony: Rabindranath and Russiar Chithi *(Letters from Russia)*

Rabindranath deepened his transformational pedagogy by increasing interaction with crisis-ridden India and Southeast Asia as well as Europe through travels, intellectual and creative interchanges, and accumulating first-hand and rapidly growing knowledge of international politics. His pedagogic project is still relevant for us as we continue to live in the socio-economic relations and aftermath of the same capitalist colonialism, which has progressed to neo-liberal imperialism. Michael Collins points out this truth when he writes:

> Both despite and because of incursions of global capitalism in its accelerated financial and commercial phases, the politics of collective identity, group belonging and nationalism show no signs of abating. From India to Europe and beyond, the politics of nationalism is manifesting itself in complex ways. In this context, Tagore's marginalized legacy, both in terms of his thinking about identity and in terms of what I ultimately see as the failure of his 'politics', seems more relevant today than ever before. (Collins 2012: 160)

Our alienation from each other, the dehumanization of people and social relations through constant wars, surplus exploitation, instrumental rationality and the destruction of the earth, only grows more intensely. So even when we do not fully share all of Rabindranath's ideas, even when we are socialists/communists, which Rabindranath was not, we still gain by becoming better acquainted with those ideas. They provide us with resources for critical reflections and judgements that hold the possibility of an effective resistance against capital's legacy in all directions. To exemplify Rabindranath's commitment to a decolonizing pedagogy, we should examine his visit to and comments on the Soviet Union.

In a letter to Dorothy Straight (Elmhirst), Rabindranath wrote a few lines about his trip to the USSR in 1930. He was particularly careful about what he wrote, as he had tried 'to persuade her to pay for one of his Indian staff at Sriniketan to visit the Soviet Union rather than the United States for agricultural training' (Dutta and Robinson 1997: 386). Though he did not receive any help, he felt obliged to give his impression to justify his recommendation:

> I cannot give you the details of my adventure in Soviet Russia. It has been a most wonderful experience for me and I assure you those people have done

> miracles in the realm of education. I implore you, do not hesitate to send Leonard to that country which is the only place where all the numerous activities of people's life are comprehended in a most intensive and intelligent form of education. My mind is humming with a swarm of suggestions for my own work – but my time is short, my resources are meagre. … [T]he proper training needed for India can only be had in Russia, where the cultivation of people's education is being carried on not [in] the soil of unlimited wealth but [by] indomitable energy and resourceful intelligence. I feel proud of the fact that the ideal which is [at] the centre of their effort is very similar to mine, only they have a very vast instrument and unobstructed perspective for their work. The titanic forces that are tremendously active over this vast country at the creation of a new world have very deeply impressed me, for the background of the manifestation of this great dream is not the limited area of national interest but all humanity. (Tagore 1997: 387)

The same sentiment is repeated in *Russiar Chithi*, emphasizing the profound socio-cultural – what I would call the hegemonic – implications of the Soviet educational project. He writes:

> I went to Russia to have a look at their method of education. It surprised me utterly. Within eight years [they have] changed the state of popular consciousness. Those who were silent have found a language of expression, for those who were uneducated the curtain over their consciousness has been lifted, the powerless have awakened into self-empowerment, those who were sunk in contempt or disrespect have emerged from within the locked spaces of society and are entitled to take their seat with others in the world. (Tagore 1931: 693)[18]

This statement reveals the depth of Rabindranath's commitment to a pedagogy of decolonization and not only praise for the emerging efforts of social transformation in the new Soviet Union.

Written from the standpoint of a colonized subject, *Russiar Chithi* is an invaluable collection that provides us with insights which are relevant even today. These letters are probably the only extensive account of the early years of the Soviet Union provided by an intellectual from any colonized part of the world. The Soviet revolution's attempts at transformation of popular consciousness and everyday life, the development of its revolutionary pedagogic philosophy and its implementation, remain to this day the grandest project for changing society from the bottom up, excepting China's. Whatever may have been the merits and demerits of Soviet hegemonic theories and practices according to western bourgeois critics, they generally amazed the contemporary world with their scale and audacity. Seeking to create a counter-feudal and a counter-capitalist hegemony at once, that is, creating a new cultural common sense among its citizens as free productive subjects, the Soviet Union aimed at a radically different society for which there was no existing template. The new Soviet state was humming like a giant beehive with innumerable socio-economic and cultural experiments. The desire to create a 'new' society and a 'new' man or woman (Fitzpatrick 1970), with all the joys and perils entailed by that and which had enlivened Europe from the era of the French revolution, had now its actualizing chance. In his reflections on the Soviet experience from the ship *Bremen* on the way back to India, Rabindranath wrote: '[T]he entire country has woven all divisions of labour into a web of nerves which by creating a huge body has taken the form of an enormous individual.' They have combined 'everyone's work, everyone's heart, everyone's spirit and created an extraordinary essence [of being]' (Tagore 1931: 699). Impressed by the gigantic scale of the Soviet ambition, covering a vast geographic territory and socio-historic diversity, Rabindranath considered the nationalist freedom project of India extremely inadequate. He remarked that India's size and diversity demanded a similar gigantic plan and boundless energy. It was not surprising then that, against the advice of some of his friends and followers, he insisted on going to Russia. As he puts it: 'I thought that at the entrance of Western civilization, rendered invisible by the power of wealth, Russia has set up a space of dedication in the pursuit of developing the power of the powerless, ignoring entirely the frowns of Western continents. If I don't go to see that for myself, who will?' (ibid.: 681). The 'I' here is definitely more than a personal subject; rather, it represents Rabindranath as a denizen of a colonized space struggling against an overwhelming force of domination and fighting an ascribed and partially internalized colonial subjectivity.

In their biography of Rabindranath, Dutta and Robinson discuss the issue of his trip to Russia at some length and what he claimed to have discovered there (1995: 296–300). Their tone is rather patronizing and indulgent regarding the value of the trip as well as the letters that he sent back. They misunderstood both his reason for the visit and his vision – not only regarding the Soviet state and the nature of its project of a fundamental social transformation, but also Rabindranath's own pedagogy and vision of decolonization which impelled him to make this trip in the first place. If they had been attuned to his social and life philosophy, of his need to create a consciousness truly free of both colonial and nationalist ones, they would not have needed to apologize for this one 'wrong' step that he took. They are relieved by and supportive of his occasional criticisms of the Soviet Union, but significantly silent about his enthusiasm and admiration. It should be noted that as late as 1940, Rabindranath compared Britain and Soviet Russia and came out in support of the latter. This trip and his responses to it would not be viewed as an aberration and an example of his misjudgement by anyone cognizant of his decolonizing pedagogy.

Though Rabindranath was not a marxist or involved with communism, he found a coherence between his own decolonizing pedagogical concerns and those of the Soviet Union. He was astute enough to get what he needed to learn from these experiments and what to reject. It is fascinating to read now how the Soviet conscientization programme and pedagogic philosophy appeared to a colonial subject who sought to overcome the double hegemony of capitalist colonialism and brahminical feudalism. Rabindranath brought to his Soviet experience a sense of recognition of a struggle for a genuine freedom which provided the ground of understanding the aim of the October 1917 revolution. He pointed out this fact when he said:

> For people like us who are British subjects, it is beyond the limits of our imagination to comprehend the great, all-pervasive, extraordinary, untiring efforts that are going into educating or enabling the nationalities and tribes of Russia. That it is possible to go so far I never thought before coming here. Because the atmosphere of 'law and order' in which we grow up since childhood makes it impossible to be cognizant of any attempt that can go anywhere near to this. (Tagore 1931: 691)

He came to the conclusion that the Soviet leadership 'have understood that education is the only way which provides strength to the weak – food, health, security all depend on this. Empty "law and order" does not fill our bellies or our hearts, yet we have become bankrupt by paying for them' (ibid.: 682).

Rabindranath's appreciation of the USSR was based not on a political ideology, but rather on his interest in creating a new liberationist philosophy. He saw that both Indian society and the individuals living in it suffered under the double yoke of the religious and feudal mores of hinduism and from the extortion and exploitation of British capitalist colonialism. The Soviet experience helped him to better articulate his ideas and forge his pedagogical practices. His letters are reflective and experiential cameos of his encounter with a society developing and implementing new ideas and practices. They simultaneously offer a critique and an analysis of British colonialism in India. In doing this Rabindranath bypasses the old stereotypes of 'east' and 'west'. His Russian experience justified his belief that education ought to comprise basic change in social consciousness and in the daily lives of people. Thus, Soviet agricultural practices involving many new changes in forms of labouring and living could all fall within such a broadly defined field of pedagogy. In his earnestness to make the matter accessible to his readers he, very uncharacteristically, provided short statistical accounts.

Although Rabindranath as an artist and a social critic was interested in the emerging Soviet intellectual and artistic strata, and the novelty and proficiency of their artistic and literary forms, such as the new modernist theatre of Meyerhold,[19] attracted him, he was keener to learn about the lives of the Russian peasantry and other common people; the measures undertaken for the upliftment of the poor of tsarist Russia interested him even more. As such, though an international literary figure and a Nobel Laureate himself, Rabindranath prioritized daily cultural activities and public education over the high culture of the elite. He compared the tsarist state and the orthodox church's repression of the Russian people with Indian feudal, hindu religious and British colonial repression of the Indian masses, particularly in the villages. Tyrannies of casteist hinduism and superstitious village customs ever occupied him. Both in their support of and disagreement with the Soviet project, *Russiar Chithi* provides a vivid and nuanced assessment of the communist experiment as it was unfolding. In that mirror, Rabindranath saw key present and future problems of India. His interest in the Soviet Union was not academic or an instance of an anti-communist critique; rather, it was a testament of an engaged, conscientizing practitioner. Throughout his life Rabindranath insisted not only on the cultivation of creative sensibilities and forms, but also on rural reconstruction and agricultural cooperatives as vital forces for an anti-colonial Indian regeneration.

The descriptions of the Soviet experience are also important because they often contained Rabindranath's own pedagogical frustrations. They prompted urgent reasons for correcting the state of literacy and social outlook. Suspicious of any justification of the status quo in the name of tradition, he supported scientific research and practical intervention in social production and reproduction of daily life. He did not expect the colonial state to care for its subjects or to even minimally fulfil their needs. The Indian middle classes, their youth and intelligentsia, he felt, mainly identified with colonial culture and were of no help in creating social conditions for truly freeing India. The same could be said of even the Indian nationalists, with their narrow chauvinism and distorted indigenism. They could not envision the nature and scope of the changes necessary to be truly free as individuals because they were distanced from the ordinary society, which lay in the poverty and superstition in Indian villages and the overwhelming urban poverty. The mentality of the colonial elite, with its fetishization of cities, instrumental education, profit-oriented industries and a culture of urbanity, obscured common people from its purview. In spite of their political profession to the contrary, they were actually self-interested and ignorant of the needs of all classes other than their own.

Having rejected institutional forms of both colonial and so-called traditional knowledge on the grounds of their destructive influence on human creativity and the development of individual personality and ethics, Rabindranath had no respect for prevalent types of education. Indian schools as they existed were for him 'factories for the production of clerks' (Tagore 1931: 685). In detailing the negative effects of this schooling, he noted not only the arrogance it bred towards the lower classes, but also the obsequious mentality towards any authority, foreign or indigenous. Schooling, the crucial vector of colonial hegemony and indigenous authoritarianism and reaction, he said, had produced two classes in Bengal: one oriented towards ruling, and the other forced or indoctrinated to be ruled. The 'educated' and the 'uneducated' were thus the equivalents of haves and have-nots. In particular, a deeply inculcated colonial mentality among the Bengali upper and middle classes, Rabindranath felt, had deprived the society at large of self-respect and intellectual and creative empowerment. Their mimicking and cringing attitude only earned the 'native' the contempt of the colonial rulers:

> The biggest price we pay for our powerlessness comes from the lack of efforts to eradicate our own contemptibleness. They serve to prove that we deserve contempt. Good education lies at the root of solving problems for humanity. The road to that education is blocked in our country because 'law and order' leaves no space for any other recourse. The treasury is entirely empty. (Ibid.: 682)

While considering the myopia caused by the internalization of colonial hegemony among the Indian higher classes, Rabindranath self-critically situated himself within its purview. He recounted how he, like the colonial rulers, had once thought that it was impossible to educate India's 330 million non-literate people, not only due to their extensive numbers and poverty, but also on account of their innate incapacity to learn. At the most, he had thought, basic literacy was all that they could hope to achieve. But the Soviet experience taught him otherwise, because they had devised a colossal and multifaceted education system consisting of both formal and non-formal schooling that aimed to educate the entire population. Education was not just a system for acquiring skills and degrees in order to function within a grid of repetitive and mindless jobs necessary for building and maintaining colonial and class power. Rabindranath's critique of the colonial capitalist education system was perhaps the earliest – and most insightful – of the critiques of colonial discourse that were to come decades later. He saw both the administrative structure and content of this system as a device for the disempowerment of Indian subjects through the ruse of education in order to reproduce relations of inequality and exploitation.

Rabindranath's own pedagogic objectives prompted him to visit a young Soviet pioneers school and popular museums for culture and the natural sciences. He enquired in detail about the daily functioning of the schools, and was pleasantly surprised by the confident and questioning tone of his young audience. His curiosity ranged from their academic syllabus to classroom interactions and their participation in community disciplining as well as in deciding their daily diet. He was highly impressed by the young peoples' knowledge of society and politics as they enacted for him the 'living newspaper' (ibid.: 696), a device he considered using with Santiniketan students. He also made direct inquiries into educational programmes for the peasants. The holistic rather than only practical nature of their education became evident to him and pleased him in face-to-face interactions with them. He says:

> One evening I went to a house that was a peasants' residence. When they come to the city upon any occasion they can live cheaply in that residence. I had a discussion with them. When I can have such a discussion with peasants of our own country, on that day I will be able to offer a proper retort to the Simon Commission. (Ibid.: 687)[20]

Rabindranath outlined three major objectives of the Soviet revolution, namely, education, agriculture and industrial production, and found an integral connection among them. He found Soviet educational philosophy and its practices useful for purposes of decolonization. Noting the Soviet educational integration of everyday life with learning, he said: 'I have always said that education should be carried on with living' (ibid.: 693). He also supported the Soviet incorporation of modernist European knowledge of science and technology within the curriculum, and their presence in the economy and social outlook. As long as a universalist humanist outlook accompanied the education of technology and skills, he accepted them. As he puts it: 'Mere technology cannot accomplish anything, if the machinist does not become human.' He felt that the Soviet 'cultivation of fields is keeping pace with mental cultivation' (ibid.). He continues: '[After] coming here I saw that they have breathed life into education. The reason for it is that they have not set apart or created a boundary between everyday life and the school. ... They teach for a holistic humanization' (ibid.).

Regarding the inclusion of the Bengal/Indian peasantry in the decolonizing endeavour, Rabindranath expressed his long regret that the Indian nationalist movements and politicians displayed such great indifference to the majority of the Indian population, namely, the peasantry. They were never offered any real representation and agency. He says: 'I remember that during the Pabna conference I told a politician who was a very important figure at that time that if we want to make real our national upliftment then we have to nurture and "humanize" those who live "below"' (ibid.: 682), but the leader ignored his suggestion.[21] As a landlord Rabindranath himself had persisted in introducing community self-empowerment schemes among the peasantry, simultaneously targeting their sense of economic self-sufficiency and dignity. These efforts on his part, somewhat similar to the Soviet attempts, resulted in two crucial and related radical realizations. He writes: 'From the point of view of justice the land should not be the possession of the landlord, it is the peasants'; secondly, if one could not consolidate the [scattered] plots for cultivation through a cooperative mode, agriculture could never be improved' (ibid.: 683). Both realizations, he felt, did not seem to be implementable under the existing capitalist colonial socio-economic circumstances in India. He had personal experience of how, through the Permanent Settlement Act[22] introduced by the colonial state, the land always devolved into the hands of the landlords, moneylenders and traders, all of whom worked in the interest of the regime and their own class power. When he spoke to Soviet peasants regarding these issues and about different types of agriculture, they understood and agreed with him. His letters also pointed out that the Bengali peasantry at that moment, due to neglect of education, lacked the necessary leadership for actualizing his improvement proposals. But being himself the landlord,

Rabindranath could not provide the leadership they needed, because to be effective it had to come from within the ranks of the peasantry.

The efforts at upliftment of the Soviet peasants revived Rabindranath's indignation as well as hopes for the Bengal/Indian peasantry. Reflecting on the peasantry and other Indian underclasses, he said:

> I remembered the workers and peasants of my own country. It [the Soviet situation] seemed the achievement of the magicians of the Arabian Nights. Even ten or so years ago they were exactly like the labourers of our country – illiterate, helpless, starving, blinded by superstition and ignorant religiosity. In their sorrow and danger they banged their heads on the threshold of [their] God, their intelligence a pawn in the hands of priests and their touts, in fear for afterlife and fear in this world [which rested] in the hands of the aristocracy, moneylenders and landlords. They shined the shoes of those who beat them with those [very] shoes. Thousands of years did not change their customs and traditions, their modes of transportation, their mills and grinders from the time of their ancestors; they stubbornly refused to handle any modern equipment. ... How this mountain of ignorance, of incapacity, has been shaken in just a few years has utterly astounded this luckless denizen of India – [but] who else would be so overwhelmed? (Ibid.: 685)

Rabindranath's response can be clarified by noting what he wrote in his novel *Gora* so many years earlier (in 1910). In this novel the eponymous protagonist went to Bengal's villages abandoning his home in the city of Calcutta, thereby expanding his social consciousness exponentially:

> For the very first time Gora saw what our country is like outside of the genteel and educated Calcutta society. How disconnected, how narrow, how weak was this village society – how unconscious of its own power, how ignorant and indifferent to its [own] well-being. A deeply ingrained social difference [lay] at the distance of every few miles, how incapacitated it was by its self-created imagined prohibitions in participating in the world's arena of action and how it had elevated every trivial and frozen custom, how dormant was its consciousness and how feeble its efforts. (Tagore 1910: 481)

Rabindranath measured the success of Soviet pedagogy in terms of the humanization of such suffering common people through the respect that this pedagogy mandates towards them:

> Here common people are not obscured by the shadows of the genteel folks. Those who were out of sight for aeons are now fully revealed. It did not take

> time to correct the mistaken view that they have merely learnt to grope through the printed letters of their children's primers. They have become 'human' in these last few years. (Tagore 1931: 686)

Ever alert to social environment, he also commented positively on the construction of public buildings that served as residential teaching-cum-meeting places for peasants and workers. These public spaces, he felt, have 'created the foundation for a socially encompassing new life' (ibid.: 688). Rabindranath accepted the view that the Soviet revolution was based on demands for equality in class relations, and to that end reminisced about the extreme exploitation of the productive classes before 1917 in Russia. He identified with their hitherto unfulfilled demands and sympathized with their grievances:

> When I was introduced to those classes of people who in our country are silent and ignorant, whose minds have been buried under piles of internal and external poverty, deprived of all life opportunities – it is then that I understood how the uncaringness of a society robs the wealth of people's hearts. What a great waste! How cruel the injustice! (Ibid.: 686)

He dubbed the neglected part of the society as 'candle-holders' who do not benefit from the very light they hold up for others (ibid.: 675). As a member of the propertied elite, he referred to his own values as those of a feudal and colonial capitalist society. He now felt embarrassed that he, along with the members of his class, had once thought that the deprived existence of the masses was a necessary and productive sacrifice for the higher cause of producing a cultural elite:

> I have thought about them [the peasants] for a long time and felt there was no other recourse or solution. One group cannot exist at a higher level if another does not stay below, and there is a social need for some to be above. … Because the richest harvest of a civilization comes from leisure – there is a need to preserve this leisure for a section of the society. … [O]thers, not only due to circumstances, but also due to their physical and mental state, must toil at a lower level. (Ibid.: 675)

Rabindranath's elite-class common sense was shaken through his increasing critical reflections on Indian and western nationalisms, through European and Asian experiences of the violence of imperialism and war, and finally by his visit to the Soviet Union. His own views on class, caste and cultural certainties became questionable by the realization that they were similar to those of the colonial elite, who looked upon Indians, irrespective of their class, caste and creative activities, as 'hewers of wood and drawers of water'. Their lives, like those of Indian peasants for the indigenous elite, were meant to be sacrificed for the civilizational and material needs of Europe. The highest classes of the colonial society were no more than 'natives' in the colonial gaze of the European ruling classes. He expressed the Indian attitude of servitude to colonial Britain and the imperialist west thus:

> Just imagine that a sustenance-deprived India has nurtured England with food. Many in England think that India's very fulfilment lies in sustaining England forever. England has achieved fame by performing a great task for humanity – and to achieve this end there is no guilt felt in enslaving a whole nation forever. What difference does it make if in this process the [Indian] people eat less or dress less well? ... All they can get is *charity,* but the limits of this charity are exposed when the self-interest of the ruler is questioned. (Ibid.)

Rabindranath's understanding of the Soviet project came from an anti-colonial perspective, and it displayed something akin to class awareness. Thus, a call for actions resembling class struggle emerged in these letters and some other writings. He contextualized the 1917 revolution in the popular immiseration produced by the accumulation of excessive wealth by a few. In fact, it is in this commonly shared misery of the masses in Russia or elsewhere that he discovered the basis for resistance, the motive force for fighting against the wealthy exploiter. The common fight against shared misery would be the source of their impetus for unity, their mutual and group identification animated by a common resolve for a better life. He referred to the Bengali labouring classes, the *shramajibi* (those living on labour), as *dukkhajibi* (those living on suffering) (ibid.: 688). He glimpsed the revolutionary possibility inhering in the extreme popular suffering, and in the following paragraph he spoke at once to the colonial and capitalist class powers – interweaving them into one:

> The powerful are arrogant, but an aspiration for power circulating among the sorrowful and the poor is making them restless. The powerful are trying to stop them, are not letting their messengers enter into their own space and are silencing their voices. But what they should fear most is the very misery of the miserable ones – but that is precisely what they have always felt contemptuous about. They have no fear of aggravating this misery in favour of their own profit making. Their hearts do not tremble when they force the hapless peasants into the grip of famines by extracting two to three hundred

per cent interest. … [But already] excessive power cannot keep increasing itself in the face of incrementally growing powerlessness. If the powerful were not so intoxicated by their own power, they would have feared this boundless inequality – because ultimately the lack of equilibrium or balance is against the very laws of universal order. (Ibid.: 680)

In these letters and in his general reflections about Russia, Rabindranath spelled out the imbrication of colonial relations to class exploitation that exists between the rich and the wretched, between Europe and its colonies. For this reason, he was able to contrast the egalitarian revolutionary aspirations of 1917 with the possessive individualism and sheer greed of capitalism:

> All other European countries have dedicated their efforts to individual profit and enjoyment. A violent agitation results from this churning, and like the [hindu] scriptural narrative of the churning of the primal ocean, this present one too has yielded both nectar and poison. But this nectar is in the possession of a [small] group, while the majority get nothing of it. This has created a perpetual unhappiness and lack of peace. Everyone considers this situation as 'inevitable'. They claim that greed lies in human nature itself and the very function of greed is to create unequal enjoyment. Competition, therefore, will continue and one must always be battle-ready. But what the Soviet people are saying is that the truth lies in human unity and social divisions are mere illusions. Through unifying social consciousness and pooling our efforts, we will reject the naturalization of disunity and ultimately the disparities will disappear as a mere dream. (Ibid.: 699)

Rabindranath drew a parallel between unequal relations between the colonized and the colonizer, and power relations between the propertied classes and the poor in India. He also drew attention to the invisibility of the colonized's repressed existence from the eyes of the world and the culture of silence regarding these issues in the colonial countries:

> All of the avenues through which our complaints could reach the world's ear are closed. On the contrary, things are said about us around the world; the modes of their diffusion lie in Western hands. This is a matter of deep humiliation for the weak nations today. … [T]he instruments of communication and information are kept by the powerful nations in their own control while they pull up the cover of infamy and vilification to obliterate the powerless. (Ibid.: 681)

Comparing the Indian situation of 'infamy' with that of the Soviet Union in the western eye, Rabindranath pointed to the animosity that the capitalist west held towards the young communist nation. He noted the exclusion and isolation of the USSR organized by the machinations of the capitalist west in order to fragment and defeat it. He repeatedly commented on the severe internal and external material constraints under which the new Soviet government laboured:

> They have a paucity of funds, they lack credit at the seats of foreign capital, lack sufficient industries and factories ... they are powerless to generate capital. For these reasons they sell the very food meant for their [own] stomachs to finance their developmental projects. Furthermore, the most unproductive department of the state – the military – has to be inevitably kept highly skilled because all the state powers of the modern capitalist era are their enemies, and their arsenals are filled to the brim. (Ibid.: 605)

In the context of the west's determination to destroy the Soviet Union, he said: 'Foreign engineers have destroyed many of their factories. The required enterprise is vast and complex, and the time at hand is very limited. They do not dare to take the time for food production because they stand or fall in the face of the entire wealthy world' (ibid.: 867). As with pejorative connotations of colonial discourse about India, Rabindranath also recognized the falsehoods and negative stereotypes articulated by the imperialist states regarding communism as such and the Soviet Union in particular. The similarity between these infamies and those of the christian missionaries and western intellectuals was not lost on him. The constant barrage of anti-communist and anti-Soviet propaganda impelled him to state that the west had developed a 'professional habit ... of finding faults; and they cannot tolerate any gesture of enlightenment, especially on the part of those whom they dislike' (ibid.). As India was vilified for trying to throw off the colonial yoke, thereby disturbing colonial capitalism's super-exploitation and accumulation and disrupting the comfortable lifestyle in the metropole, so was the Soviet Union hated for rejecting capitalism and its colonialist logic. Nothing could be worse for them than an anti-capitalist and anti-colonial world-view, a philosophy and praxis of social equality.

Rabindranath's own urgency towards ridding India of colonialism led him to the desire for positively engaging with post-1917 Russia. Through his eyes we can get a strong sense of how titanic and disruptive the Russian revolution appeared to both the west and to the subject-populations of colonized countries. While the capitalist west panicked at the simultaneous assault against feudalism and capitalism coming from a largely underdeveloped semi-Asiatic country, the colonized peoples of the world, irrespective of their particular political ideologies, applauded its scale and its audacity as well as the political possibilities inherent in the revolution. For them it gave hope and could mean that India too might overturn its colonized reality. To be colonized could no longer seem predestined. But the Soviet example revealed to Rabindranath some other aspects as well, namely, that underdevelopment could not be the sole cause of Indian susceptibility to colonial rule. After all, pre-revolutionary Russia was not socio-economically much better situated than India before 1917. He writes: 'Every sin of poverty, servitude and deprivation, religious bigotry and anti-Semitism attended them' (ibid.: 703). Yet they attempted and to a large extent succeeded in making a radical change. Rabindranath tried to work out the lowest common denominators existing in the conditions of the two countries: both Russia and India were village-based societies with primarily agricultural economies and peasant labour, and thus, societies with limited urban, industrial and working class development; both had long existed in the throes of feudal and monarchical oppression, though India was in an even worse condition because it was also prey to British capitalist colonialism; both suffered from religious bigotry and the tyranny of tradition, but in the case of India these were further incentivized by hegemonic machinations of the colonial power. Rabindranath felt that the Indian freedom struggle, its nationalist attempts at decolonization, should have had the peasantry as the primary agent of social change. Agricultural labourers rather than white collar and industrial workers should have been the determining labour force mobilized for transformation.

However, having said the above, we need to note that *Russiar Chithi* is not a univocal text. It swings between a genuine admiration for the Soviet audacity and achievement, and some criticism of the central bolshevik revolutionary tenets and their particular modes of implementation. This sense of ambivalence and its reasons are scattered in these letters and throughout Rabindranath's correspondence and social writings. His admiration of the Soviet project was tempered by his perception of a dividing line between his own transformational philosophy and the Soviet Union's political programmes and their objectives. Some of his criticisms were similar to ones directed at Indian nationalism. The major point of difference lay in his attitude towards the vital role accorded to the state in what he felt was a counterproductive value attributed to it. For, unlike the nationalists and the communists, he did not primarily aim towards the formation of an all-pervading, indigenous postcolonial state. The state for Rabindranath was neither the major site for resistance nor the primary goal for a radical transformation, as it was for the bolsheviks or the Indian nationalists. The site of liberationist and emancipatory agency, he thought, must lie within society itself, making society the beginning and the endpoint of decolonization. While he felt that Indian nationalists could learn much from the Soviet system about how to deal with ignorance, superstitions and ritualism brought on by poverty and the oppressions of tradition, they should stay away from an obsession with the state. He praised the Soviet Union where he thought praise was due. Describing the pre-revolutionary condition of the Russian common people, he said: 'The old religious traditions and antiquated statecraft overwhelmed their intelligence and nearly drained their life-force for centuries. The Soviet revolutionaries have uprooted both of these; [my] heart rejoices at seeing that such a shackled population has been offered such a great liberation' (Tagore 1931: 702). After all, he asked, how did the ignorance and superstitions, such as of witch-burning, torture of heretics and other forms of violence, come to an end in Europe or in the Soviet Union? His answer was: by means of education (ibid.: 703). If the Russians could achieve this much success in these areas, and if Japan or Turkey could also do more than India, why could India not go beyond a mere alphabetization of its people to a higher level of knowledge, thus bringing about a deeper social conscientization?

In order to build his argument, Rabindranath provided an idealized civilizational template of ancient Indian civilization:

> Once the Indian society was primarily a village society. In this intimacy of the village society lay a balance between private and social property. The influence of social opinion was such that the wealthy felt the condemnation for consuming their entire wealth for their own enjoyment. ... In that society in order to maintain their very own social status the prosperous had to put forward a large amount in tribute to the society as a whole. (Ibid.: 730)

This imagined society of ancient India provided him with a representational figure which would be the standard of measurement in the evaluation of the current degrading actuality. An iconic figure rather than a factually accurate history was what he sought for this enterprise. This idealized version of India was meant to serve as an inspiration for a better society. His schema claimed that '[i]n this situation the voluntary [individual] participation merged with the wishes of the society [as a whole]', and 'this exchange was not through the state machinery' (ibid.). This society created by all, instead of one consisting of the ruler and the ruled, one not driven by power struggles, stood for him as a truly liberated society.

Drawing from a relatively closer historical period, Rabindranath described the decline of Indian villages over the past two centuries and contrasted this with the rise of the cities and urban societies in Europe. He traced the process of urbanization through different stages of development, starting with the emergence of 'the mercantile community' whose 'primary business is in putting their wealth to work' (ibid.). This enterprise, however, did not make the reign of the wealthy merchants legitimate or respected, because no matter how rich they were, they lacked the required intellectual and cultural status within the social hierarchy: in terms of their social status 'they were the fallen ones. . For this reason, the gap between wealth and non-wealth was not so big' (ibid.). Into this feudal world of merchants and landlords there entered other economic and social forces, but unlike in Europe, the developmental changes wrought by them were not found in India; they would not be organic to Indian society. The introduction to India of socio-economic forces of capitalism proper by the British was for their own enrichment and in no way to benefit India. Furthermore, unlike in Europe, capitalism in colonial India was not industrialized but rather remained agricultural, as urbanization and science and technology were not an indigenous outgrowth, nor did the colonizers seek to foster these. Rabindranath compared modern Europe with the current reality of Indian villages, further stagnated by inappropriate introduction of a distorted colonial capitalism, which could not produce an organic urban industrial development and a scientific world-view: 'European civilization focused on the emergence of cities. In cities, people's opportunities expand and their social relationships contract. The city is very large; in them people are scattered everywhere, individual difference becomes of the essence, and the churning or upheaval of competition dominates the space' (ibid.: 731).

Emphasizing the dynamic nature of European capitalist economy and the social alienation of European capitalism and life in the cities, in contrast to the stagnation and isolation of Indian villages and the scarce presence of urban cultural centres, Rabindranath sought a postcolonial future for India that could bypass the human/social and moral costs incurred by Europe:

> [T]here appeared [in Europe] the age of machine and industry, profit rose to an unbelievable level. When this epidemic of profit[-making] started to spread over the world, then those who lived afar, those who were not rich, had recourse

> to nothing. China had to swallow opium, India dispersed all she owned and ever-oppressed Africa had to cope with even greater oppression. (Ibid.)

His acute awareness of how colonialism and the greed of industrial capitalism were mutually constitutive gave him an insight into the rise of bolshevism in Russia. He felt that the destructive and alienating conditions that obtained mainly in industrial Europe were also to be found to a larger extent in Russia than in India, where they were not totally lacking however:

> The main point is that the individual accumulation of wealth in modern times which has bestowed on the rich their enormous wealth cannot be the cause of joy or dignity for all. On the one side there is an infinite greed and, on the other, a deep envy. Between them lies an unbridgeable gap. This facilitates competition far more than co-operation. The competition is between one class and another – internally within the country, and externally between them. There is no way to reduce their intensity. (Ibid.: 731–32)

To describe the capitalist and colonial relations of violence between the haves and the have-nots, where deprivation of the most creates the enrichment for a few, he used the metaphor of the vampire. He wrote of 'foreigners who pacify the hunger of the demon of luxury whose anaemic wasting away only increases through the ages' (ibid.: 731). The Russian revolution and the bolshevik ideology, Rabindranath said, were the 'natural' outcomes of an 'unnatural' imbalance:

> In this inhuman condition of the current civilization arose the Bolshevik ideology. ... Because the equilibrium of the human society had broken down, this unnatural revolution arrived. Because individualism's contempt for the collective [spirit] was ever increasing, there arose the suicidal idea of only appealing to the people [as an abstract collective subject]. (Ibid.: 732)

The agency for 'this unnatural revolution' devolved upon the wretched of the earth, 'those who suffer ceaselessly, those unfortunate ones are the mainstay of the messengers of the god of suffering – the fire of apocalypse is smouldering in their starvation' (ibid.: 731–32).

In the last analysis, Rabindranath's final criticism of the Soviet project arose from the same interest in devising a transformational pedagogy which in the first place drew him to the Russian revolution. On balance he found the Soviet project to be rich, but also wanting in humanist terms because its political collectivism reduced individual subjects into an abstraction. Its state-centred social vision particularly denuded individuality. But he expressed these disagreements with the same openness with which he praised the bolsheviks for having embarked on an unprecedented experiment meant to empower the poor and the dispossessed and make them the protagonists of history-making. The Soviet policy of agricultural collectivization and the scheme for eradication of private property in land and produce, however, drew words of caution from Rabindranath.[23] Indeed, his criticism extended to the communist approach of total denial of private property. The goal of the bolshevik revolution seemed to him to be 'unnatural', as it entailed a radical negation of the affective aspects of private property, the sources of which he found in 'human nature': 'Love for one's property is a matter of affection and attachment, not a matter of argument. It is customary or traditional for us. We want to express ourselves, having property is one way of doing that' (ibid.: 690). He expanded on this idea:

> For common people their ownership of property is the language of their individuality – if they lose that, it is akin to becoming dumb. If property were only a means of livelihood, not a form of self-expression, then it would have been easy to convince through reason that only by forfeiting private property would their lives and livelihood improve. Higher modes of self-expression – for example, of intelligence, skill, or expertise – cannot be robbed by force, but private property can be. It is for this reason the division of and the threat to enjoyment of property can produce such cruelty, deceit and unending discord in society. (Ibid.)

For Rabindranath, the policy-makers and planners of the Soviet state had ignored these emotional and expressive aspects of proprietorial human nature by reducing the issue of ownership of property to one of a rational, state-initiated economic arrangement, a matter of wealth accumulation. Instead, he advocated a compromise, suggesting that the 'solution to this cannot be anything [categorically exclusive] but something that lies midway' (ibid.). Human nature, as Rabindranath understood it, consists of two parts – an introvertive one, involved with the self, and another which seeks an involvement with others and is extrovertive in its sociality. Emphasizing any one aspect of this nature at the cost of the other would mean either an unending greed, self-interest and subservience to an all-engrossing particularity, as evident in western colonial capitalism, or a coerced submission to an abstract artificial and administrative mechanical state form as the only embodiment of a collective good. Both options would deny the centrality of the human subject/agent, the individual with a will and a desire to give their life a social form. Since Rabindranath saw the state as primarily a device for governing and accumulating, he rejected the top–down constructive and command relations between the state and society. He also questioned the humanistic aspects of bolshevik pedagogic philosophy. He thought that Soviet economic and social planning emanated from a totalizing rationality of the state based on a political party, which mistook a social engineering approach for the task of emancipatory transformation. And so it de-emphasized the required cultivation of the individual imaginative and creative/expressive self emanating from universalist humanism. Rabindranath, therefore, was in a state of ambivalence and could not adopt the Soviet method as suitable for his own conscientizing pedagogy. In conformity with his rejection of the state as the source of radical social transformation, he criticized the Soviet dictatorship of the state in the name of the proletariat, which term he found to be both urban and one-dimensionally political. Though this state was meant to embody the will and well-being of the people as a whole through a unitary representation by the Communist Party of the Soviet Union (CPSU), he did not consider it to be ultimately a genuine people's state.

But some similarities between his criticism and those of pro-capitalist Europeans notwithstanding, Rabindranath's critique has to be distinguished from them and from the American anti-communism prevalent even before the cold war. We should note that his stance against a state-centric approach and support for an individual-based civil society far pre-dated the Russian revolution. They developed during the days of his participation in and quitting of the Indian *swadeshi*/nationalist movement (1905–08). From that period onwards, Rabindranath honed his critique of politics as a cult of power severed from the lives and experiences of common people. Indeed, since that time he began to question what freedom actually means, and how a true decolonization might be possible without nationalist politics which fetishized the state and relations of power.[24]

Rabindranath's novels, such as *Gora*, *Ghare Baire* and *Char Adhyay*, present his problematic of freedom and individual development within the perspective of universal humanism. Much of this writing came before he went to the Soviet Union. What he saw there made a difference in his outlook. It affirmed his criticism of a state-dominated society, but it rid him of a binary approach between the individual and social collectivity. The trip also clarified for him the nature and needs of Indian society. Though he persisted in keeping a space between the state, economy, and everyday life and culture, this was a liminal space he considered necessary for the evolution of a transformational pedagogy. He thought that a wider social learning would be conducive to individual development and give rise to a new consciousness which could penetrate the state apparatus. Europeans, he felt, had become absorbed into the ethos of the state, deriving from the state its norms and values, and sought from it society's general welfare, which the state by the logic of its organization is unable to provide. He was prescient in being able to detect the routine micro-management of the civil society by the capitalist state, an interpellating tactic similar to what came to be called the 'ideological apparatus of the state' (Louis Althusser) and 'governmentality' (Michel Foucault). This would be the opposite of the process entailed in a real decolonization, as it would convert participation in the making of a new society into a passive object of the state's social engineering. European culture for some centuries, he thought, had morphed into a culture of the state, into a capitalist ethic which emphasized relations of order and submission among the populace. Rabindranath predicted a disastrous outcome from this situation in Europe, and he was proven right by both the first and second world wars. The modern nation states, he felt, in spite of the claims of liberal democracy, were essentially dictatorial. Competition, acquisition and ethnic rivalry ruled the day, eliciting in many ways popular consent. But in the Soviet case he saw the state's legitimation exercise as meant for the diffusion of social good outside the purview of capitalist accumulation and possessive individualism. There was a danger that some amount of non-voluntary popular participation might vitiate the good intentions of both the state and communist social organization. Rabindranath felt that an element of instrumental rationality and mechanical materialism, as found in a capitalist society, might taint the Soviet project. He warned against interpreting the dictatorship of the proletariat in the same sense of the dictatorship of industrial capitalism. He said: 'If the people's destinies are not created or nurtured by their combined will, then they create a cage. One might get fed well there, but it is not a home. Living long in it paralyses the wings' (Tagore 1931: 727).

But Rabindranath's criticism of the workings of the Soviet state was qualified by his sympathy for the sufferings and attacks undergone by the new state. His positive response also lay in his perception of the collectivist goal of the state, of an opening in the state armour for popular participation, without which it would collapse. He found this opening in the extensive multilayered pedagogic dimension of the Soviet state itself. In its early stages, he even felt that the communists might require a form of dictatorship in its infancy, but not in the long run. He said: 'I accept that dictatorship is a great evil. I believe that much repression in Russia flows from that. The negative side of this coercion is a sin, but its positive side lies in education – the exact opposite of coercion' (ibid.). He saw a contradiction between long-term dictatorship and a socially transformative pedagogy. This contradiction is exemplified by the following comparison with the tsarist state:

> [T]hose who wish to keep a dictatorship in place cannot afford to educate people. Neither the tsar's rule nor the orthodox faith tried to free people from ignorance and superstition. This ignorance could be easily manipulated to serve the tsar's purpose – for example, to get the Christians to attack the Jews or to set the Muslims against the Armenians – these were grotesque intrusions in the name of religion. (Ibid.)

Rabindranath considered that these tsarist intrusions and distortions were not the final goal of the equalist ideology of the Soviet state. The great, necessary push towards an immediate and total transformation had produced some negative results which would be corrected in time, but not until the overwhelming pressure from outside of the Soviet Union and inside from its lingering class divisions, pressures that drove the state into a perilous condition, had abated. But he believed, or perhaps hoped, that this phase of dictatorship would be a transitional one, because new social agents and ways of thinking had unleashed an irreversible educational process among the social majority. 'Its generalization of education is extraordinary', wrote Rabindranath; 'this state does not have a lust for personal and factional power or greed for money. There is an unstoppable urge to initiate common people into an economic view in order to nurture them irrespective of their race, colour or class' (ibid.). Though he complained that '[i]n the Soviet Union there is an attempt to shape everybody's judgment in the same mould of the Marxian economic system … [and f]ree discussion has been forcibly closed down in the face of this obdurateness' (ibid.), he is still hopeful regarding the value of communist economic planning. His final and considered opinion was that '[t]he time has not yet come to say whether that economic view is wholly acceptable or not because until now this economic approach was primarily wandering around on pages of books and had not been released so courageously in such a vast arena' (ibid.).

Rabindranath's views on the USSR should be seen as generally positive, as well as wisely cautious and richly ambiguous. His feelings and judgments were in a state of fluidity, both admiring and critical, congratulatory and corrective. This confusion was in no way out of sync with the situation then obtaining in the Soviet Union. When he identifies the 'normal' life of revolutionary Russia as in 'a state of war' against internal and external political and military forces, he captures the turmoil of an emerging socio-historical reality that was still unshaped. His sympathy and concern for this fledgling, beleaguered and besieged state targeted as an object for destruction by the bourgeois west are undeniable. He informs the reader: 'The condition of Russia is that of a time of war, with enemies on the inside and outside. Much plotting and deception is happening to ruin the experiments undertaken there. So, they have to solidify the foundation of their construction as fast as possible [and] for this they do not hesitate to use force' (ibid.). Rabindranath obviously admired the philosophy and the scale of the Soviet revolutionary pedagogy, which aimed beyond literacy and skills training towards a universalist outlook. Though he could condone the use of state force in a temporary manner for implementing socio-economic equality, he was fearful that it might compromise the necessary universality of the intent of a humanist education. He feared that, in the face of overwhelming adverse reactions on the part of the west and its own internal propertied classes, the content of Soviet education stood in danger of becoming prematurely hardened before having enough time to grow, and thus might lose touch with the necessary lessons of flexibility that history could teach. He observed the irony in the fact that those who denied the absolutism of any religion seemed to offer their own political ideology as a dogma: '[They] who do not obey the scriptures are resting implacably on their scriptural approach to an economic system' (ibid.: 728–29).

The Soviet experience in its positive and negative aspects held up a mirror to Rabindranath's own ideas and aspirations, and gave him new insight and some hope. It affirmed his belief that education was not simply an institutional matter but a powerful, perhaps the most powerful, source of social transformation. It confirmed to him the hazards of depending completely on the state. He saw how it could be mechanized, transforming a holistic philosophy into a political ideological programme. His decolonizing vision admired the Soviet pedagogical project for its ambition to reinforce a peoples' sense of self and the growth of individuality and freedom, and to promote their desire for knowledge, creativity and innovation, all with the intent of overturning class relations. But he felt that there was always a need for vigilance, lest a dream of social regeneration and encouragement of individuality turn into a collective coercion. The principle of social cooperation which he cherished as the core of a fundamental social transformation, expressed in freedom of thought and artistic endeavours, could not be compressed. It called for a synthesis of the private and externally directed creative and rational aspects of the mind. His notion of social cooperation has some resemblance to the idea of Soviet agricultural collectives based on peasant *obschinas*.[25] He concluded *Russiar Chithi* by saying:

> I desire the victory of the law of co-operation in the villages of our country to create wealth and conduct our affairs. Because the co-operation implied in this process does not reprimand the participant's desires, it thus accepts human nature. If there is coercion against this nature it will not work. ... I desire that the villages of our country should not live on the leftovers and wastes of the cities; they should enjoy their prosperity. It is my faith that only through the processes of co-operation will the villages be able to retrieve [their] full potential from [the present] sunken condition. (Ibid.: 732–33)

Conclusion

Rabindranath's reflections in *Russiar Chithi*, though made in connection with a specific visit to the Soviet Union, should be treated as basic to his social thought. I offer, therefore, a few tentative remarks which may broaden the concerns contained in these letters. The commonality that I have been talking about between Rabindranath's pedagogical philosophy and praxis, Gramsci's ideas on hegemony and common sense, Freire's pedagogy of the oppressed, and Fanon's critical distinction between 'false' and 'true' decolonization, should by now be evident. In the Indian context, the complexity of Gandhi's social and political thought and vast scope of his vision for Indian independence notwithstanding, Rabindranath's ambitious praxis for changing the life-culture of a colonized or any oppressed people should be considered as the first attempt to assert universalist humanism to overcome exploitative and oppressive hegemony. Though Gandhi was a great theorist of political and moral philosophy, and one whose thinking helped to mobilize India's freedom struggle, it was much less socially critical and ethically reflexive than Rabindranath's. Unlike Rabindranath's universalist humanism, Gandhi's political project relied on particularist, religiously derived concepts of hindu tradition as a unifying principle of Indian society. Rabindranath found Gandhi's acceptance of caste, albeit in a modified form, and the centrality of hinduism objectionable. He also found Gandhi's overemphasis on tradition and rejection of scientific outlook destructive to the purpose of genuine decolonization. This difference between them is well captured in the oft-noted *charkha* (spinning wheel) controversy. In a letter to Rani Mahalanobis dated 16 October 1929, Rabindranath expressed the following opinion while commenting on spinning one's way to freedom, as Gandhi recommended:

> The *charkha* does not require anyone to think: one simply turns the wheel of the antiquated invention endlessly, using the minimum of judgement and stamina. In a more industrious, vital country than ours such a proposition would have stood no chance of acceptance – but in this country anything more strenuous than spinning would be rejected. Just think what would happen if instead of spinning Mahatma were to rule that each cultivator must grow at least two *seers* of produce per *bigha* of land; that such a target should be his sole aim and a mark of his piety; and that his patriotism would be judged by the extent to which he achieved this aim – then everyone would argue that such a programme would require intelligence, knowledge, drive and commitment to productive agricultural techniques. Indeed it would – and those are precisely the means whereby a country may be liberated; a country cannot be awakened by the inane enthusiasm of ignorant minds. That the cultivators who form three-quarters of this country's population should receive advice on how to spin with a *charkha* like an imbecile rather than on how to become better farmers, is an insult to their humanity. (Dutta and Robinson 1997: 365)

Gandhi's social vision was contradictory and compromised by his ethnicist culturalism, similar to what we have come to call 'identity politics'. This put religion in the centre of Indian polity. Thus, Gandhi's national imaginary created anti-colonial political agency and identity through the balancing of hinduism with islam, and by accepting the existing social hierarchies of caste and other differences. Unlike Gandhi, Rabindranath's decolonizing praxis is articulated outside of conventional politics and premised on a universal humanism beyond the civilizational binaries of colonial discourse. He stood for the right and the necessity for all humans to develop a full and expressive selfhood and individuality. While Gandhi's conscientizing trajectory consisted of a movement from the particularities of nationalism and the goal of a nation state, Rabindranath began by considering the self and the world in a mutually formative relation and history as world history – a world history in which India plays a role. The content of their correspondence is evidence of the difference between them.

Though he considered India's freedom from colonial status as imperative, Rabindranath's criticism of nationalism grew ever-more trenchant, and his universalist humanism became unshakeable in the face of the world's crises.

Rabindranath's opus displays the integrity of anti-colonial and class struggle. Though not a marxist and thus lacking a systemic understanding of capitalist colonialism, he called for a generally equitable distribution of wealth and well-being. In his all-round criticism of techno-rationalism, greed for money and power, commodity fetishism, dehumanization and the destruction of nature, Rabindranath's social thought evokes Marx's critique of capitalist alienation. The languages of *The Economic and Philosophical Manuscripts of 1844* (Marx 1964) and Rabindranath's essays and literature resonate with each other. Both Rabindranath and Marx were master readers of feudalism, of the hypocrisy and cruelty of institutional religion, and capitalism's deformation of vital and creative human capacities. Both emphasized the disorientation of people's 'natural' desires by a developmental process which puts accumulation of wealth and profit before people. If Rabindranath had read Marx's critique of alienation – of how, through a socio-economic system grounded in exploiting labour for boundless profit, 'man' is alienated from nature, from other 'men', from his own productive capacities and creations, and, finally, from himself – he would have agreed with him. Knowingly or unknowingly, these theorists of radical social transformation in the quest for freedom, equality and creativity share critical epistemological and ethical premises and imperatives. Rabindranath's pedagogy or philosophy of decolonization or true human freedom is entirely consonant with the anti-colonial and anti-imperialist thinkers who followed him. It is regrettable that from the period prior to the second world war he has been shrouded in either silence or occasional hagiographies – a veil of mysticism surrounds him. A large majority of readers, Bengalis in particular, along with orientalist non-Indians, continue to eclipse his trenchant social criticism and liberationist pedagogic praxis.

I will conclude with a brief attempt at situating Rabindranath in his own time. Extraordinary as were his creative and critical abilities, he was not alone or eccentric in thinking as he did. He shared with many contemporaries a lineage of social criticism and reform. His transformational ideas descended as much from the Indian Upanishads as from brahmo reformers such as Raja Rammohan Roy or his own father, Debendranath Tagore. The popular and elite syncretic thought of India partook of both the European enlightenment and the enlightening philosophy of Indian and Perso-Arabic traditions (not necessarily religious ones). His life was lived at the centre of reform movements mounted by the philosophers and educationists of eighteenth- and nineteenth-century Bengal/India as well as of Europe. His aspirations for a holistic pedagogy were also shared by others in Europe and India. Even those who were more engaged in institutional schooling, as well as liberal social and political thinkers of the time, were deeply perceptive of the wider scope of pedagogy, some with social and others with revolutionary implications. Their preoccupation extended from designing new curricula to the architecture of schools and classrooms. Social consciousness and advocating for change were central to educational philosophy, both in India and abroad. The two centuries of Europe preceding Rabindranath, as well as the nineteenth century in Bengal, could easily be called 'centuries of pedagogy', enlivened by a passion for creating a 'new man', a 'new society' and a 'new age'.[26] The works of Rousseau, Locke, Helvetius, the European Encyclopaedists and the philosophers of the French revolution, all began with the idea of redesigning society and the diffusion of education on a broad social basis. This was also the case with Fourier, Saint-Simon, John Stuart Mill and Marx, among others. Their pedagogic philosophies and political ideologies may have differed, but all of them had something to tell us about changing society through cultivation of reason and imagination.

The fact that Rabindranath's pedagogy is a composite of Indian philosophical thought and European enlightenment should not be read as a gesture of submission to colonial discourse. In all cases the aim was change of consciousness and the protagonist was 'man', who is naturally endowed with multiple practical and intellectual capacities, which enable him to survive and develop and to be motivated by the desire to create a better world. This subject 'human' or 'man' is also the central figure in the Indian Upanishads, and contains the idea of a knowing and reflective self. All of these ideas and their practical renditions were present in cultures across the world and were philosophical rather than religious. Secularism overtook or accompanied a spiritual dimension, though from the seventeenth century on, a secular perception of human capacities became gradually dominant. In Europe, the idea of refashioning the existing society on universalist humanist principles became particularly important, and reason and action began to be implicated in each other. Their practical forms manifested in the creation of representative government and institutions which would meet emerging new social needs. These conscious attempts to educe and enlighten went far beyond the restricted and elite intellectual circles, including in them revolutionary popular thinkers. As such, the Jacobinism of French politics was in large part an expression of the radical common sense of the time. Seen thus, Marx and Engels' *The Communist Manifesto*, Marx's *The Poverty of Philosophy*, or J.S. Mill's *On Liberty and Civil Government*, as much as Mary Wollstonecraft's *A Vindication of the Rights of Women* and her daughter Mary Shelley's *Frankenstein*, should be considered as much more than political and literary texts – which is to say, as multidimensional pedagogical texts. The nature and role of human consciousness in socio-political life were central topics of the debates of the time, which ranged from women's and anti-slavery movements and the philosophies of child-raising to the development of the proletarian consciousness for a communist revolution. Obviously, Rousseau's Émile and *The Social Contract*, Hegel's *Phenomenology of Mind*, and the poetry of the romantics ranging from Schiller, Goethe and Heine to Wordsworth, Shelley and Browning, shared similar philosophical and pedagogic premises with innate transformative impulses. In order to do justice to Rabindranath, his readers must de-particularize his thought and place him in this grand tradition of radical and visionary philosophers and educators, many of whom he had read. They all undertook projects of widening conscious intervention based on 'humanity' and 'truth', rather than on rigid 'fact' and obedience to order.

The central figure of Rabindranath's decolonizing imaginary was a free and creative individuated self who is neither an oppressed nor an oppressor. *Manab* (the iconic human) or '*mahamanab*' (the quintessential human, rather than a heroic man) is his central metaphor, an ideal type congealed with varied human possibilities. Not an empiricist construction, this 'new man' could be seen as a modern Prometheus who rises from the flow of history and is not a 'found' or pre-scribed figure. Nor are we likely to treat him as a conclusive figure with a fixed identity. Rabindranath finds in this 'human' or 'man' an echo of our own humanity, but he is also as new-born as a poem – a *nabajatak*.[27] This becoming of the 'human' is an adventure, from the state of a biological and sentient beginning to what is created by the interaction with history and society. It is this human person who is degraded and reified by colonial and other relations and devices of power. Awareness of this preoccupied Rabindranath throughout his life as an artist, as a transformative social critic and as a practitioner of humanist pedagogy.

As an indigenous subject of colonial rule, Rabindranath performed a most difficult ideational and practical task by fashioning a universalist, humanist social subject, a source and a result of changing consciousness.

Rejecting parochial nationalism as a distorted version of real passion for freedom from any kind of domination, he tried to imagine a different kind of 'freedom' which is entirely inclusive, because it rests in a common humanity, a shared condition with all others. This individual imaginary would eschew any thirst for power to acquire individuality or any hateful self–other relation, epitomized by colonialism. In the novel *Ghare Baire*, Rabindranath tore apart the false sense of freedom which self-centredness in many of its guises offers at the cost of human dignity and desire for sociality. In the very idea of the nation he found the source of the destructive behaviour of a state and a society which would relinquish humanity, once more waging a war of each against all.

Reified identities central to any nationalism were abjured by Rabindranath, who upheld an open-ended, flexible idea of the self and a socially grounded personality or individuality. As political struggles, he thought, were waged under a banner of a fixed identity, he sought one that unites people. The identity for a real decolonization at all social levels must resort to a sense of self which implicates its freedom with those of others, namely, the idea of 'the human,' an encapacitated and creative individual. Rejecting an empiricist interpretation of the idea of the human, Rabindranath converted it into a category of desire and social imagination. This 'human' is always an approximation, and it depends on drawing from sources of commonality between diverse and dispersed peoples. Thus, he projected the vision of a 'world-literature', a 'world university', a 'world-society' and a 'world home'. Needless to say, the universal magnitude of the concept of 'the human' borders on pure idealism and has provided the opportunity to treat Rabindranath as a spiritual/mystical thinker, as a romantic in a simplistic sense. While he is an idealist, and his metaphor of the universal 'man' is based on idealism, it still resonates with the imperative of human coexistence in history. The physiognomy of this human of course has to be drawn with the changing concrete social particulars of experiences and emotions and creations of the time. But the more concrete the face of this human becomes, the more forceful is this human's humanity. Even though idealism is the basic component of Rabindranath's conception of being human, this idealism is complemented and concretized by the ensemble of continually developing human capacities. Therefore, this figure of 'man' is a full complex of the biological, the social and the aesthetic. The 'new' man is an embodiment of the social, rather than an anti-social *übermench* fixed at the top of the mountain (Nietzsche). Rabindranath's universalist individual is thus a 'being' always in the process of 'becoming'. His pedagogy of decolonization is therefore a process of freeing one's self, of witnessing and awaiting the emergence of the truly 'human' in us for the creation of a 'humane' society.

Notes

[1] Often used interchangeably, these two Bengali words overlap in meaning, but also have their specificties. *Swa* means 'of one's own' and *raj*, 'rule' – thus *swaraj* is translated as 'self-rule', amounting to independence. *Desh* means 'country', among other things, so *swadesh* means 'one's own country'. Both words are connected to the ideology and politics of Indian nationalism.

[2] Gramsci and Rabindranath arrive at similar ideas, though Rabindranath was only tangentially connected with a political organization (the Indian National Congress) and Gramsci, in contrast, was a founder of the Communist Party of Italy (PCI) and a major organizer of trade unions in Italy. Perhaps because Gramsci saw the political import of culture and change in consciousness, and is retrospectively reflecting on the failure of the PCI and the rise of fascism, his conclusions are less politically strategic and more philosophical in the years of his imprisonment. For 'structures of feelings', see Williams (1985): 128–35; Williams connects social experiences with feelings which develop emotional structures in conjunction. He says: 'The term is difficult, but "feeling" is chosen to emphasize a distinction from more formal concepts of "world-view" or "ideology". It is that we are concerned with meanings and values as they are actively lived and felt. ... We are talking about characteristic elements of impulse, restraint and tone, specifically affective elements of consciousness and relationships: not feelings against thought, but thought as felt and feeling as thought: practical consciousness of a present kind, in a living and interrelated continuity' (ibid.: 132).

[3] In Gramsci's political thought, the concept of hegemony came to be associated with consciousness and production of consent among the ruled.

[4] On what it means to say that everyone is a philosopher, see Gramsci's 'The Study of Philosophy', in his *Prison Notebooks* (1971); see also Thomas (2009).

[5] Regarding people's participatory role in fashioning their own social consciousness, as compared to the conventional portrayal of the consciousness of the masses as externally shaped, see the 'Preface' in Thompson, *The Making of the English Working Class* (1966).

[6] For ideas underlying Santiniketan (founded 1901) and Sriniketan (founded 1921), his two educational institutions, see Dutta and Robinson (1995), chapters 22 and 23.

[7] Regarding debates on Rabindranath's 'cosmopolitanism' and internationalism, see Collins (2012). On difficulties involved with the issue of 'cosmopolitanism', see 'Introduction' and 'Conclusion' in Brennan (1997); Brennan discusses Rabindranath especially in connection with Martha Nussbaum's use of Rabindranath in defence

of cosmopolitanism (Nussbaum 1994). On Rabindranath's internationalism, see Sehanabis (1983) and Dutta and Robinson (1995).

[8] Authors such as Partha Chatterjee do not entirely let Rabindranath off the hook of 'nationalism', but rather place him in a 'modernist' camp of nationalist thought derived from the European enlightenment and liberalism. Many such authors place him with Jawaharlal Nehru and other 'progressives' as a thinker in the tradition of colonial or bourgeois modernism. See Chatterjee (1993b); Muthu (2000); Sartori (2008).

[9] For Rabindranath's other significant writings on nationalism, see also his essays 'India and Europe' and 'East and West', in Sisir Kumar Das (1996b).

[10] See also Pradip Kumar Datta (2003).

[11] There are debates about placing Rabindranath within a political spectrum of 'nationalism', 'cosmopolitanism' and 'internationalism'. A question remains whether these are versions of the same 'better' nationalism that Uma Dasgupta attributes to him – or can we accept that it makes better sense to see 'nationalism' and 'patriotism' as qualitatively distinct from each other, as Tanika Sarkar does? In this connection, Timothy Brennan's comments on Martha Nussbaum might provide an insight: 'Martha Nussbaum faced off against an impressive array of intellectuals by defending the cosmopolitan ethos against a contemporary American "patriotism". Dissenting from Richard Rorty's appeal to patriotism as "shared national identity", she invokes Rabindranath Tagore's novel *The Home and the World*, endorsing the message of that novel's central drama that "patriotic pride is morally dangerous". Rorty, she charges, "substitutes a colorful idol for the substantive universal values and rights", for the point is to find what we all "share as both rational and mutually dependent human beings" rather than as citizens [of the United States]' (Brennan 1997: 24).

[12] The first chapter of *The Wretched of the Earth* (1968) begins with Fanon saying that '[d]ecolonization is a violent process', and he proceeds to examine the notion of violence in its different socio-historical and political contexts and contents. The violence that Fanon approved of is a decolonizing one. It is conducted in the process of erasing the impacts of colonialism and changes forms in the process of the struggle for decolonizing. For him, violence is not only directed towards colonizers, but is also something within the subjective identities of the colonized. As the colonized are not free of the mentality of power and greed for wealth, thereby creating a culture of domination in their space, this situation became a continuation of colonialism. In this state the elite of the colonized subjects control and direct the economy and society. Thus the postcolonial state becomes a neo-colonial one, continuing its entanglement with the colonial power. On this type of postcolonial condition, see A. Mbembe, *On the Postcolony* (2001).

[13] Cited in Sekyi-Otu (1996): 103–04; cf. Fanon (1968): 36.

[14] See, for example, 'Samaj' (Society) in *Kalantar*, Tagore (1933a): 31, 372.

[15] On the state-centred versus community-centred approach to social transformation, see also Nandy (1983, 1994). In contrast to Nandy, who tried to appropriate Rabindranath for his own community-centred approach, Rabindranath shunned

identification with community, seeing this as ethnicist and communal. His was a socially centred approach, inclusive of all communities.

[16] In *Gora, Ghare Baire* and *Kalantar,* among other numerous texts, Rabindranath described, lamented and excoriated the deformations to be found in Indian society and its villages, caught at the axis of feudalism and colonialism; see Tagore's '*Palli Prakriti*' (Nature in the Village) (1915–40) and *Kalantar* (1933a: 502). Rabindranath felt that India was imprisoned by its own history and then strangled by colonial rule.

[17] There is a vast array of books on this subject. Of particular importance, see the anthology of Sangari and Vaid (1989) on women's oppression in India and patriarchy as social oppression.

[18] This and all subsequent translations in this chapter of the letters and essays are mine, though another translation exists (Tagore 1960).

[19] Vsevolod E. Meyerhold (1874–1940), an early Soviet theatre director.

[20] The Simon Commission, 1928, was a British commission to study Indian constitutional reform. It was met with massive resistance on the part of the people of India.

[21] The Pabna Conference was held after the peasant uprising between 1873 and 1876.

[22] The 1793 Permanent Settlement of Bengal imposed by Charles, Earl Cornwallis, chief administrator of the East India Company administration. This legislation created and empowered a class of landlords in Bengal who were largely loyal to British rule.

[23] For Rabindranath's economic views and his thoughts on cooperatives, see Chakrabarti and Dhar (2008).

[24] A passage from Tagore's '*Samaj*' demonstrates his view of the relationship between the state and society. 'I have stated before that ours is not a unity centred on the state. We did not experience a one-ness for any length of time by attacking [our] enemies or defending ourselves against them, or lived under the same state's rule protecting mutualities of interest or well-being or the lack of it. We were always fragmented into territories and societies bounded by narrow provincialism or chauvinism' (Tagore 1933b: 31).

[25] Russian peasant practice of common agricultural cultivation which attracted Marx in his last years and which he considered a likely form of production for a communist state. See Musto (2020).

[26] See Rabindranath's essay, '*Nutan Jug*' (New Age), in *Kalantar* (Tagore 1933a).

[27] 'Newborn', the title of his poem written in 1940.

6

Beyond the Binaries

Notes on Karl Marx's and Rabindranath Tagore's Ideas on Human Capacities and Alienation

> The chief defect of all hitherto existing materialism ... is that the thing, reality, sensuousness, is conceived only in the form of the *object or of contemplation*, but not as *sensuous human activity, practice*, not subjectively. Hence, in contradistinction to materialism, the *active* side was developed abstractly by idealism – which, of course, does not know real, sensuous activity as such.
>
> – Marx and Engels (1970; emphasis in original)

It is not a usual practice to place Karl Marx and Rabindranath Tagore side by side to draw out their commonalities in any sustained fashion. If anything, there has been an assumption of radical difference between them. But in the last two decades, there have been some attempts to relate Marx and Tagore positively, though much more work still needs to be done. This chapter, avoiding oversimplification and reductionism, depicts their similarities without losing sight of specificities in their epistemologies and practices. Similarities and differences are explored in their world-views, social understanding, and ideas of subjectivity and agency, within the framework of their commitment to creative human capacity and their general sense of aesthetics. If the idea of their common concerns is lost sight of, we do a disservice to them and to their readers.

Our present turn to a comparative assessment of the social and political thought of Marx and Rabindranath is linked to the current crises of socialism and the rise of right-wing ideologies globally. These crises offer both a problem and an opportunity, as they impel us to examine and refine our understanding of socialism. If we are to go beyond tinkering with different versions of liberalism towards the formulation of a fundamental social transformation, we would do well to re-examine their philosophic, and social and political thought. Marx's goal of communist revolution and Rabindranath's of a basic transformation of colonial consciousness towards decolonization cannot be sealed away in separate boxes. Instead of rigidly differentiating among their epistemologies, socio-political critiques and aesthetics, we need to situate Marx's and Rabindranath's calls for a social and historical awakening within the knowledge parameters to which they had access, both European and Indian. We need to remember, however, that the tenets of the enlightenment, later termed modernism, were not univocal. They comprised a constellation of ideas used for different ends according to the social and political visions and practices that they were articulated to. On the one hand, they had an egalitarian goal positing a universalist humanism, a rationalist critique applicable for an overall social transformation; and on the other, the same ideas modified through the imperatives of capitalist colonialism negated the universalist aspect. Thus, in the latter context the universalist connotation of the concept 'human' became an exclusive and repressive one when solely attributed to Europeans (Williams 1976). Modernity therefore developed two faces: one pro-liberationist, the other of capitalist-colonial domination.

In the works of Marx and Rabindranath we find a commitment to the universalist humanist version of modernity. While their epistemologies, conceptual content and practices of social transformation did not always coincide, their overall philosophical and social outlook resonated with a desire for a 'new age', a 'new society', a 'new man' and 'new art forms'.[1] This chapter attempts to capture the humanist enlightenment/modernist aspects of these two thinkers and their times. Those times, as we know, were alive with efforts at social analyses and critiques aspiring to changes in social consciousness, social reform and, ultimately, for communist revolution. This chapter especially scrutinizes Marx's and Rabindranath's ideas of the universal human. While universalist humanism has been identified as a basic characteristic of Rabindranath's idealist thought, it has been a matter of dispute as to how Marx, as a historical materialist, could also have a humanist dimension to his critical thought. The first part of the chapter concentrates on Marx and the second on Rabindranath.

The debate on Marx's humanism is old and continuing. But the most contentious moment of this debate was introduced by Louis Althusser in *For Marx* (1969: 21–86).[2] Imputing an 'epistemological break' between the young 'philosophical' and the older 'scientific' Marx, with a new 'theoretical' consciousness as opposed to the earlier metaphysical one carried over from Feuerbach, Althusser wrote:

> There is an unequivocal '*epistemological break*' in Marx's work ... which is a critique of his erstwhile philosophical (ideological) conscience ... This 'epistemological break' concerns conjointly *two distinct theoretical disciplines*. By founding the theory of history (historical materialism), Marx simultaneously broke with his erstwhile ideological philosophy and established a new philosophy (dialectical materialism). (Ibid.: 33; emphasis in original)

Through this new 'scientific' 'theory of history', *For Marx* presents grounds for a rejection of Marx's humanism. Many who worked on the problematics of alienation, reification, labour and social history have opposed Althusser.[3] The two most rewarding sources for understanding Marx's 'humanism' and its connection with a historicized 'universalism' are István Mészáros' *Marx's Theory of Alienation* (1978) and Bertell Ollman's *Alienation: Marx's Conception of Man in Capitalist Society* (1976).[4] The notion of 'scientific' marxism as elaborated by Althusser, however, originated from a positivist, structuralist perspective rather than from Marx's own use of the notion 'science', for example in *The German Ideology*, in which 'science' is not connected to a structuralist or empiricist understanding of either history or materialism.[5] Althusser's notion of science, as in Auguste Comte's idea of a science of society, may have more to do with the thought of Friedrich Engels and V.I. Lenin, as well as with the established tenets of communist parties over time which morphed into structuralist marxism.[6] Positivist or rational-choice marxists have further developed this structuralist, non-agentic and subject-less version of Marx's method, which calls for a base and superstructure approach to social understanding.

In order to see Marx as a 'humanist' and accepting universalism, the conventional, purely idealist understanding of the concepts 'human' and 'humanism' have to be discarded, and these notions must themselves undergo an epistemological shift. This requires that we treat both notions articulated upon universality as conceptual constellations, as assemblages of critical and discursive practices, rather than as discrete and overdetermined concepts. We cannot treat them as signifiers of a fixed 'human essence' or of 'human nature'. The idea of the 'human', therefore, cannot be seen as having a pre-defined, unchanging body of content generated outside of social history and organization, a content outside of modes of production and the reproduction of human life and society. In making this epistemological shift, we need to delink the concept 'human' from its purely idealist epistemology and engage it with a method of inquiry which incorporates in its universalism the actuality of physical and mental capacities possessed by human beings. These formative human capacities become concrete or gain their substance through historical and social interactions as well as through what they inherit and find around them, which provide the basis for changes in people's ways of seeing and doing. Thus understood, the notion of the human implies the existence of physically and mentally enabled conscious social subjects, and their practices and needs. The point of departure for a useful social inquiry lies, as Marx noted, in the endurance of human lives and societies through time, generating different histories. The claim of materiality of creative/productive human capacities is evidenced by the ability of human beings to build and sustain life at physical, mental, socio-cultural and political levels. Production and reproduction of lives and increasingly growing complex needs, resulting in multifaceted social forms, norms and relations, all comprise a continuum and concreteness of historical existence. Expressivity and practical as well as aesthetic object-making are essential to this. An incremental development of human capacities and production and reproduction of physical and mental objects continue unabated. This exercise and development of human capacities is necessarily formatively connected to what lies both within and outside of each person, and is thus susceptible to and creative of all human experiences and social phenomena, including the modification of nature. As such, the notions of alienation and reification must be understood in a complex manner. Alienation as necessary externalization and reification as the creation of objects for any kind of use are not negative or destructive phenomena. Under particular circumstances involving relations of power and exploitation, they are destructive of the development of human capacities, of human subjectivity, and aspirations of creativity and freedom. But under other social and political aspirations and struggles, they become revolutionary – that is, they eliminate the kind of alienation and objectification that is destructive to being fully human. The 'human' conceived in these terms is neither an idealist fiction, a rational abstraction, nor an empiricist entity, a fixed idea of human essence, but rather an aspiration to the creation of a new and dynamic concrete human being.

This chapter, therefore, is an effort to validate an understanding of being 'human' and humanism as social and ethical engagement that can include Marx and Rabindranath in a general purview. My interpretation relies on the epistemological method provided by Marx in *The German Ideology* and its aphoristic presentation in the eleventh 'Theses on Feuerbach' (Marx and Engels 1970), as evident in the epigraph to this introduction from the first thesis. As stated there, neither a solely object-oriented materialism nor a purely subjectivist idealism can provide us with the right tools for framing a social problematic necessary for a humanist critique. What is needed is an epistemological device which builds into the problematic the socio-historical and political ground of conceiving an individual subject–agent in a given society. This will allow us to think of manifold forms of consciousness, practices and objects of (re)production in terms of '*sensuous, human activity, practice*' Marx's idea of 'real sensuous activity' in *The German Ideology* comprehends and uncovers the socio-historical basis of consciousness and locates individual experience and its deployment within such consciousness, which holds an inter-constitutive relation to reality. Asserting such an informing relationship between ideas and reality allows for a kind of materiality to be introduced into humanism and the concept 'human' without erasing either the specificities of or the commonalities between Marx and Rabindranath. In Marx's case the concept of the human is accomplished in such an integrated manner through his employment of the concept of labour, both as the concrete particular labour of individuals and as a general human productive activity. Seen thus, his idea of human labour becomes a transformative notion signalling the past, the present and the future.

At the present time the concepts and uses of 'human' and 'humanism' are tarnished. Critiques of racializing/otherizing colonial discourse emanating from the violence of capital's expansion have rightly subjected the enlightenment notion of the 'human' and the epistemology of humanism to condemnation. The idea of the 'human' articulated through capitalist colonialism has branded Europe's 'others' through negative fixations, relegating them to a lesser human status, with humanism seen as an exercise of this absolutist knowledge/power relation. It has been rightly observed that in the context of capitalism's patriarchal, racist and generally negatively differentiated world history, the universalist potentials of the 'human' and humanism and the administrative mode of creation of ruling through 'difference' have been thoroughly compromised. The enriching potentials of the 'human' and humanism have not been experienced in any effective sense so far in either the ideologies or the practices of capitalism. They have served instead as devices for marginalizing, degrading and erasing those whom capitalism has preyed upon. Individuality, humanity and civilization have been denied to them. It is not surprising, therefore, that so many critiques of anti-colonial, anti-capitalist resistance have proudly taken up the cause of anti-humanism.[7]

Why, then, should this chapter pick up these repudiated notions and treat them as positive and even liberatory? I try to answer this question, suggesting that something important may be gained through rethinking them. I attempt to go beyond the colonial and racializing use of these notions and explore why, how or to what extent the 'human' and its profession in 'humanism' can serve us. Not that any concept or 'ism' can be used as a talisman against the violence of colonialism, imperialism, genocide and ethnocide in the name of civilization, democracy, development, nation or god. But it might still be worth testing and retooling these notions that allow us to think beyond an irreducible self–other relation of fragmented, atomistic and self-serving particularisms and so see the 'other' not solely as an enemy, pointing out that the 'other' has a mobile trajectory. We need to create, therefore, different forms of identification that can be termed 'universal' in a historical and materialist sense. It becomes our challenge to the mutilation of the social subject in order to imagine and create a world of fully encapacitated and expressive humans. The idea here is to resituate and rework these notions in such a way that instead of the violence of abstracting one big homogeneous 'us' and its 'them', without losing the identifying specificities, we may create an 'us' and 'them' forged in actual historic, socio-cultural, political struggles. It is my belief that a nuanced exploration of Marx and Rabindranath even in a limited way may help us get a grasp of the processes of shaping transformative subject–agents.

Our first task in this rethinking is to understand the human and humanism in ways that will avoid treating them as empty or abstract universalist and romantic wish-images, even when they contain implicit utopian ideas. We have to connect the ideal with the existing reality. The idea of the 'human' should be fashioned in such a way that it can acquire concreteness as a social individual with a body, a self-consciousness and a world awareness. Humanism will then be dislocated from its metaphysical ideological status and shifted from idealist pious platitudes, and therefore not presented in terms of ineluctable binaries of body and mind, emotion and reason, nature and culture, the 'self' and 'other', and so on. Doing this will entail the disclosure of actual existing connections between 'real, existing individuals' and their forms of consciousness. The idea of the 'human' will then encompass the historical and social lives of people in terms of their basic sensuous, creative and receptive capacities. The epistemological standpoint for this critical approach is found in the following lines of Marx and Engels:

> We set out from real, active men, and on the basis of their real life-process we demonstrate the development of the ideological reflexes and echoes of this life-process. ... Morality, religion, metaphysics, all the rest of ideology and their corresponding forms of consciousness, thus no longer retain the semblance of independence. They have no history, no developments, but men, developing their material production and their intercourse, alter, along with their real existence, their thinking and products of their thinking. Life is not determined by consciousness but consciousness by life. (Marx and Engels 1970: 47)

The imagination for fashioning our social ideals is not independent of our socio-historical circumstances. On this note we will begin our exploration by first addressing some aspects of the social thought of Marx, and then move on to a discussion of Rabindranath.

Marx

> Estrangement is manifested not only in the fact that *my* means of life belong to *someone else*, that *my* desire is the inaccessible possession of *another*, but also in the fact that everything is itself something *different* from itself ... all is under the sway of *inhuman* power.
>
> – Marx (1964: 156; emphasis in original)

Some marxists and many anti-marxists have both presented us an economistic Marx who places consciousness as secondary to economic structures and separates them from each other. This is the Marx of 'the base and superstructure', of 'correspondence' and 'reflective' relations between consciousness and reality.[8] This dualist Marx is the Marx of the 'epistemological break', the social scientist of ideology presented by Althusser in *For Marx*. A non-economistic or a non-scientistic and non-structuralist reading, however, reveals a different Marx, one who does not radically 'break' with either his past epistemology or his transformative goals, but rather materializes and deepens his theorization and critique over time. The claim that 'we begin from real life', from actually existing individuals, their activities and societies, is elaborated thus by Marx and Engels:

> The premises from which we begin are not arbitrary ones, not dogmas, but real premises from which abstraction can only be made in the imagination. They are the real individuals, their activity and the material conditions under

> which they live, both those they find already existing and those produced by their activity. (Marx and Engels 1970: 42)

This new method of knowing is constantly developed throughout all of Marx's opus, and *The Communist Manifesto*, first published in 1848, presents for the first time the political consequences of the fusion of knowing and doing. In this communist revolutionary vision which is intrinsic to class struggle, consciousness of and concerns for the 'human', the idea of universally shared human capacities for a sensuous life of producing and consuming/enjoying are not left behind, but rather are given an increasingly fuller and practical articulation. From *The Economic and Philosophical Manuscripts of 1844* through to *The Communist Manifesto* to *Capital*, Vol. 1 of 1867 and beyond, Marx keeps intact his quest for an integral social and self-emancipation, for human liberation. This is expressed in his famous statement in *The Eighteenth Brumaire of Louis Bonaparte*, written in 1852, in which he says: 'Men make their own history, but they do not make it just as they please; they do not make it under circumstances chosen by themselves, but under circumstances directly found, given and transmitted from the past' (Marx 1978: 595).

The call for ending the eternal return of the past at the cost of a genuine social transformation and the individual self is at the core of Marx's revolutionary thought. Otherwise, as he says, we are doomed to a situation where '[t]he tradition of all the dead generations weighs like a nightmare on the brain of the living' (ibid.), and accomplishing any real change is rendered impossible. Throughout, Marx's emphasis is on the conscious, creative, active subject, an agent who is in an emancipatory, mutually transformative relation with society, nature and history. The communist revolution, for Marx, is not the function of self-shifting economic structures which use human subjects to get to different economic stages. The relative unimportance of the human subject as the key actor in the process of social change and structural overdetermination amounts to objective idealism. This is explicitly disputed in the above quotation from *The Eighteenth Brumaire*, in which people *do make* their own history. History is not imposed upon them from an external structure. Any view of history that uses 'ideology' or functions of 'structures' as the motive force for historical social change implies that history happens to people 'behind their backs' without some involvement on their part.[9] And even if it were the case that people were unaware of their own role in politics, the possibility of conscious politics is always present. The communist revolution as projected by Marx is just such a conscious attempt at history-making. It is simultaneously a self- and socially emancipatory project. It involves a consciously organizing collective consisting of individuals.[10] As Georg Lukács remarks in *History and Class Consciousness* (1971), individual subjects act as classes both *in* and *for* themselves, and when they realize this they become *conscious* subject–agents in the process of class struggle, the basic force of history. They are *embodied*, experiencing, socially related real people, not abstract collectivities of a structurally driven and ideologically possessed consciousness. Nor is the development of class/communist consciousness centrally dependent on the intelligentsia, who claim to occupy a superior vantage point for 'knowing' the 'science' of revolution and who claim that they can teach workers their 'true' proletarian consciousness, thus resulting in a hierarchic relationship between leaders and the led.[11]

Social and self-emancipation as conceived by Marx involves a change 'inside' people through reflected-upon practices and experiences. Thus, they become revolutionary subjects in their consciousness as well as in their organizational practices. They act on the objective historical world 'outside'. Each moment of class and social struggle implies an inter-constitutiveness between the individual and society involving a changing consciousness, a consciousness beyond the binaries of bourgeois thought consisting of an atomized competitive conception of the individual self and the 'other'. It becomes apparent that the individual is actually individuated *in* and *through* society, and is immersed in constant sensuous and practical engagements.[12] Exposing the distinction between the bourgeois and historical-materialist notions of the individual while talking about Robinson Crusoe, Marx debunks the myth of man alone, of an asocial entity non-reliant upon socio-historically collective development of his human capacities (Marx 1973: 83).

Marx spent his entire life in analysing the riddle of the psycho-social formations vitally necessary for the political organization of communist revolution and possibilities of counter-revolution. For this reason, the notions of 'human capacities', of sensuousness possessed by every individual universally, occupy a central position in Marx's revolutionary theory.[13] A *social* ontology of human consciousness with its multifaceted productive/creative abilities provides the forces and the vehicle of social transformation. The 'universality' of this human consciousness with its relational, practical and reflexive capacities allows the subject to move from the local to a larger perception of the social, from the past to the present, and from the individual to the collective. This, according to Marx, distinguishes 'man' from animals and is man's 'species being' – an old philosophical concept that he reworks through historical materialism. The kind of 'species being' that Marx attributes to man or humankind is found in *The Economic and Philosophical Manuscripts of 1844*. It is that of a conscious universal producer, a creator. He says:

> In creating a *world of objects* by his practical activity, in *working-up* inorganic nature, man proves himself a conscious species being, i.e., a being that treats the species as its own essential being, or that treats itself as a species being. Admittedly animals also produce. They build themselves nests and dwellings, like the bees, the beavers, ants, etc. But an animal only produces what it immediately needs for itself or its young. It produces one-sidedly, while man produces universally. … [M]an produces even when he is free from physical needs and only truly produces in freedom therefrom. (Marx 1964: 113; emphasis added)[14]

Marx sees the extent and content of productive human consciousness implicated in each aspect and change of society and history. This is the source of new and future forms of all things social. Both revolution and reaction of the individual and society may result from this interactivity and susceptibility. Therefore, the work of social transformation and that of individual consciousness become one. These mutually formative interactions simultaneously form, externalize, shape and are shaped by historical changes. Regarding this phenomenon of productive involvement Marx writes:

> [M]an also possesses 'consciousness', but, even so, not inherent, not pure consciousness. From the start the 'spirit' is afflicted with the curse of being 'burdened' with matter, which here makes its appearance in the form of agitated layers of air, sounds, in short, of language. Language is as old as consciousness, language *is* practical consciousness that exists also for other men, and for that reason alone it really exists for me personally as well; language, like consciousness, only arises from the need, the necessity, of intercourse with other men. (Marx and Engels 1970: 50–51; emphasis in original)

Consciousness, Alienation and Labour in Marx

What, then, constitutes the alienation of labour?

> First, the fact that labour is *external* to the worker, i.e., it does not belong to his essential being; that in his work, therefore, he does not affirm himself but

> denies himself, does not feel content but unhappy, does not develop freely his physical and mental energy but mortifies his body and ruins his mind. The worker therefore only feels himself outside his work, and in work feels outside himself. He is at home when he is not working, and when he is working he is not at home. (Marx 1964: 110; emphasis in original)

Let us now consider Marx's ideas on the involvement of consciousness with labour, and frame the reading through the lens of all human activities as being social, as 'sensuous human activity, practice'. Seen thus Marx's concept of labour has an expressive dimension, as the same human capacities are involved in all forms of production, making no active distinction between industry and art. Such integrity of labour and consciousness shows an internal and formative relationship between them, no matter how this labour is employed. We are aware that different historical modes of production give rise to different types of social relations and forms of alienation, and, in fact, a kind of alienation is involved in any object creation (Mészáros 1978). It is evident that if labour is understood as *any* or *all* conscious productive activity, the very fact of creating objects will involve a form of *alienation*, as any humanly produced object implies externalization in and through a form. It is alienated or separated as it arises from being submerged in the inner life of the creator/producer. An object is thus necessarily an external–internal entity and a phenomenon of *alienation*.

Marx further points out that the larger the social scope, the more complicated and indirect are the relations between production and consumption. The immediacy found between them in the very early productive stages of society is complicated through varied mediations, thus providing room for mystification. As production and consumption occur in the context of *property relations* and of changing modes of appropriation, the objects of labour, machinery or art now enter a labyrinth of a kind of alienation through which they, and labour itself as a commodity, are appropriated by the owners of the means of production and controllers of the market. The social circumstances of this phenomenon are presented in *The Economic and Philosophical Manuscripts of 1844*, among other texts, and in the explicitly materialist analysis of *Capital*, Vol. 1, centred on the 'commodity' as a social relation. Any act of object-making within any productive process obviously involves a transformation of nature and available material resources through labour, and results in a form of alienation and re-formation as well as innovation. But this transformation does not necessarily entail a negative aspect or exploitation. The relations between the producer, nature and other resources, including human capacities, enter into affirmative and enabling social relations and into objects which meet human needs, including those for beauty and other pleasures. This process confirms for humans the 'external' status of nature and their internal connection within it. Thus a state of consciousness results which is self- as well as 'other'-conscious, including of nature. Over time, significant changes in the mode of production result in andro/anthropocentrism, in which a proprietorial attitude sees nature's main purpose as serving 'man'. This, with the development of science and technology, calls for domination of nature. Nature eventually becomes the 'other' of the human, and people become 'others' of each other, entailing exploitation of labour and accumulative relations of property.

Marx offers a highly nuanced account of alienation in his analysis of the *fetishism* of commodities:

> A commodity appears, at first sight, a very trivial thing, and easily understood. Its analysis shows that it is, in reality, a very queer thing, abounding in metaphysical subtleties and theoretical niceties. So far as it is a value in use, there is nothing mysterious about it, whether we consider it from the point of view that by its properties it is capable of satisfying human wants, or from the point that these properties are the product of human labour. It is as clear as noon-day that man, by his industry, changes the forms of the materials furnished by Nature, in such a way as to make them useful to him. The form of wood, for instance, is altered, by making a table out of it. Yet, for all that, the table continues to be that common everyday thing, wood. But, so soon as it steps forth as a commodity, it is changed into something transcendent. It not only stands with its feet on the ground, but, in relation to all other commodities, it stands on its head and evolves out of its wooden brain grotesque ideas, far more wonderful than 'table-turning' ever was. (Marx 1954: 76)

What we find is that at the very foundation of the capitalist mode of production are workers deprived of control over their own labour, the means to sustain life except through the market and money, which enchain them in the first place. Thus, the dispossessed sell their own labour power, their very being and capacities to make. Systemic integrated 'alienation' emerging from earlier property relations achieves its perfection in the capitalist mode of production. Thus, basic productive human capacities are reified and commoditized to sustain existence itself. This commodity regime is wholly one of subjection to capital either directly or in/through processes of articulation. The labouring subject is trapped in the mechanics of capitalist production, its flow of technological and social dynamism, caught within a process of repetition. This alienation lies at the heart of social existence and has profound consequences for social transformation.

As mentioned earlier, productive capacity is foundational, in Marx's thought, to being human. From the beginning of history it meets the needs of daily life and creativity, and itself needs to be daily renewed. The creation and transforming of objects are as such inescapable aspects of the human condition. Conscious labour from times immemorial has created functional objects, skills, tastes and aesthetics. Need for beauty, intellection and inquiry marks our patterns of productive consumption. These productive activities, with their motive force and enjoyment, involve all our senses and practical capacities, and even give rise to our structures of feelings (Marx 1964; Williams 1985). Alienation takes a systemic and deadly turn in capitalism as the works of our own hands, our feelings, our 'others' and nature itself turn against us. As Marx says in his de-mystification of the myth of self-sufficient individuals isolated from the world, or Robinsonades, the mode of production sustains and shapes our very being. He writes:

> Individuals producing in society – hence socially determined individual production – is, of course, the point of departure. The individual and isolated hunter and fisherman, with whom Smith and Ricardo begin, belongs among the unimaginative conceits of the eighteenth-century Robinsonades, which in no way express merely a reaction against over-sophistication and a return to a misunderstood natural life, as cultural historians imagine. (Marx 1973: 83)

We carry within us creative/productive capacities, skills and tastes which develop over time. But as capitalism generalizes socio-historically, modalities of doing and being become so naturalized that we can only, with great effort, imagine an opposite world with other ways of being and doing. This captivated mind-set is the largest success of 'alienation', and we consequently consider those who still live partly outside of capital's social sway with their own, even if residual, pre- or non-capitalist practices and values as 'primitive' or 'savage' and in need of 'development', that is, of being incorporated within capitalism. This justified colonialism as a 'civilizing mission' or 'modernization'. The first struggle against capitalist alienation is to *de-naturalize* and historicize capital so as to open the doors of other social and conceptual possibilities. Knowledge of history comes to our aid by showing how other social and productive organizations declined, and that this too would be the fate of capitalism.

Wage labour indicates the self-alienation that characterizes capital in that there is a price for everything, even for capacities and energy that reside in our bodies and minds. All social relations are accomplished through capital's modalities, thus alienating us from ourselves and from those among whom we live. The more we talk about being an individual, a possessive individual, about possessing the freedom of our 'personal' life, the less we have of individuality. Though we crave a full personal life, our insistent desire only indicates an absence of it and creates an illusion of a divided reality called the 'private' and the 'public', which, in actuality, turns out to be isolation – living as a 'thing' among 'things'. Yet, it is also true that this existential situation holds contradictory possibilities and thus those of reflection and critique. Other premises of expressive desires project imaginaries and objective practices, a craving for a sense of self and cooperative/positive interaction with others, pointing to a way out of alienation. Thus, through making and experiencing art, though we cannot *have* the 'whole', we can imagine an experience of a state of non-alienation, a self-coherence which enlivens our way to another world, to the opposite of isolated, exploited and hostile lives. European art theories and philosophy of art, for example, are replete with ideas regarding the making of the self, counterposing loss of the self and the 'other' to a paradise regained.

Marx's Humanism and Alienation

Many marxists, for example Althussarians, and certainly anti-marxists, deny an ethical basis to Marx and marxism, thus disputing the enduring presence of the idea of the 'human' in his life's works. To see Marx as a humanist would be, for these marxists, to render him a Hegelian, an idealist in the last instance. In this context, it is important to quote Althusser:

> In the text entitled 'Marxism and Humanism', dating from 1963, I have already interpreted the present inflation of the themes of Marxist or socialist 'Humanism' as an *ideological* phenomenon. ... I criticized the *theoretical* effects of ideology which are always a threat or a hindrance to scientific knowledge. And I pointed out that the inflation of the themes of 'Marxist humanism' and their enchantment on Marxist theory should be interpreted as a possible historical symptom of a double inability and a double danger. An inability to read the specificity of Marxist theory, and, correlatively, a revisionist danger of confusing it with pre-Marxist ideological interpretation. (Althusser 1969: 11–12)

Althusser's interventions have dogged the development of marxist theories to this day. He drew a 'line of demarcation' between marxist 'theory' and 'forms of philosophical subjectivism' (ibid.: 11). This reading of Marx in dualist terms and the so-called materialist interpretations have created a rift between the humanist and the communist Marx, thereby denying a motive for communist revolution. This split, upon scrutiny, seems to be a spurious one, an attribution of one-dimensionality to Marx's complex project of a revolutionary social transformation. A historical-materialist understanding of the definition and usage of the concepts of 'the human', 'universal' and 'man', and of 'science', 'humanism' and 'communism', captured in *The German Ideology* and *The Communist Manifesto*, would help us to get beyond this aporia. After all, the very point of departure for Marx's historical-materialist epistemology is laid bare in the 'Eleventh Thesis on Feuerbach': '[P]hilosophers have so far merely interpreted the world, the point is to change it' (Marx and Engels 1970: 122). Marx devoted himself to developing an epistemology arising from social ontology which does not 'merely' interpret, but also roots this interpretation in actual lives of people. In the societies, cultures and economies they have created and inherited, and in the histories that texture their present, we find both the reasons for and the paths to 'change'. Thus, he posits a coincidence of self- and human emancipation. This intention is certainly 'humanistic'.

Marx insists that the communist revolution, at once human and self-emancipation, is the end to alienation. In bringing it about, lost and distorted human capacities are resuscitated. These human capacities are universal, they hold the very nature of the human species, and they are vitalized and refined by socially interactive organizational practices. The subject–agent of this revolution is dramatized in *The Communist Manifesto* as the proletariat. Alienation becomes visible through and resisted by their lives and politics. Through this agency, utopian imagination and liberationist desires are connected. By radically challenging the existing circumstances they call for radical transformation, the realization of which requires all the resources of human knowledges and capacities. By bringing together social interactions, analytical/critical thinking and creative/imaginative capacities, Marx breaks through the solipsism of alienation inherent in capitalism with its rigid division of labour and the extensive mediations existing between production, consumption and distribution. After all, if not for this, what would be the purpose of pursuing a knowledge that cannot enlighten a fuller life for humanity? Why would we need a revolution at all, through ongoing 'open' and 'hidden' struggles of classes, if not to liberate ourselves and the world we live in (Marx 1964; Marx and Engels 1985)? Otherwise, in a disengagement of human capacities and with an erasure of the active subject–agent, revolution itself would become an event occurring behind our backs through functions of structures.

In his concern about universal human emancipation, Marx is in the company of many thinkers dating back centuries, from Greek and Roman times to his own. He could well discern the shortcomings of, and even reversals brought about by these attempts. The failures of the French revolution, of 1848 and even of the Paris Commune (1871) were critically studied by Marx, but he never lost faith in people's need for making revolutionary history. Throughout his life, he saluted the Promethean spirit that emerged from the vortex of inchoate, short-lived moments of class struggle (Marx 1968). He too, with other revolutionaries and romantics of his time, awaited the dawn of a new age, the birth of a new society and the appearance of a new 'man' cleansed of the marks of centuries of alienation. His revolutionary inspiration, only apparently dissimilar, had a qualitative commonality with that of Walter Benjamin, with its messianic language of revolution, and with those predecessors who, in Christopher Hill's appraisal, wanted to turn the world upside down (Hill 1975). Himself a romantic poet, a lover of literature, Marx was not immune to the poetry of revolution, even though he refused to recycle the poetry wholly from the past. It is as though Aristotle's idea of the 'good life' expanded and materialized itself through the dialectical relation between individual consciousness, a sense of history and the creation of the *polis*. It also needs to be emphasized that Marx's revolution against alienation and reification is not just one for a 'better life', an improved version of the present, but for a qualitatively 'different' one which dares to demand radically oppositional premises and outcomes.

Enter Rabindranath

> Man's social world is like some nebulous system of stars, consisting largely of a mist of abstractions, with such names as society, state, nation, commerce, politics and war. In their dense amorphousness man is hidden and truth is blurred. The one vague *idea of war* covers from our sight a multitude of miseries, and obscures our sense of reality. The *idea of the nation* has created forms of slavery without number, which we tolerate simply because it has deadened our consciousness of the reality of the personal man. In the name of religion deeds have been done that would exhaust all the resources of hell itself

> for punishment, because with its creeds and dogmas it has applied an extensive plaster of anaesthetic over a large surface of feeling humanity.
>
> – Tagore (2005: 27–28; emphasis in original)

Now we should move to Rabindranath and explore the critique of nationalism he made from an overtly humanist standpoint. I claim that Marx and Rabindranath held common assumptions regarding the social character of the relations of individuals, and attributed to them productive/creative capacities connected to this. For both, humans possess physical and mental capacities peculiar to their species, with which they incrementally create and participate in society. Their sociality manifests itself in recreating multifaceted symbiotic relations which give rise to extensive and contradictory socio-economic and cultural formations. There is, however, a difference in their attitude to nature. For Rabindranath, 'nature' is not an antithesis to the human, but rather a source of symbiosis for a universal consciousness and aesthetic production. Though for both the 'human' is situated *in* nature, Marx emphasizes labour over nature in that it has the capacity to transform and transcend it, and he sees this capacity of labour as integral to human nature. But they share the belief that such creative and reflexive capacities are lacking in other species in any fundamental way. In this sense, human beings can consciously work upon nature and create a 'second' nature. Like Marx (1954, Chapter 7), Rabindranath in his essay 'What Is Art?' makes a sustained comparison between human and animal productive/creative capacities (Tagore 2005: 14). He subscribed to what Marx called the 'species being' of the human, consisting of conscious, creative labouring/making capacities, as compared to insects and animals. However, his observations expand and make explicit Marx's idea of use value to emphasize the pleasure of making and sensuous enjoyment of the objects made. In contrast to Marx's emphasizing the object-producing aspect of relations and uses of labour and the afterlife of the object, Rabindranath emphasizes the artistic and aesthetic aspects of this production. He says:

> I shall not define Art, but question myself about the reason of its existence, and try to find out whether it owes its origin to some social purpose, or the need of caring for our aesthetic enjoyment, or whether it has come through some impulse of expression, which is the impulse of our being itself. (Tagore 2005: 12)

But they both concur in the belief that there is a human need for giving an aesthetic expression to objects produced, though Marx sees that as a matter of historically developed 'taste', a refinement in the mode of consumption.

Some of these differences notwithstanding, Rabindranath and Marx concur that be-ing human is not something passive, but an imaginative, inquiring and incrementally developing process which creates art and simultaneously engages in the transformation of nature, self, society and aesthetic processes and objects. These transformative and inter-constitutive faculties are formed in interaction with nature over time and developing social complexities. But because Rabindranath made a conceptual separation between 'useful' productive labour and 'creative' processes of art, he used the word 'labour' in functional and economic terms, and 'use' for him signified the fulfilment of physical and practical necessities. Thus, he accepted the bourgeois distinction or division between labour and activities of consciousness, such as art and philosophy. He however sought to add an aesthetic and imaginative side to daily labour. Even mundane domestic acts in homes and institutions, for example in Santiniketan, had to go beyond functional sparseness and convey a touch of beauty. Rabindranath demonstrated through his own creative process and preoccupation with aesthetics what he meant by be-ing and becoming 'human'. Like Marx, he too noticed the tragedy of alienation inflicted upon the human subject, condemning basic deformations of human capacities brought about by negative conditions and uses of labour and simultaneously the destruction of nature, both within 'man' and in the world. He also connected these alienating conditions to histories and experiences of power relations culminating in the colonial capitalism he saw in India. Mental and physical deprivations brought on through systematic economic exploitation of 'free' and forced labour provided the central themes of his social thought. In fact, all 'labour' became 'forced' labour in the context of power relations.

Rabindranath's rejection of alienation and resulting dehumanization is evident throughout his opus. The profit motive, greed, competition and reification brought about by the market are castigated as sources of human deformation and the death of the creative principle. He identifies industrial colonial capitalism as the most violently exploitative, dehumanizing system to date. He commented frequently on the difference between science as a project of knowledge and human welfare, and science's servitude to capitalism and the nation state with their projects of militarization and wars of annexation. His letter to Leonard Elmhirst dated 7 November 1926 is a case in point:

> This time I have been able to see the state of things in Europe that has filled my mind with misgivings. ... But today all the big nations seem to have gone

> half seas over in their reckless career of political ambition and adventures of greed. None of them has the natural privilege today to stand for the right when any great wrong is done to humanity. ... Europe has got her science not as complimentary to religion but as its substitute. Science is great, but it only affords us knowledge, power, efficiency, but not an ideal of unity, no aspiration for the perfect – it is nonhuman, impersonal, and therefore is like things that are inorganic, useful in many ways but useless as our food of life. If it is allowed to go on extending its sole dominion in the human world, then the living flesh of man will wither away and his skeleton will reign supreme in the midst of his dead wealth. (Dutta and Robinson 1997: 340–41)

In a later letter to Elmhurst dated 3 September 1932, Rabindranath offers another example of an alienating use of science:

> The Ideal, which I cherish in my heart for the work I have been struggling to build up through the best portion of my life [does] need qualifications that are not divided into compartments. It was not the Kingdom of the Expert in the midst of the inept and ignorant which we wanted to establish—although the experts' advice [is] valuable. The villages are waiting for the living touch of creative faith and not for the cold aloofness of science which uses efficient machinery for extracting statistics, the statistics that deal with *fragments of dissected life.*[15]

We can assume from such views that if Rabindranath had read Marx's *Economic and Philosophical Manuscripts of 1844*, he would have generally agreed with what Marx had to say. Marx's concern for the liberation of 'man' from oppressive existential conditions or for the full and increasing development of 'human' capacities, his sense of urgency for eliminating distortive modes of production, and his opposition to social relations of power and inequality can be supported by Rabindranath's writings. In numerous plays, novels, short stories and poems, Rabindranath portrayed both alienation and resistance.

It should be repeated, however, that in his condemnation of alienation Rabindranath showed neither a simple, one-sided rejection of modernity nor an appeal to tradition. Thus we find that in his view of science and technology he made a strong distinction. He concentrated on the social relations of industrial colonial capitalism through which they developed and the uses they were put to, rather than rejecting the scientific spirit and technology. He shared Marx's interest in science and technology, and approved of the use of machines for augmenting productive and social well-being. His discerning attitude contradicts Gandhi's one-dimensional approach to science. Acceptance of the use of science on non-instrumental and exploitive bases is evident in Rabindranath's rebuttal of Gandhi's advocacy for retreat to a non-industrial rural past.[16] While rejecting the mechanical, anti-nature cultural institutions and environment articulated through the instrumental rationality of capitalism and the acquisitiveness of nationalism, Rabindranath appreciated the spirit of inquiry, adventure and the human potential of science.

Neither he nor Marx were moral and epistemological relativists who reject the idea of 'truth' both in relation to social reality and in imaginative and personal terms. For both of them this 'truth', beyond its socio-historical and empirical dimensions, included the reality, indeed materiality, of thought, of the creative and critical nature of human consciousness. Though for Marx the emphasis lay in a nuanced historical-materialist method of inquiry and critique, Rabindranath awarded imagination and intuition central roles in apprehending the 'truth' about self and society. They derived ethical imperatives from this 'truth', though they differed epistemologically. And while Marx conceded the value of imagination, he differed from Rabindranath's explicitly spiritual and poetic metaphysics of truth. For Marx, 'truth' was arrived at through educated sensibilities and a secular method of social inquiry which combines social ontology, historical anthropology and critical epistemology.[17] Rabindranath accepted these intellectual aspects, but awarded a great role to experience, feeling and imagination in seeking and finding 'truth'. Rabindranath was not a methodological thinker who created a systemic mode of social inquiry, one whose critique of social and political thought emanated from a world-view which incorporated into his philosophy a scientific spirit connecting knowledge with imagination. Marx, conversely, conferred on the creative capacity an important role, but concentrated more on analysing the capitalist mode of production in its historical materialist and economic dimensions. But both saw 'truth' everywhere as historically gleaned from our antecedents and internalized creative forms, technology, skills and scientific insights into the workings of nature.

Thus they also made a distinction between truth, facts and information. Marx's anti-positivist view of the ideas of 'use' or 'use value', therefore, which is radically different from the views of the utilitarians and empiricists, compares well with the holistic world understanding of Rabindranath. But Rabindranath prioritizes 'man' as a seer or a creator over 'man' as a 'producer' in the immediate sense and as a 'knower' in a systemic logical sense: '[M]an, as a knower, is not fully himself – his *mere information* does not reveal him' (Tagore 2005: 11; emphasis added). He continues:

> But we live in an age when our world is turned inside out and when whatever lies at the bottom is dragged to the surface. Our very process of living, which is an unconscious process, we must bring under the scrutiny of our knowledge – even though to know is to kill our object of research and to make it a museum specimen. (Ibid.)

Rabindranath felt that the joy of creation was essential to being human and could not be kept alive by tearing apart the created object through scientific analysis or reduction, but rather that it needed to be holistically approached, and that science was incomplete without imagination and art. The root and goal of art, he felt, is life itself, and a factual truth, however useful, had to acquire a deeper dimension of reality through imagination and experience.

Despite their differences, Marx and Rabindranath coincide in their delight in the enjoyment of art. A sensuous enjoyment-making/production, the development of taste through the creative process itself, and the fulfilment in the 'consumption' or reception in a refined sense are elaborately discussed by Marx in *Grundrisse* (Marx 1973: 9). And if we confuse Rabindranath's view of art with the aesthetic elitism of 'art for art's sake', we would be making a serious mistake. We need to realize that 'art' for him encoded the very vitality and core of human sociality, and, therefore, the source of morality. Thus, the pursuit of art was to be for 'life's' sake, for ethical relations with others. This ethics is to be contrasted with a narcissistic morality, as neither Marx nor Rabindranath was an advocate of 'puritanism' and 'austerity'. Sensuous enjoyment was essential in their world-views and illuminates Marx's idea of consumption. The 'good' that creativity or art does for us/for humans is not a didactic precept, but a sensuous and enhancing experience of the pleasure principle inherent in life. Rabindranath calls this feeling *ananda* or joy, simultaneously present in being, knowing and making (Tagore 2005: 13). Rabindranath as an artist understood the transformative capacity of enjoyment in contrast to being stagnated and imprisoned by barriers of mere facts and social prohibitions, of repressive institutions. A world composed of such things was devouring of the human, as amply demonstrated by the wars brought on by the imperialisms and nationalisms of his time.

Life within a creative and dynamic society was the central goal for both Marx and Rabindranath. Throughout, Marx's poetry of revolution resonates with the passions of the past and of his contemporaries. This matches Rabindranath's literature, music and painting, replete with his concern for universal humanism. This universal humanism, the wholeness of Rabindranath's vision, his self-proclamation as a universal human subject and not a colonial object, is a necessary daring gesture proclaiming freedom. The context of a pre-existing class/caste society and colonialism redeems Rabindranath's claim of the universal 'man' from being a cliché of the European enlightenment. Considered by Europe as a lesser human, Rabindranath took upon himself the task of human liberation on behalf of not only Indians, but of the entire oppressed humanity. He articulated the necessity for all humans, not just the colonized, to participate in the project of overthrowing forces of alienation. Colonization here serves as a homology for all forms of domination imposed upon humanity, putting obstacles in the path of full human potential. This is the main reason why Rabindranath rejected the idea of the nation and the ideological practices of nationalism, feeling that this paradigm reinvented social relations and ethical and cultural mores of colonialism. He deplored the substitution of native rulers for the foreign ones. His ambition was to fashion a *new* human subject and a hitherto unforeseen and non-alienating world.[18]

Thus Rabindranath fought alienation in the name and language of the human or 'man', leaning on Upanishadic philosophy and the European Enlightenment equally to forge his idea of the self and an individual.[19] He especially shunned the mores of a market society and the commodity fetishism diffused by it. He substituted this subject with the moral and aesthetic ideal of a free and dynamic one. The fetishism expressed through capitalist consumption and the fixation on machines and commodities, he felt, needed to be replaced by a new kind of universalist social being. But speak as they often did in the singular discourse of 'man', neither Marx nor Rabindranath thought of 'man' as a homogenized abstraction; rather, 'man' served as the metaphor for a fully realized human person. 'Man' was a figure or an icon of an emancipated, encapacitated human in creative harmony with the self and the other, made in equal parts of similarity and difference. Conceived in this way, the idea of 'man' becomes a poetic transcreation of historic and social reality.[20]

When we step out of the binary mode in which the human and the social, the human and the natural, the self and the other are treated as segregated categories, and speak instead of the self, the social and the human in the same breath, we overthrow centuries-old dualisms in which the subject and the object, the body and the mind, emotion and reason ever stand in variance. This integrative sense of a complex wholeness was shared by Marx and Rabindranath. It challenges the conventional approach in which the whole is either a generalized or idealized abstraction, or a serialized aggregation of particulars. We shift here to another way of understanding reality in the idea of the dialectical *wholeness* of our personal social being. This desire for wholeness, of an unbounded and constitutive reality, provides the first premise of the idea of the universal human that we find in the writings and social projects of both Marx and Rabindranath.

Rabindranath and Alienation of the Colonial Capitalist Subject

Marx's theory of alienation as an intrinsic moment of capitalism receives an extra dimension in the context of its expansion into colonialism. The colonized society and subject suffer a double burden of unequal indigenous social formation and of foreign domination and exploitation. The violence of 'primitive accumulation' and 'forced surplus production and appropriation' are more deeply intensified in colonization than in the rise of wage labour in Europe (Marx 1954: 667–724). The sense of self of the colonial subject becomes the site of compounded alienation of self-division and unhappy consciousness, a phenomenon that is not a feature of the Marxist conception of the relation between the bourgeoisie and proletariat.[21] In *Chhelebela* (My Boyhood) and other memoirs, Rabindranath narrates his childhood and presents us with this problem of identity or subject formation even among the wealthy. Reminiscing on his suffering in educational and other institutions and at the hands of the English language, he speaks of how this repressed a child's imagination and hindered self-expression. In many literary works and essays he provides us with an understanding of the self-developmental process of a child in an elite household in colonial Bengal. In these texts, he recounts and explores distortions inflicted on the growing self and personality through colonial and class–caste-based social norms and practices infused with feudal social mores. He captures both explicit and subtle pervasive diffusion of colonial culture in Bengal, including in his purview the colonial state's hegemonic influence through the promulgation of laws and modes of governance. Thus, the elite colonial subject is both ruled and ruling, and it smarts from the insult of being forced into the shoes of the inferior classes.[22] This double consciousness works to the advantage of the elite, in so far as this elite feels it can legitimately represent the colonized society as a whole and become the agent of nationalism. But for the colonized subjects of lesser status the oppression is further complicated, as they suffer under both local and foreign masters.

The subject formation of the colonized is extensively explored by Rabindranath. He reflects upon the conditions not only of the middle-class subject, but of poor and rent-dominated peasantry in Bengal. He uncovers the process of continual alienation created by evictions from land, by taxation and rent, by the neglect of the landlords and traditional casteist indoctrination, all of which are ultimately connected to the colonial land tenure system of the Permanent Settlement (1793).[23] The peasantry and the land-poor, he argues in his numerous discourses on village life and communities, are often reduced to a sub-human existence, especially as landless labour.[24] He also shows how the mores of both local and foreign domination are internalized and legitimated throughout the colonized society. The colonial subjects' self-confidence, agency and self-image are in a crisis along with their economic well-being and productivity. In his novels such as *Gora*, *Ghare Baire* or *Jogajog*, he ponders over the identity or sense of self of middle-class colonial subjects caught between spaces of submission and resistance. A real decolonization, he felt, could not come about through nationalism, through a simple inversion of masters and subjects. The point of departure, he assumed, would involve the concept of a universal subject to serve as an agent for change. In this view, the enclosed and stultified existence of the inhabitants of the colonized space needed a new vitality, initiation and practice of both imaginative and critical thought. Based on his readings and first-hand knowledge of Europe and North America, Rabindranath offered a trenchant critique of the physical and mental alienation of the inhabitants of the colonies as well as of those living in industrialized, imperialist nations. With respect to Indian industrial workers, he relied on his knowledge of jute mills, coal mines and other aspects of British Indian capitalist ventures which involved his own extended family. He was also aware of instances of industrial workers' actions in Europe and India, as well as of Indian plantation workers. He sustained a lifelong communication with European intellectuals, some of whom – for instance, Romain Rolland – were involved in anti-fascist movements, and which drew him into the orbit of progressive writers' and artists' associations.

As did Marx, so does Rabindranath explore the effects of alienation in the economic regime, but he goes further in considering the psychological and cultural alienation produced in Bengal as well as in the heartland of imperialism. He notices astutely the ubiquitous presence of colonial discourse in Indian life and how Europe, Britain in particular, abounded in constantly reproducing tropes of degradation, savagery and decayed civilization. As his letters from the United States of America indicate, he was not only aware of the treatment of the indigenous peoples of the colonies, but also of the legacy of slavery and the oppression of black Americans. He saw the same logic of colonial capitalism working there as well. He felt keenly the insult of the physicalization of Europe's subject-peoples and the obscuring of their intellectual, creative and critical capacities. He denounced the domination of nature enjoined by industrial capitalism and science's servitude to capital, as well as the perception that individuals living in the colonies were incapable of a universalist consciousness. This latter schema wholly denied the humanity of the colonized and attributed to them an essential particularism. These insights of Rabindranath into the processes of colonization and other forms of domination help us to understand the typologies of the European Man of Reason, such as Prospero and his indigenous island subject, Caliban, a man-and-animal hybrid figure found in Shakespeare's *The Tempest.*[25] Rabindranath's understanding resonates with that of Marx, who shows how a bourgeois view denigrates human labour and the labouring body, how dehumanizing is the rigid separation between mental and manual labour – and, ultimately, a dualist understanding of the mind and the body.

Colonial capitalism essentially relied on racialization through both a cultural and pseudo-scientific assumption about 'others' of Europe. Rabindranath understood this and deepened his critique by adding to it his criticism of caste-ridden hinduism, which saw underclasses and women as lesser beings. His insight about 'race' and racialization is ubiquitously present, even in his children's stories.[26] Interestingly Marx, in spite of his criticism of colonialism and African slavery, is less sustained in connecting 'race', class and gender. From Rabindranath's standpoint as a colonized subject, however, 'race' was only too visible both in India and abroad, as were, of course, caste and ethnicity. He repeatedly noted, especially when writing on nationalism, how the ideology of 'race' organized the colonial knowledge so-called and the administrative apparatus, especially through law-and-order-legitimated colonial rule. His entire opus shows the violence of the ideology of 'race' in the actuality of colonialism. We see how a potent technology for alienation manifests in the internalization of a racialized colonial discourse into the self of a colonized subject, breaking it up into a self and other. Thus, the discourse of 'race' serves as an alibi for the subjugation of non-European 'others.' This insight alone makes Rabindranath's declaration of universal subjecthood of the colonized person a revolutionary act.

Rabindranath shows how 'race' and economic subjection are inseparably articulated in colonialism. 'Race', in a broad sense of negative difference, signifies a disempowerment of colonized subjects, and serves as an impediment to universal subjecthood of the colonized and empowerment for the colonizer in material and psychological terms.[27] Even the working classes of the west experience an identification with the ruling classes while fighting against them. As such, they become parties to colonialist and imperialist ventures and games. Rabindranath sees this same racializing ideology of imperialism internalized in an inverted fashion by the nationalist discourses of India and elsewhere in the colonies, serving a mobilizing and legitimating function and drawing common people into war, conquest, and a phoney sense of cultural superiority and a false independence. In this context, he remarks on a constitutive relationship between capitalism, colonialism, nationalism, caste and race. All this adds up to a quintessential alienation in which the idea of racial purity stands in for the caste purity of brahmanical hinduism. This is explicit in *Gora* (Tagore 1910), in which the eponymous hero arrives by the end of the novel to a 'human' identity by jettisoning caste and racial identity. In Gora's struggle to achieve a universal human identity, Rabindranath captures the process that the colonized subject must undergo to move beyond the antagonistic dualism of the 'self' and the 'other'. The Europeans too, he felt, must go through a similar 'humanizing' process by shedding imperialist identity. It is only then that the idea of the human would achieve its unalienated universal definition.

Overcoming alienation for Rabindranath was not only a matter of moral and aesthetic judgment, but of creating the necessary social and cultural practices from this consciousness. This idea was simultaneously expressed in his philosophy of education and his actual practices of pedagogy. He propounded what we would call a theory of counter-hegemony when he said that a major mechanism for incorporating Indian subjects into the colonial project was education in institutional and non-institutional senses. For him, the structures of formal schooling, the diffusion of the English language and attempts to displace the vernacular, and the practice of English in governance comprised this hegemony and alienated Indians from their very selves, their experiential lives, and from others. Thus, compulsory English literacy, English institutional forms of knowledge production and general cultural diffusion through print and other media could also be counted as hegemonic devices. The Indian middle class arising in this terrain was alienated from the common people.

As Rabindranath developed from a nineteenth-century Bengali poet to a twentieth-century international personality, becoming a critic of politics and society in India and the West and a poet and philosopher of universalist humanism, he arrogated to himself the right and the responsibility to speak as the harbinger of the universal 'man', demanding life conditions for the growth of full human potential. This is the challenge he offers to European colonial capitalism's modernization, and through this he sought to break Europe's monopoly on modernity by defining the true meaning of enlightenment. He felt that Europeans had lost the distinction between the modernist values of enlightenment and modernization called for by capitalism. Rabindranath's ability to articulate this difference, his resisting voice, rose from his colonized subject experience. Mainstream European thought buried this truth in both its 'civilizing' and rationalist discourse. Rabindranath rejected the alienating categories of power and possessive individualism, and sought a resolution through critical and aesthetic mediation of the concept of the 'human'. The idea of the 'human', not an individualist entity, was for him a discursive constellation with universalist connotations which embodied the creative and intellectual capacities of all. In his use the categories 'man' and 'human' cease to be empty idealist abstractions because he grounded them in the shared sensuous empirical dimensions of existing human beings. Through this device, while accepting what 'is', he opened an ideal passage for what could be or ought to be. Thus 'the human' or 'man' was made to serve as a mediatory device transcending the distorting binary relations between the self and the other, 'man' and nature, individual and society. This mode of connection and transcendence offered Rabindranath an unrestricted space for identification of all human beings, which was a shift to a third space of universalist humanism, opening the door to new creative and ethical possibilities. He posited a relationship between 'is' and 'ought' that is both constitutive and fluid, spelling out an internal relationship between them. Even when he could not disclose the full extent of the mediation, he relied on a poet's sensuous capacities and imagination to capture the actual and the ideal in their concreteness in a work of art.

If we were to look for a socially concrete 'is–ought' dialectic among different determinations, going beyond a work of art, it would not be possible for us to find a consistent view of it in Rabindranath's thought.

The major reason for this is that his idealist epistemology separated creative capacities and 'art' from social production. Unable to contain materiality in his epistemology, he separated social production from the production of art and creativity from the labour process in the making of objects of 'art'. This shows that his idea of 'labour' was an intrinsically physical and mechanical activity, a making process not relevant to art. The faculty of imagination, the process of making (poesis), was set apart from production considered mainly in economic and practical terms. This left him with two options: that of retaining a set of binaries articulated upon a sustained division between mental and manual labour, or that of subsuming social concreteness in an imaginative–spiritual consciousness. He fluctuated between these two options without coming to a clear conclusion. In his idealist aesthetic there was little conceptual room for seeing labour as being involved in any act of production, and not necessarily an act which does not involve imagination. Marx, on the other hand, understood 'labour' differently. For him 'labour' developed a general sense as 'conscious, sensuous practical human activity' involved in all kinds of production as an exertion of human capacities. He could thus see all forms of object-making as connected with imagination and practical usefulness, which did not exclude aesthetic pleasure. For Rabindranath, creativity was a qualitatively different set of mental capacities and activities distinct from those involved in 'productive' labour. For Marx, alienation meant a disarticulation and disembodiment of labour from the materiality of life production implying a secular socio-historical ontology. Rabindranath, however, saw alienation primarily as an event in human consciousness, mainly as a psychological, individually experienced phenomenon, as after-effects of relations of power rooted in mercantile-industrial, money-making activities. While he assumed and partially conceded a kind of reflective relation between art and society, he could not or did not want to sufficiently materialize or socialize creativity. The modalities of interpenetration between the spiritual or the ideal and the actual or existential reality necessary for overcoming alienation were left unconsidered. Lacking such mediatory modes, Rabindranath perceived the mind or the spirit as overdetermining or even erasing the material aspects of lives and societies when he engaged in theorization, while in his literary works he grasped them concretely. Thus, Rabindranath's treatment of the encapacitated human body, its sensuousness and emotions, remains ambiguous and unreconciled with a socially grounded consciousness.[28]

Though an artist drawing essentially on experience and feelings,

Rabindranath in his most idealist mood sees the body as a 'cage' for the soul – a nameless bird that flies in and out of this cage with the breezes of birth and death. The human body, in many of his creative writings, is often on the brink of vanishing by bringing to the fore transcendent emotion which submerges the self. The body remains static, while imaginative consciousness ranges freely. But in his creative practice, while providing concreteness in his art, he shows us how the spirit can only be apprehended through physical life and emotional social interaction. This feat is accomplished by his poetic vision and craftsmanship, which in its need for an expressive form, turns to resources of images, metaphors, similes, allegories – the whole arsenal of art-making. This need for figuration inherent in expressiveness, in the concreteness of the art object, provides an embodiment – that is, materiality – for his spiritual and moral abstractions. As a creator of expressive objects, he needs the positivity of difference and specificity to provide his audience's experience of art, without which they are left unconnected either to the world or the text. This difference and specificity are often found in his creative writings in the plenitude of nature, and in the nuanced differences between man and woman in the varieties of moods and sensibilities. There is, in his writings, a sensuous-emotional struggle or fusion – for example, between an ambiguous depiction of masculinity and femininity, reason and emotion, consciousness and nature. Possibilities of alienation residing in the division of the body and the mind, in spite of his own distinction of mind and matter, also provide him with some of the central problematics of his novels and short stories.[29] In *Chaturanga* (Tagore 1916a) or *Char Adhyay* (Tagore 1934), for instance, the women protagonists search for an authentic identity and self-expression, and they aspire to overcome a dualist existence. Though this self-quest is usually a preoccupation attributed to men, Rabindranath's women subjects reach out beyond their usual ascription to transcend nature and dwell in the realm of consciousness. In the process, they have to leave behind the socially signified woman's 'body' and sacrifice physical and social emotions in the name of reason and desired spirituality. These dualities or self-abnegations prevent women's entry into the subject position of the universal 'human', thus setting up a contradiction between being a woman and a human at once. The same might be said of men. Generally, Rabindranath does not resort to any significant resolution in these binaries, and he shares with his readers an awareness of the absence of a comfort zone of reconciliation. An irresolution is almost present between being forced to be and wanting to be, thus making power a basic ingredient in his project of freedom.

In the last decades of his life, Rabindranath's vision of decolonization, of fundamental social transformation, was overwhelmed by industrial capitalism's power of creating alienation through commodity fetishization, as also by the nationalist impulse within Europe which manifested itself as imperialism. The terrible destructiveness of capitalism with its technology for mass killing was bringing European and other civilizations to rubble. Rabindranath wrote to Yone Noguchi, Japan's imperial poet, regarding Japan's invasion of China and its broader dominating ambitions:

> Humanity, in spite of its many failures, has believed in a fundamental moral structure of society. When you speak, therefore, of 'the inevitable means, terrible it is though, for establishing a new great world in the Asiatic continent' – signifying, I suppose, the bombing of Chinese women and children and desecration of ancient temples and universities as a means of saving China for Asia – you are ascribing to humanity a way of life which is not even inevitable among the animals. … [Y]ou are building your conception of Asia which would be raised on a tower of skulls. (Tagore 1997: 497)

The culmination of his critique and denunciation of imperialist aggression is found in his last public piece, 'The Crisis in Civilization' (Tagore 1996b). Alienation had reached its ultimate and maximum sense. Europe's self-devouring annexations and wars caused a deep despair in Rabindranath. He questioned Europe's 'civilizing' claims:

> Such is the tragic tale of the gradual loss of my faith in the claims of the European nations to civilization. In India the misfortune of being governed by a foreign race is daily brought home to us not only in the callous neglect of such minimum necessities of life as adequate provision for food, clothing, educational and medical facilities for the people but in an even unhappier form in the way the people have been divided among themselves. The pity of it is that the blame is laid at the door of our own society. (Ibid.: 725)

In spite of such catastrophe, Rabindranath maintained the principle of hope. In the face of the devastation of Europe by nazi-fascist forces as well as the destruction of China by imperial Japan, he wrote:

> As I look around I see the crumbling ruins of a proud civilization like a vast heap of futility. And yet I shall not commit the grievous sin of losing faith in man. I would rather look forward to the opening of a new chapter in his history after the cataclysm is over and the atmosphere rendered clean with the spirit of

> service and sacrifice. Perhaps that dawn will come from the East where the sun rises. A day will come when unvanquished man will retrace his path of conquest, despite all the barriers, to win back his lost human heritage. (Ibid.: 726)[30]

The death camps for the enemies of the nazis and the fascists, the ultimate expressions of alienation, were run with the most efficient technologies, and their beginnings were already evident by the first world war. As Europe moved closer to the second world war, Rabindranath, who closely followed newspaper and other reports, became increasingly angry and depressed. On 14 April 1938, he wrote to E.P. Thompson: 'It is a torture for me to have to witness, in the last chapter of my life, the nauseating sight of maniacs let loose making playthings of all safeguards of human culture' (Dutta and Robinson 1997: 493). In August of 1941 Rabindranath died, not as a happy man. Alienation surrounded him on all sides. The conception of the universal human was all that was left for him. He had forged it with his life experience, and it was his wish-image for a redeemed world. He knew that this 'human' did not yet exist as an embodied way of be-ing, but rather as a figure of desire containing the potential fullness for all human capacities. He held on to his hope, which came from his faith in the human with its spirit of oneness, in human empathy and sympathy enabling creative capacities. In this way he sought to transcend the alienation, fragmentation and enslavement of humanity to power by imagining the iconic figure of the universal human. He left behind his immense creative and critical opus and a sense of oneness with life and nature as a legacy for others. Marx, on his part, socialized and politicized the problem of alienation, and conveyed as well the revolutionary poetry of its overcoming. His concept of 'the human', asserted from the early stage of his life, escapes the trap of an empty idealism to become a concrete imaginary through the convergence of the many determinations of history, society, and struggles and experiences of myriads of men and women.

Conclusion

The goal of creating a society and forms of critical and creative individual consciousness that eliminate alienation brings Marx and Rabindranath together in spite of their epistemological differences. It is obvious that Marx's historical materialism and Rabindranath's radical idealism rely on different theoretical premises. But this difference notwithstanding, they assert similar beliefs along the way in what they observe about human capacities and creative potentials, and those forces that destroy or distort them. Their desire for a truly human world where 'man' becomes the subject and the agent of history, and not merely the object of external forces, makes their paths coincide. While Rabindranath is a keen and feeling observer of history and social relations of power, and shares aspects of Marx's social critique and ethical impulse, Marx equally shares with Rabindranath a utopian moment of human and historical redemption. Though phrased through a metaphysical language, Rabindranath's social and spiritual concerns resonate with Marx's view that the human, as described in *The Economic and Philosophical Manuscripts of 1844*, is the measure of all things. And Rabindranath speaks of the divinity in man – 'which is his humanity' (Tagore 1966: 16).

The ways to explore the revolutionary or visionary redemptive moments for Marx and Rabindranath need different compasses, but their 'true North' lies in the same direction. While Rabindranath offered a trenchant criticism of social injustice and degradation anywhere, denounced alienation arising from greed for wealth and commodities and an aggressive masculinist self-image, and stressed empathy, creativity and the aesthetic experience, Marx shared this criticism and distilled his own critique in the context of human labour/productivity. Marx could not do without the poetry that lay in the desire for a 'new man' and a 'new society', nor could Rabindranath imagine the 'human' without responding to and engaging with the actual conditions of colonized India, oppressive landlord–tenant relations, and imperialism in Europe and Asia, as well as the dangers of nationalism, even that of the colonized. Unless we are going to be dogmatic about the 'right' theory and epistemology and thus fall into the schismatic and barren counterposing of idealism and materialism, we can accept that for both Marx and Rabindranath the universal human stands in for a living, breathing, creative social being – the best that human capacities can aspire to. Without this belief in the 'human', all theory is lifeless and all creativity a fetishized aestheticism.

Notes

[1] Himani Bannerji (2011); see also Draper (1978).

[2] See also Althusser and Balibar (1970).

[3] See E.P. Thompson (1978).

[4] See also Derek Sayer (1979).

[5] On Marx's use of the term 'science' in this regard, see Marx and Engels (1970).

[6] See Williams (1985): 75–114; also Margaret A. Majumdar (1995).

[7] Fanon (1965, 1967); Gilman (1985); Stoler (1995). These are some key works

from among innumerable sources that can be cited as evidence of what I am saying. The most trenchant anti-humanist theoretical impulse, however, came from the works of Michel Foucault, which pushed aside much of the 'humanist' tradition espoused by different disciplines.

[8] Williams (1985): 73–82; see especially the sections on 'Ideology' and 'Base and Superstructure'.

[9] The idea that history happens to people, or that reality is a self-reflection of the Idea/demi-urge, entails a long discussion of Hegel's philosophy of history. This is an antithetical approach to Marx's own historiography, found for example in *The German Ideology* (specially the first thesis on Feuerbach). See also *The Communist Manifesto* (Marx and Engels 1985), for a socially concrete version of his philosophy of history. See Marcuse (1941) for an excellent discussion on these points.

[10] See *The Communist Manifesto*, where Marx and Engels (1985) outline the different typologies of class politics that are found in attempts to change/make history. See also the explorations in Draper (1978) of different types of revolution as conceived by Marx and Engels.

[11] On the middle-class intelligentsia and the embourgeoisement of revolutionary social thought, see Marx (1978a): 555. In 'The Critique of the Gotha Programme' (Marx 1978b: 525–41) and the 'Circular Letter to Bebel, Liebknecht, Bracke, and Others' (Marx 1978a: 549–55), we find Marx's stern rejection of elite, bourgeois and petty-bourgeois leadership in the task of revolution. He says, for example, in the latter: 'As for ourselves, in view of our whole past there is only one path open to us. For almost forty years we have stressed the class struggle as the immediate driving power of history and in particular the class struggle between the bourgeoisie and proletariat as the great lever of the modern social revolution. ... When the International was formed we expressly formulated the battle cry: The emancipation of the working class must be the work of the working class itself' (Marx 1978a: 555).

[12] This is evident in Marx's humorous critique of 'Robinsonades', of the fiction of the solitary man in nature. See Marx (1973).

[13] For Marx's understanding of communist revolution and counter-revolution, see also Marx (1978d, 1978c).

[14] For Marx, the difference between animal and man lies in conscious making/productive and aesthetic capacities. See also Baxandall and Morawski (2006). Consider also his concept of 'freedom', which is not the type of 'freedom' found in the doctrine of *laissez faire* or the Hobbesian one of war of each against all, but rather a freedom that embraces the freedom of 'humanity', not a survivalist struggle.

[15] Dutta and Robinson (1997): 413 (emphasis added). On this deadening, violent and instrumental use of science, see also Tagore (1966).

[16] In a letter to Rani Mahalanobis dated 16 October 1929, he astutely comments on Gandhi's advocacy of the *charkha* or the spinning wheel as an 'ideology', not just a practice: 'The *charkha* does not require anyone to think: one simply turns the wheel of the antiquated invention endlessly, using the minimum of judgement

and stamina. In a more industrious, vital country than ours such a proposition would have stood no chance of acceptance – but in this country anything more strenuous than spinning would be rejected. Just think what would happen if instead of spinning Mahatma were to rule that each cultivator must grow at least two *seers* of produce per *bigha* of land; that such a target should be his sole aim and a mark of his piety; and that his patriotism would be judged by the extent to which he achieved this aim – then everyone would argue that such a programme would require intelligence, knowledge, drive and commitment to productive agricultural techniques' (Dutta and Robinson 1997: 365).

[17] In his introduction to *Capital*, Vol. 1, Marx (1954) gives us an account of his method by positively relating and contra-distinguishing his method from that of Hegel.

[18] On the formation of the 'self' of the colonial subject as the site of compounded alienation and strategies of decolonization, numerous authors have produced a wide variety of writings in literature, politics, social psychology and philosophy. Some notable examples are Frantz Fanon, Aimé Césaire, Achille Mbembe, Sembene Osmane, N'gugi waThiongo and George Lamming, among others.

[19] Rabindranath wrote extensively on the Upanishads and the notion of the self they contain; see, for example, his *Santiniketan* (Tagore 1994).

[20] For a proper understanding of this, we need to understand Rabindranath's world-view and its creative connections with Bauls, Sufis and other popular Indian saints, as well as with the aforementioned Upanishads.

[21] In the context of social and subject formation under capitalist colonialism, Marx's concept of class and his analysis of capital and capitalist society have to be stretched. This is apparent from Fanon's first chapter, 'On Violence', in Fanon (1968), and somewhat less but also importantly from Albert Memmi (1967). Marx himself modified his views in the later part of his life (see Musto 2020).

[22] See Partha Chatterjee, Dipesh Chakrabarty and other members of the Subaltern Studies group. It is probably such a perception that directed them to include the colonial middle class in the category of the 'subaltern'. Rabindranath, however, had harsh words for the middle class, for example in his novels, essays in *Kalantar* (1933a), and his letters, explicitly in *Russiar Chithi* (1931).

[23] On the Permanent Settlement specially, see Ranajit Guha (1981); Ramakrishna Mukherjee (1957).

[24] Rabindranath's concern for the plight of the Bengal peasantry is so pervasive that it exceeds the need of citations. But it is still worthwhile to remember *Russiar Chithi* (1931), *Palli Prakriti* (1915–40), *Samaj* (1996c), *Gora* (1910), *Ghare Baire* (1916b) and *Jogajog* (1929b). Rural upliftment was his life's ambition, and he gave this an institutional and practical form in establishing Sriniketan.

[25] The racism/colonialism inherent in Shakespeare's view is challenged by numerous anti-imperialist writers, such as Aimé Césaire in *A Season in the Congo* (1966) and *A Tempest* (1986).

[26] Rabindranath's insight on 'race' and on the self 'whitening' of and by the colonized subject herself/himself is beautifully expressed in a parable in *Shey* (1937a), in

which there is a pathetic and futile effort made by a fox to become 'human' by cutting off his tail, shaving his fur, and tottering on his hind legs and speaking in the human tongue. This transformation leads to the creation of a sad and hideous identity which is the inevitable result of the British colonial 'civilizing' or 'humanizing' project. The issues of racism and self-racialization resonate in every aspect of Rabindranath's writings, extending from his essays, letters, children's writings and novels, from *Gora* (1910) to *Sesher Kabita* (1929c).

[27] Rabindranath's letters from the United States on the condition of the Afro-Americans, on the issue of 'race', a phenomenon expressive of alienation and domination in the self–other relation with its own discursive mechanism for reproduction of such power relations, need to be remembered in this regard. See, for example, his letter to C.F. Andrews, in which he shows how the European civilizing discourse of the west and the east are racialized categories for ruling relations and hegemony (Tagore 1997: 332–36). Caste, a social organization analogous to 'race' with some common elements between them, was severely criticized by Rabindranath. See, for example, his musical play, *Chandalika* (1933).

[28] This is evident in his treatment of sexuality, for example, in Sachish's uncanny sexual experience with Damini in the cave in *Chaturanga* (1916a), where he experiences her touch as reptilian, or in the relationship between Atin and Ela in *Char Adhyay* (1934) or between Bimala and Sandip in *Ghare Baire* (1916b).

[29] See Chapter 4 in this volume.

[30] It should also be noted that, as Krishna Dutta and Andrew Robinson mention, 'In 1937, in a public appeal for the republican side in the Spanish civil war, Rabindranath wrote that "this devastating tide of International Fascism must be checked ... come in your millions to the aid of democracy to the succour of civilization and culture" – and earned a public rebuke from Joseph Goebbels, speaking at the Nazi Party's Nuremburg rally' (Dutta and Robinson 1997: 492–93).

Bibliography

Entries and in-text citations for works of Rabindranath Tagore from *Rachanabali* (Collected Works) reference the date of first publication of the particular work by Tagore, not the publication date of the collection itself. Those for works appearing in anthologies and translations follow standard bibliographic practice.

Agarwal, Bina (1994), *A Field of One's Own: Gender and Land Rights in South Asia*, Cambridge: Cambridge University Press.

Ahmad, Aijaz (1992), *In Theory: Classes, Nations, Literatures*, London: Verso.

——— (1996), *Lineages of the Present: Political Essays*, New Delhi: Tulika Books.

Alloula, Malek (1987), *The Colonial Harem: Images of Subconscious Eroticism*, Manchester: Manchester University Press.

Althusser, Louis (1969), *For Marx*, translated by Ben Brewster, London: New Left Books.

Althusser, Louis and Étienne Balibar (1970), *Reading Capital*, London: New Left Books.

Amin, Samir (1976), *Unequal Development: An Essay on Social Formations of Peripheral Capitalism*, New York: Monthly Review Press.

Anderson, Benedict (1983), *Imagined Communities: Reflections on the Origin and Spread of Nationalism*, London: Verso.

Ariès, Philippe (1965), *Centuries of Childhood: A Social History of Family Life*, New York: Vintage.

Aronson, Alex (1991), *Brief Chronicles of the Time: Personal Reflections of My Stay in Bengal 1937–46*, Calcutta: Writers Workshop.

Bagchi, Amiya Kumar (1982), *Political Economy of Underdevelopment*, Cambridge: Cambridge University Press.

——— (2006), *Perilous Passage: Mankind and the Global Ascendancy of Capital*, Delhi: Oxford University Press.

Bagchi, Amiya Kumar and Nirmala Banerjee, eds (1981), *Change and Choice in Indian Industry*, Calcutta: K.P. Bagchi.

Bagchi, Barnita (2005), 'Introduction', in Rokeya Sakhawat Hossain, *Sultana's Dream and Padmarag: Two Feminist Utopias*, New Delhi: Penguin India.

Bagchi, Jasodhara (1985), 'Positivism and Nationalism: Womanhood and Crisis in Nationalist Fiction – Bankim Chandra's *Anandamath*', *Economic and Political Weekly*, 20 (43 WS).

——— (1993a), 'Representing Nationalism: Ideology and Motherhood in Colonial Bengal', *Economic and Political Weekly*, 24 (41).

——— (1993b), 'Socializing the Girl Child in Colonial Bengal', *Economic and Political Weekly*, 28 (41).

——— (1996), 'Secularism as Identity: The Case of Tagore's Gora', in *The Nation, the State and Indian Identity*, edited by Madhusree Dutta, Flavia Agnes and Neera Adarkar, Calcutta: Samya.

——— (2003), '*Anandamath* and "The Home and the World": Positivism Reconfigured', in *Rabindranath Tagore's 'Home and the World': A Critical Companion*, edited by Pradip Kumar Dutta, New Delhi: Permanent Black.

——— (2017), *Interrogating Motherhood*, New Delhi: Sage.

Bandyopadhyay, Manik (2002), 'Sarisreep' [The Reptiles], in *Shreshtha Galpa*, Kolkata: Bengal Publishers.

Bannerji, Himani (2001a), 'Pygmalion Nation: Towards a Critique of Subaltern Studies and the "Resolution of the Women's Question"', in *Of Property and Propriety: The Role of Gender and Class in Imperialism and Nationalism*, edited by Himani Bannerji, Shahrzad Mojab and Judith Whitehead, Toronto: University of Toronto Press.

——— (2001b), 'Fashioning a Self: Educational Proposals for and by Women in Popular Magazines in Colonial Bengal', in *Inventing Subjects: Studies in Hegemony, Patriarchy and Colonialism*, New Delhi: Tulika Books.

——— (2001c), 'Writing "India", Doing Ideology: William Jones' Construction of India', in *Inventing Subjects: Studies in Hegemony, Patriarchy and Colonialism*, New Delhi: Tulika Books.

——— (2001d), 'Age of Consent and Hegemonic Social Reform', in *Inventing Subjects: Studies in Hegemony, Patriarchy and Colonialism*, New Delhi: Tulika Books.

——— (2011), *Demography and Democracy: Essays on Nationalism, Gender and Ideology*. Toronto: Canadian Scholars' Press.

——— (2016), 'Patriarchy in the Era of Neoliberalism: The Case of India', *Social Scientist*, 44 (3–4).

——— (2018), 'Rabindranath Tagore's Postcolonialism: A Vision of Decolonization and a Modernist Idealism', in *History, Imperialism, Critique: New Essays in World Literature*, edited by Asher Ghaffar, New York: Routledge.

——— (2020a), 'Women, Gender and the Family in Tagore', in *The Cambridge Companion to Rabindranath Tagore*, edited by Sukanta Chaudhuri, Cambridge: Cambridge University Press.

——— (2020b), *The Ideological Condition: Selected Essays on History, Race and Gender.* Leiden: Brill and Chicago: Haymarket.

Bannerji, Himani, Shahrzad Mojab and Judith Whitehead, eds (2001), *Of Property and Propriety: The Role of Gender and Class in Imperialism and Nationalism*, Toronto: University of Toronto Press.

Barlow, Maude (2002), *Blue Gold: The Battle Against Corporate Theft of the World's Water*, Toronto: Stoddart.

Basu, Tapan, Pradip Datta, Sumit Sarkar, Tanika Sarkar and Sambuddha Sen (1993), *Khaki Shorts and Saffron Flags: A Critique of the Hindu Right*, Delhi: Orient Longman.

Baxandall, Lee and Stefan Morawski, eds and trans. (2006), *Karl Marx and Frederick Engels on Literature and Art*, Nottingham: Critical, Cultural and Communications Press.

Benjamin, Walter (1969a), 'Theses on the Philosophy of History', in *Illuminations*, edited by Hannah Arendt, New York: Schocken.

——— (1969b), 'The Work of Art in an Age of Mechanical Reproduction', in *Illuminations*, edited by Hannah Arendt, New York: Schocken.

——— (1969c), 'The Image of Proust', in *Illuminations*, edited by Hannah Arendt, New York: Schocken.

Berman, Morris (1988), *All that Is Solid Melts into Air: The Experience of Modernity*, New York: Penguin.

Bhabha, Homi (1994), *The Location of Culture*, London: Routledge.

Bhattacharya, Malini (2003), '*Gora* and *The Home and the World*: The Long Quest for Modernity', in *Rabindranath Tagore's 'Home and the World': A Critical Companion*, edited by Pradip Kumar Datta, Delhi: Permanent Black.

Bhattacharya, Malini, ed. (2004), *Perspectives in Women's Studies: Globalization*, New Delhi: Tulika Books.

Bhattacharya, Sabyasachi (1997a), 'Introduction', in *The Mahatma and the Poet: Letters and Debates Between Gandhi and Tagore 1915–1941*, Delhi: National Book Trust.

Bhattacharya, Sabyasachi, ed. (1997b), *The Mahatma and the Poet: Letters and Debates Between Gandhi and Tagore 1915–1941*, Delhi: National Book Trust.

Bouche, Teryn and Laura Rivard (2014), 'America's Hidden History: The Eugenics Movement', www.nature.com/scitable/forums/genetics-generation/america-s-hidden-history-the-eugenics-movement-123919444/.

Brecht, Bertolt (1973), *The Threepenny Opera*, London: Eyre Methuen.

Brennan, Timothy (1997), *At Home in the World: Cosmopolitanism Now*, Cambridge, MA: Harvard University Press.

Chakrabarti, Anjan and Anup Kumar Dhar (2008), 'Development, Capitalism and Socialism: A Marxian Encounter with Rabindranath Tagore's Ideas on the Cooperative Principle', *Rethinking Marxism*, 20 (3).

Chakrabarty, Dipesh (1998), 'The Difference-deferral of (a) Colonial Modernity: Public Debates on Domesticity in British India', in *Subaltern Studies VIII*, edited by David Arnold and David Hardiman, Delhi: Oxford University Press.

——— (2000), *Provincializing Europe*, Princeton, NJ: Princeton University Press.

——— (2004), *Habitations of Modernity: Essays in the Wake of Subaltern Studies*, New Delhi: Orient Blackswan.

Chakravarti, Uma (1989), 'Whatever Happened to the Vedic Dasi?' in *Recasting Women: Essays in Colonial History*, edited by Kumkum Sangari and Sudesh Vaid, New Delhi: Kali for Women.

——— (1998), 'The Myth of "Patriots and Traitors": Pandita Ramabai, Brahminical Patriarchy and Militant Hindu Nationalism', in *Embodied Violence: Communalising Women's Sexuality in South Asia*, edited by Kumari Jayawardena and Malathi di Alwis, London: Zed Press.

Chatterjee, Partha (1989), 'The Nationalist Resolution of the Women's Question', in *Recasting Women: Essays in Colonial History*, edited by Kumkum Sangari and Sudesh Vaid, New Delhi: Kali for Women.

——— (1993a), *The Nation and Its Fragments: Colonial and Postcolonial Histories*, Delhi: Oxford University Press.

——— (1993b), *Nationalist Thought and the Colonial World: A Derivative Discourse?* London: Zed Press.

Chattopadhyay, Kunal, ed. (2002), *Genocidal Pogrom in Gujarat: Anatomy of Indian Fascism*, Kolkata: Inquilabi Communist Sangathan.

Chaudhuri, Supriya (2003), 'A Sentimental Education: Love and Marriage in *The Home and the World*', in *Rabindranath Tagore's 'The Home and the World': A Critical Companion*, edited by Pradip Kumar Datta, Delhi: Permanent Black.

Chaudhuri, Sukanta, ed. (2020), *The Cambridge Companion to Rabindranath Tagore*, Cambridge: Cambridge University Press.

Chowdhury, Indira (1998), *The Frail Hero and Virile History: Gender and the Politics of Culture in Colonial Bengal*, SOAS Studies on South Asia, Delhi: Oxford University Press.

Churchill, Ward (1998), *A Little Matter of Genocide: Holocaust and Denial in the Americas, 1492 to the Present*, Winnipeg: Arbeiter Ring.

Cipris, Zeljko (2007), 'Seduced by Nationalism: Yone Noguchi's "Terrible Mistake"', *Asia-Pacific Journal*, 5 (11), 30 November.

Cohen, Bernard S. (1996), *Colonialism and Its Forms of Knowledge: The British in India*, Princeton, NJ: Princeton University Press.

Coletti, Lucio (1972), *From Rousseau to Lenin: Studies in Ideology and Society*, London: New Left Books.

Collins, Michael (2012), *Empire, Nationalism and the Post-colonial World: Rabindranath Tagore's Writings on History, Politics and Society*, New York: Routledge.

Communalism Combat: Genocide (2002), year 8, no. 76, Mumbai: Sabrang.

Conrad, Joseph (1965), *Heart of Darkness*, Harmondsworth: Penguin.

Coquereau, Elise (2014), 'Modernism and Modernity in Rabindranath Tagore', in *Planeta Literatur: Journal of Global Literary Studies*, 2014/3.

Das, Sisir Kumar (1996a), 'Introduction', in *The English Writings of Rabindranath Tagore*, Vol. 3, edited by Sisir Kumar Das, New Delhi: Sahitya Akademi.

Das, Sisir Kumar, ed. (1996b), *The English Writings of Rabindranath Tagore*, Vol. 3, New Delhi: Sahitya Akademi.

Das Gupta, Uma, ed. (2009), *Tagore: Selected Writings on Education and Nationalism*, New Delhi: Oxford University Press.

Datta, Manjira, dir. (1992), *Seeds of Plenty, Seeds of Sorrow*, British Film Institute.

Datta, Pradip Kumar (1999), *Carving Blocs: Communal Ideology in Early Twentieth Century Bengal*, Oxford: Oxford University Press.

Datta, Pradip Kumar, ed. (2003), *Rabindranath Tagore's 'The Home and the World': A Critical Companion*, Delhi: Permanent Black.

Davis, Angela Y. (1983), *Women, Race and Class*, New York: Vintage.

Davis, Mike (2006), *City of Quartz: Excavating the Future of Los Angeles*, London: Verso.

Devi, Mahasweta (1979), '*Nun*', in *Nairite Megh*, Kolkata: Karuna Prakashani.

Draper, Hal (1978), *Karl Marx's Theory of Revolution, Volume II: The Politics of Social Classes*, New York: Monthly Review Press.

Du Bois, W.E.B. (1996), *The Souls of Black Folk*, Harmondsworth: Penguin Classics.

Dutta, Krishna and Andrew Robinson (1995), *Rabindranath Tagore: The Myriad-minded Man*, London: Bloomsbury.

Dutta, Krishna and Andrew Robinson, eds (1997), *Selected Letters of Rabindranath Tagore*, Cambridge: Cambridge University Press.

Fanon, Frantz (1967), *Black Skins, White Masks*, New York: Grove.

——— (1968), *The Wretched of the Earth*, translated by Constance Farrington, New York: Grove.

Federici, Silvia (2018), *Witches, Witch Hunting and Women*, Oakland, CA: PM Press.

Fitzpatrick, Sheila (1970), *The Commissariat of Enlightenment: Soviet Organization of Education and the Arts Under Lunacharsky, October 1917–1921*, Cambridge: Cambridge University Press.

Foucault, Michel (1978), *History of Sexuality*, vol. 1, translated by Robert Hurley, New York: Pantheon.

——— (1980), *Power/Knowledge*, edited by Colin Gordon, Brighton: Harvester Press.

——— (2004), *Abnormal*, translated by Graham Burchell, New York: Picador.

Freire, Paulo (1970), *Pedagogy of the Oppressed*, New York: Continuum.

Gay, Peter (1966), *The Enlightenment: An Interpretation*, New York: Knopf.

Gellner, Ernest (1983), *Nations and Nationalism*, Oxford: Oxford University Press.

George, Susan (1977), *How the Other Half Dies*, Harmondsworth: Penguin.

——— (1988), *A Fate Worse than Debt*, New York: Grove.

Gilman, Sander (1985), *Difference and Pathology: Stereotypes of Sexuality, Race and Madness*, Ithaca, NY: Cornell University Press.

Gohain, Hiren (2011), 'Two Roads to Decolonization: Tagore and Gandhi', *Economic and Political Weekly*, 46 (31).

Goldberg, Daniel T. (1993), *Racist Culture: Philosophy and the Politics of Meaning*, Oxford: Blackwell.

Gould, Stephen Jay (1996), *The Mismeasure of Man*, rev. edn, New York: Norton.

Gramsci, Antonio (1971), *Selections from the Prison Notebooks of Antonio Gramsci*, edited and translated by Quentin Hoare and Geoffrey Nowell Smith, New York: International.

——— (1973), *Letters from Prison*, edited by Frank Rosengarten, translated by Raymond Rosenthal, New York: Harper Colophon.

Golwalkar, M.S. (1939), *We, Or, Our Nationhood Defined*, Nagpur: Bharat.

Guha, Ranajit (1981), *A Rule of Property for Bengal: An Essay of the Idea of Permanent Settlement*, New Delhi: Orient Blackswan.

Habib, Irfan (1995), *Essays in Indian History: Towards a Marxist Perception*, New Delhi: Tulika Books.

——— (2011), *The National Movement: Studies in Ideology and History*, New Delhi: Tulika Books.

Habib, Irfan, ed. (2007), *Religion in Indian History*, New Delhi: Tulika Books.

Harding, Sandra (1993), *The 'Racial' Economy of Science: Towards a Democratic Future*, Bloomington: Indiana University Press.

Harvey, David (1989), *The Condition of Postmodernity: An Enquiry into the Origins of Cultural Change*, Oxford: Blackwell.

——— (2003), *The New Imperialism*, New York: Oxford University Press.

——— (2005), *A Brief History of Neoliberalism*, Oxford: Oxford University Press.

Hardt, Michael and Antonio Negri (2000), *Empire*. Cambridge, MA: Harvard University Press.

Hegel, G.W.F. (1977), *Phenomenology of Spirit*, translated by A.V. Miller, Oxford: Oxford University Press.

Herf, Jeffrey (1985), *Reactionary Modernism: Technology, Culture and Politics in Weimar and the Third Reich*, Cambridge: Cambridge University Press.

Heywood, Colin (2018), *A History of Childhood: Children and Childhood in the West from Medieval to Modern Times*, Cambridge: Polity Press.

Hill, Christopher (1975), *The World Turned Upside Down: Radical Ideas During the English Revolution*, London: Penguin.

Hobsbawm, Eric J. (1990), *Nations and Nationalism Since 1780: Programme, Myth, Reality*, Cambridge: Cambridge University Press.

Hobsbawm, Eric J. and Terrence Ranger, eds (1983), *The Invention of Tradition*, Cambridge: Cambridge University Press.

Hochschild, Adam (1998), *King Leopold's Ghost: A Story of Greed, Terror and Heroism in Colonial Africa*, Boston: Houghton Mifflin.

Hossain, Rokeya Sakhawat (2005), *Sultana's Dream and Padmarag: Two Feminist Utopias*, introduced and translated by Barnita Bagchi, New Delhi: Penguin India.

Huntington, Samuel (1996), *The Clash of Civilizations and the Remaking of World Order*, New York: Simon & Schuster.

Inden, Ronald (1990), *Imagining India*, Bloomington: Indiana University Press.

Jayawardena, Kumari (1986), *Feminism and Nationalism in the Third World*, London: Zed Press.

Ilaiah, Kancha (1996), *Why I Am Not a Hindu: A Sudra Critique of Hindutva Philosophy, Culture, and Political Economy*, Calcutta: Samya.

Joshi, V.C., ed. (1975), *Rammohun Roy and the Process of Modernization in India*, Delhi: Vikas.

Kaiwar, Vasant and Sucheta Mazumdar, eds (2003), *Antinomies of Modernity: Essays on Race, Orient, Nation*, Durham, NC: Duke University Press.

Kant, Emmanuel (1967), 'What is Enlightenment?' in *Kant: A Collection of Critical Essays*, edited by Robert Paul Wolff, New York: Anchor.

Kapur, Geeta (2000), *When Was Modernism: Essays on Contemporary Cultural Practice in India*, New Delhi: Tulika Books.

Kaufmann, Walter (1974), *Nietzsche: Philosopher, Psychologist, Antichrist*, Princeton, NJ: Princeton University Press.

Koonz, Claudia (2013), *Mothers in the Fatherland: Women, the Family and Nazi Politics*, Abingdon: Routledge.

Kumar, Radha (1993), *The History of Doing: An Illustrated Account of Movements for Women's Rights and Feminism, 1800–1990*, Delhi: Kali for Women.

Kumar, R. Siva (1997), *Santiniketan: The Making of a Contextual Modernism*, New Delhi: National Gallery of Modern Art.

Larrain, J. (1989), *Theories of Development: Capitalism, Colonialism and Dependency*, Cambridge, MA: Blackwell.

Lewontin, Richard C., Steven P.R. Rose and Leon J. Kamin (1984), *Not in Our Genes: Biology, Ideology and Human Nature*, London: Pelican.

Levine, Philippa (2016), *Eugenics: A Very Short Introduction*, Oxford: Oxford University Press.

Liddle, Joanna and Rama Joshi, eds (1986), *Daughters of Independence: Gender, Caste and Class in India*, London and New Delhi: Zed Press and Kali for Women.

Loomba, Ania (2005), *Colonialism/Postcolonialism*, second edn, Abingdon: Routledge.

Lovejoy, Arthur O. (1948), *Essays in the History of Ideas*, Baltimore: John Hopkins Press.

Lukács, György (1971), *History and Class Consciousness: Studies in Marxist Dialectics*, translated by Rodney Livingstone, Cambridge, MA: MIT Press.

Lyotard, Jean-François (1984), *The Postmodern Condition: A Report on Knowledge*, Manchester: Manchester University Press.

Macpherson, C.B. (1962), *The Political Theory of Possessive Individualism: Hobbes to Locke*, London: Oxford University Press.

——— (1973), *Democratic Theories: Essays in Retrieval*, Oxford: Clarendon Press.

——— (1977), *The Life and Times of Liberal Democracy*, Oxford: Oxford University Press.

Majumdar, Margaret A. (1995), *Althusser and the End of Leninism?* London: Pluto Press.

Majumdar, Ramesh Chandra (1962–63), *History of the Freedom Movement in India*, 2 vols, Calcutta: K.L. Mukhopadhyay.

Mamdani, Mahmood (1996), *Citizen and Subject: Contemporary Africa and the Legacy of Late Colonialism*, Princeton: Princeton University Press.

Marcuse, Herbert (1941), *Reason and Revolution: Hegel and the Rise of Social Theory*, London: Oxford University Press.

Marx, Karl (1954), *Capital: A Critique of Political Economy*, vol. 1, edited by Frederick Engels, translated by Samuel Moore and Edward Aveling, Moscow: Foreign Language Press.

——— (1964), *The Economic and Philosophic Manuscripts of 1844*, edited by Dirk J. Struik, translated by Martin Milligan, New York: International.

——— (1973). *Grundrisse: Foundations of the Critique of Political Economy*, translated by M. Martin Nicolaus, Harmondsworth: Penguin.

——— (1978a). 'Circular Letter to Bebel, Liebknecht, Bracke, and Others', in *The Marx–Engels Reader*, second edn, edited by Robert C. Tucker, New York: W.W. Norton.

——— (1978b), 'The Critique of the Gotha Programme', in *The Marx–Engels Reader*, second edn, edited by Robert C. Tucker, New York: W.W. Norton.

——— (1978c), 'The Civil War in France', in *The Marx–Engels Reader*, second edn, edited by Robert C. Tucker, New York: W.W. Norton.

——— (1978d), *The Eighteenth Brumaire of Louis Bonaparte*, in *The Marx–Engels Reader*, second edn, edited by Robert C. Tucker, New York: W.W. Norton.

Marx, Karl and Frederick Engels (1970), *The German Ideology*, Part 1.1, edited by C.J. Arthur, New York: International.

Marx, Karl and Friedrich Engels (1985), *The Communist Manifesto*, translated by Samuel Moore, London: Penguin.

Mbembe, Achille (2001), *On the Postcolony.* Berkeley and Los Angeles: University of California Press.

McClintock, Anne (1995), *Imperial Leather: Race, Gender and Sexuality in the Colonial Contest*, London: Taylor and Francis Group.

McNally, David (2001), *Bodies of Meaning: Studies on Language, Labor, and Liberation*, Albany, NY: State University of New York Press.

——— (2006), *Another World is Possible*, second edn, Winnipeg: Arbeiter Ring.

Memmi, Albert (1967), *The Colonizer and the Colonized*, Boston: Beacon Press.

Mészáros, István (1978), *Marx's Theory of Alienation*, London: Merlin Press.

Mies, Maria (1986), *Patriarchy and Accumulation on a World Scale: Women in the International Division of Labour*, London: Zed Press.

Mill, James (1968), *The History of British India*, 2 vols, New York: Chelsea House.

Mitter, Partha (2007), *The Triumph of Modernism: India's Artists and the Avant-garde, 1922–1947*, London: Reaktion Books.

Mitter, Swasti (1986), *Common Fate, Common Bond: Women in the Global Economy*, London: Pluto Press.

Mohan, Pankaj (2010), 'Tagore's Idea of Pan-Asian Solidarity and Its Influence in East Asia', Globalization, Localization and Japanese Studies in the Asia-Pacific Region: Past, Present, Future, International Symposium in Sidney, 2003, http://doi.org/10.15055/00001326.

Mukherjee, Ramakrishna (1957), *The Dynamics of a Rural Society: A Study of the Economic Structure in Bengal Villages*, Bombay: Popular Prakashan.

Mulvey, Laura (1989), *Visual and Other Pleasures*, Hampshire: Palgrave Macmillian.

Musto, Marcello (2020), *The Last Years of Karl Marx: An Intellectual Biography*, Stanford: Stanford University Press.

Muthu, Sankar (2000), *Enlightenment Against Empire*, Princeton, NJ: Princeton University Press.

Naipaul, V.S. (1961), *A House for Mr. Biswas*, London: André Deutsch.

——— (1967), *The Mimic Men*, London: André Deutsch.

Nandy, Ashis (1983), *The Intimate Enemy: Loss and Recovery of Self under Colonialism*, Delhi: Oxford University Press.

——— (1994), *The Illegitimacy of Nationalism: Rabindranath Tagore and the Politics of the Self*, Delhi: Oxford University Press.

Nietzsche, Friedrich (1961), *Thus Spoke Zarathustra*, translated by R.J. Hollindale, Harmondsworth: Penguin.

Noorani, A.G. (2014), *Destruction of the Babri Masjid: A National Dishonour*, New Delhi: Tulika Books.

Norris, Christopher (1993), *The Truth about Postmodernism*, Oxford: Wiley-Blackwell.

Nussbaum, Martha C. (1994), 'Patriotism and Cosmopolitanism', *Boston Review*, 19 (5), October–November.

O'Connell, Kathleen M. (2002), *Rabindranath Tagore: The Poet as Educator*, Kolkata: Visva-Bharati.

Ollman, Bertell (1976), *Alienation: Marx's Conception of Man in a Capitalist Society*, second edn, Cambridge: Cambridge University Press.

Patnaik, Utsa (1999), *The Long Transition: Essays on Political Economy*, New Delhi: Tulika Books.

——— (2003), 'Global Capitalism, Deflation and Agrarian Crisis in Developing Countries', *Journal of Agrarian Change*, 3 (1–2).

——— (2004), 'The New Colonialism: Impact of Economic Reforms on Employment and Food Security in India', in *Perspectives in Women's Studies: Globalization*, edited by Malini Bhattacharya, New Delhi: Tulika Books.

Ramachandran, V.K. and Madhura Swaminathan, eds (2002), *Agrarian Studies: Essays on Agrarian Relations in Less-Developed Countries*, New Delhi: Tulika Books.

Raychaudhuri, Tapan (1988), *Europe Reconsidered: Perceptions of the West in Nineteenth-century Bengal*, Delhi: Oxford University Press.

Rothschild, Emma (2002), *Economic Sentiments: Adam Smith, Condorcet and the Enlightenment*, Cambridge, MA: Harvard University Press.

Rousseau, J.J. (1968), *The Social Contract and Discourses*, translated by G.D.H. Cole, New York: Everyman's.

Said, Edward (1979a), *Orientalism*. New York: Vintage.

——— (1979b), *The Question of Palestine: A Political Essay*, New York: Times Books.

——— (1981), *Covering Islam*, New York: Random House.

——— (1995), *Peace and Its Discontents: Essays on Palestine in the Middle East Peace Process*, New York: Vintage.

Sainath, P. (1996), *Everybody Loves a Good Drought*, New Delhi: Penguin India.

Sangari, Kumkum, and Sudesh Vaid, eds (1989), *Recasting Women: Essays in Colonial History*, New Delhi: Kali for Women.

Sarkar, Sumit (1973), *Swadeshi Movement in Bengal, 1903–1908*, New Delhi: People's Publishing House.

——— (1983), *Modern India, 1885–1947*, New Delhi: Macmillan India.

——— (1985), *A Critique of Colonial India*, Calcutta: Papyrus.

——— (2003), '*Ghare Baire* in Its Times', in *Rabindranath Tagore's 'Home and the World': A Critical Companion*, edited by Pradip Kumar Datta, Delhi: Permanent Black.

Sarkar, Susobhan (1970a), 'Rabindranath Tagore and the Renaissance in Bengal', in *Bengal Renaissance and Other Essays*, New Delhi: People's Publishing House.

——— (1970b), *Bengal Renaissance and Other Essays*, New Delhi: People's Publishing House.

Sarkar, Tanika (2001a), 'Rhetoric Against Age of Consent: Resisting Colonial Reason and the Death of a Child-wife', in *Hindu Wife, Hindu Nation: Community, Religion and Cultural Nationalism*, Delhi: Permanent Black.

——— (2001b), *Hindu Wife, Hindu Nation: Community, Religion and Cultural Nationalism*, New Delhi: Permanent Black.

——— (2003), 'Many Faces of Love: Country, Woman and God in *The Home and the World*', in *Rabindranath Tagore's 'The Home and the World': A Critical Companion*, edited by Pradip Kumar Datta, New Delhi: Permanent Black.

——— (2009), 'Questioning Nationalism: The Difficult Writings of Rabindranath Tagore', in *Rebels, Wives, Saints: Designing Selves and Nations in Colonial Times*, New Delhi: Permanent Black.

Sartori, Andrew (2008), *Bengal in Global Concept History: Culturalism in the Age of Capital*, Chicago, IL: University of Chicago Press.

Sassen, Saskia (2014), *Expulsions: Brutality and Complexity in the Global Economy*, Cambridge, MA: Belknap Press.

Sastri, Sivanath (2016), *Ramtanu Lahiri – Brahmin and Reformer: A History of Bengal Renaissance*, Delhi: Wentworth.

Saul, John S. (2006), *Development after Globalization: Theory and Practice for the Embattled South in a New Imperial Age*, Gurgaon: Three Essays Collective.

Savarkar, Vinayak Damodar (1923), *Hindutva: Who is a Hindu?* Pune.

Sayer, Derek (1979), *Marx's Method: Ideology, Science and Critique in 'Capital'*, Brighton: Harvester Press.

Sehanabis, Chinmohan (1983), *Rabindranather Antarjatik Chinta*, Calcutta: Baatigar.

Sekyi-Otu, Ato (1996), *Fanon's Dialectic of Experience*, Cambridge, MA: Harvard University Press.

——— (2018), *Left Universalism, Africacentric Essays*, London: Routledge.

Sen, Asok (1977), *Iswar Chandra Vidyasagar and His Elusive Milestones*, Calcutta: Riddi-India.

Sen, Gita and Caren Grown (1987), *Development, Crisis, and Alternative Vision: Third World Perspectives*, New York: Monthly Review Press.

Sharma, Nandita (2006), *Home Economics: Nationalism and the Making of 'Migrant Workers' in Canada*, Toronto: University of Toronto Press.

Sinha, Mrinalini (1995), *Colonial Masculinity: The 'Manly' Englishman and the 'Effeminate' Bengali in the Late Nineteenth Century*, Manchester: Manchester University Press.

Smith, Anthony D. (1983), *Theories of Nationalism*, London: Harper and Row.

Smith, Dorothy E. (1995), 'Women's Experience as a Radical Critique of Sociology', in *The Conceptual Practices of Power: A Feminist Sociology of Knowledge*, Toronto: University of Toronto Press.

Soyinka, Wole (1972), *The Interpreters*, New York: Africana.

Sprinker, Michael (2003), 'Homeboys: Nationalism, Colonialism and Gender in *The Home and the World*', in *Rabindranath Tagore's 'The Home and the World': A Critical Companion*, edited by Pradip Kumar Datta, Delhi: Permanent Black.

Stiglitz, Joseph (2003), *Globalization and Its Discontents*, New York: Norton.

Stoler, Ann Laura (1995), *Race and the Education of Desire: Foucault's History of Sexuality and the Colonial Order of Things*, Durham, NC: Duke University Press.

Stolte, C. and Harald Fischer-Tiné (2012), 'Imagining Asia in India: Nationalism and Internationalism (ca. 1905–1940)', *Comparative Studies in Society and History*, 54 (1), Cambridge Core, 5 January.

Tagore, Abanindranath (2004), *Raj Kahini*, New Delhi: Katha.

Tagore, Rabindranath (1881), *Yurop Prabasirpatra*, Kolkata: Saradaprasad Gangopadhyay.

——— (1908) *Katha o Kahini*, Kolkata: Visva Bharati Granthanbibhag.

——— (1910), *Gora*, in *Rabindra Rachanabali*, vol. 7, Calcutta: West Bengal Education Department, 1980–96.

——— (1912a), *Jibansmriti*, in *Rabindra Rachanabali*, vol. 10, centenary edn, Kolkata: Visva-Bharati, 1961.

——— (1912b), *Dakghar*, in *Rabindra Rachanabali*, vol. 5, Calcutta: West Bengal Education Department, 1980–96.

——— (1915–40), *Palli Prakriti*, in *Rabindra Rachanabali*, vol. 13, centenary edn, Kolkata: Visva-Bharati, 1961.

——— (1916a), *Chaturanga*, in *Rabindra Rachanabali*, vol. 8, Calcutta: West Bengal Education Department, 1980–96.

——— (1916b), *Ghare Baire*, in *Rabindra Rachanabali*, vol. 8, Calcutta: West Bengal Education Department, 1980–96.

——— (1918), *Tota Kahini*, in *Rabindra Rachanabali*, vol. 26, Kolkata: Visva-Bharati, 1939–present.

——— (1921), *Nationalism*, London: Macmillan.

——— (1922a), *Muktadhara*, in *Rabindra Rachanabali*, vol. 5, Calcutta: West Bengal Education Department, 1980–96.

——— (1922b), *Achalayatan*, in *Rabindra Rachanabali*, vol. 5, Calcutta: West Bengal Education Department, 1980–96.

——— (1925), *Red Oleanders*, London: Macmillan.

——— (1926), *Raktakarabi*, in *Rabindra Rachanabali*, vol. 6, Calcutta: West Bengal Education Department, 1980–96.

——— (1929a), *Samabayniti*, in *Rabindra Rachanabali*, vol. 13, centenary edn, Kolkata: Visva-Bharati, 1961.

——— (1929b), *Jogajog*, in *Rabindra Rachanabali*, vol. 9, Calcutta: West Bengal Education Department, 1980–96.

——— (1929c), *Shesher Kabita*, in *Rabindra Rachanabali*, vol. 10, Calcutta: West Bengal Education Department, 1980–96.

——— (1931), *Russiar Chithi*, in *Rabindra Rachanabali*, vol. 10, centenary edn, Kolkata: Visva-Bharati, 1961.

——— (1933a), *Kalantar*, in *Rabindra Rachanabali*, vol. 12, centenary edn, Kolkata: Visva-Bharati, 1961.

——— (1933b), *Samaj*, in *Rabindra Rachanabali*, vol. 12, centenary edn, Kolkata: Visva-Bharati, 1961.

——— (1933c), *Chandalika*, in *Rabindra Rachanabali*, vol. 25, Kolkata: Visva-Bharati, 1939–present.

——— (1934), *Char Adhyay*, in *Rabindra Rachanabali*, vol. 8, Calcutta: West Bengal Education Department, 1980–96.

——— (1937a), *Shey*, in *Rabindra Rachanabali*, vol. 9, Calcutta: West Bengal Education Department, 1980–96.

——— (1937b), *Visva Parichay*, in *Rabindra Rachanabali*, vol. 15, Calcutta: West Bengal Education Department, 1980–96.

——— (1940), *Chhelebala*, in *Rabindra Rachanabali*, vol. 10, centenary edn, Kolkata: Visva-Bharati, 1961.

——— (1941), *Sabhyatar Shankat*, in *Rabindra Rachanabali*, vol. 13, Calcutta: West Bengal Education Department, 1980–96.

——— (1960), *Letters from Russia*, translated by Sasadhar Sinha, Calcutta: Visva-Bharati.

——— (1966), *The Religion of Man*, Boston: Beacon Press.

——— (1980–96), *Rabindra Rachanabali*, Calcutta: West Bengal Education Department.

——— (1994), *Santiniketan*, Kolkata: Visva Bharati Granthanbibhag.

——— (1996a), 'Nationalism', in *The English Writings of Rabindranath Tagore*, vol. 2, edited by Sisir Kumar Das, New Delhi: Sahitya Akademi.

——— (1996b), 'Crisis in Civilization', in *The English Writings of Rabindranath Tagore*, vol. 3, edited by Sisir Kumar Das, New Delhi: Sahitya Akademi.

——— (1996c), 'Society', in *The English Writings of Rabindranath Tagore*, vol. 3, edited by Sisir Kumar Das, New Delhi: Sahitya Akademi.

——— (2005), 'What is Art?' in *On Arts and Aesthetics: A Selection of Lectures, Essays and Letters*, edited by Prithwish Neogy, Kolkata: Subarnarekha.

——— (2009a), *Of Myself: Atmaparichay*, edited and translated by Devadatta Joardar and Joe Winter, Kolkata: Visva-Bharati.

——— (2009b), 'Letter to C.F. Andrews', 14 January 1921, in *Tagore: Selected Writings on Education and Nationalism*, edited by Uma Das Gupta, New Delhi: Oxford University Press.

Taylor, Charles (1989), *Sources of the Self: The Making of Modern Identity*, Cambridge, MA: Harvard University Press.

——— (1992), *Multiculturalism and 'The Politics of Recognition'*, Princeton, NJ: Princeton University Press.

Teltumbde, Anand (2018), *Republic of Caste: Thinking of Equality in the Era of Neoliberalism and Hindutva*, New Delhi: Navayana.

Thapar, Romila (1992), *Interpreting Early India*, Oxford: Oxford University Press.

——— (2017), 'Syndicated Hinduism', in *The Historian and Her Craft: Collected Essays and Lectures*, Vol. IV, Delhi: Oxford University Press.

Tharu, Susie and K. Lalitha, eds (1993), *Women Writing in India, II: The Twentieth Century*, New York: Feminist Press.

Thomas, Peter (2009), 'Gramsci and the Political: From the State as "Metaphysical Event" to Hegemony as "Philosophical Fact"', *Radical Philosophy*, 153, January–February.

Thompson, E.P. (1966), *The Making of the English Working Class*, New York: Vintage.

——— (1978), *Poverty of Theory and Other Essays*, London: Merlin Press.

——— (1993), *Witness Against the Beast: William Blake and the Moral Law*, New York: New Press.

Vanaik, Achin (2017), *The Rise of Hindu Authoritarianism: Secular Claims, Communal Realities*, London: Verso.

Walia, Harsha (2021), *Border and Rule: Global Migration, Capitalism, and the Rise of Racist Nationalism*, Chicago: Haymarket.

Williams, Raymond (1976), *Keywords: A Vocabulary of Culture and Society*, New York: Oxford University Press.

——— (1985), *Marxism and Literature*, Oxford: Oxford University Press.

——— (1992), *A Modern Tragedy*, Middlesex: Penguin.

Wood, E.M. (1986), *The Retreat from Class: A New 'True' Socialism*, London: Verso.

——— (2003), *Empire and Capital*, London: Verso

Yuval-Davis, Nira (1997), *Gender and Nation*, London: Sage.